A Modern Book on Art and Culture

A Modern Book on Art and Culture

Manohar Bhardwaj

CYBER TECH PUBLICATIONS
4264/3, Ansari Road, Daryaganj, New Delhi-110002 (India)
Ph.: 011-23244078. Fax: 011-23280028
E-Mail: cyberpublicationsdelhi@yahoo.com

A MODERN BOOK ON ART AND CULTURE

Manohar Bhardwaj

First Edition 2009

Published by :

G.S. Rawat for **Cyber Tech Publications**
4264/3, Ansari Road, Daryaganj, New Delhi-110002 (India)
Ph.: 011-23244078. Fax: 011-23280028
E-Mail: cyberpublicationsdelhi@yahoo.com

Printed at : Asian Offset Printers

Preface

The Universal Soul is the basis of the world, as the horse is the basis of the entire sacrifice. It is the substratum; and every activity-name, form, action-is something like a wave in the ocean. But the wave is the ocean. The wave is in the ocean, or on the ocean, as you may think of it. Likewise, all actions, name and form, rise and subside within the bosom of the universal Soul, so that you may say, just as waves are the ocean, actions are the Universal Soul. So the universe is the ocean, or rather, the Universal Soul is the ocean. That is the deepest and the nearest associate. The greatest friend of man is God.

This book is meant to explore the modern trends of art and culture with religious realm, I hope that this book will be appreciated by the readers.

— *Author*

CONTENTS

1

Ancient Indian Rituals

THE QUEEN-HORSE COPULATION RITUAL OF THE ASVAMEDHA YAJNA

The *asvamedha yajna* was the grand horse sacrifice which Aryan (Hindu) kings conducted to celebrate their supremacy and for the prosperity & fertility of their kingdoms. The queen-horse copulation ritual was sometimes conducted during this sacred rite; the relevant Hindu scriptural quotes are presented below.

I. The sexual ritual of the *asvamedha yajna* quoted from the Vedas (*Satapatha Brahmana*).

II. Lord Rama's mom & co-moms participate in the queen-horse sexual ritual of the *asvamedha* in the Valmiki Ramayana.

The Sexual Ritual of the Asvamedha Yajna Quoted from the Vedas

The priests supervising the *asvamedha*: the efficient (*adhvaryu*), overseer (*brahman*), cantor (*udgatri*) and the invoker (*hotri*). The king's wives which participate in the queen-horse copulation ceremony of the *asvamedha*: the chief wife (*mahishi*), favourite wife, rejected wife and the fourth wife. The *Satapatha Brahmana*, quoted below, offers clear instructions on how the queen-horse copulation ritual of the *asvamedha* is to be conducted; the king's chief wife (the *mahishi*) is to copulate with the carcass of the horse while the priests and all the participants curse each other in degenerate language:

> *"A cloth, an upper cloth, and gold is what they spread out for the horse, and on that they 'quiet' him. When the sacrificial*

animals have been 'quieted', the (king's) wives come up with water for washing the feet—four wives, and a maiden as the fifth, and four hundred women attendants. When the water for washing the feet is ready, they make the chief queen (Mahishi) lie down next to the horse, and they cover the two of them up with the upper cloth as they say the verse, 'Let the two of us cover ourselves in the world of heaven', for the world of heaven is where they 'quiet' the sacrificial animal. Then they draw out the penis of the horse and place it in the vagina of the chief queen, while she says, 'May the vigorous virile male, the layer of seed, lay the seed'; this she says for sexual intercourse. While they are lying there, the sacrificer insults the horse by saying, 'Lift up her thighs and put it in her rectum.' No one insults (the sacrificer) back, lest there should be someone to act as a rival against the sacrificer.

The efficient (Adhvaryu) then insults the maiden: 'Hey, maiden, hey, maiden, the little female bird...' and she insults him back: 'Hey, efficient, hey, efficient, that little bird....' And then the overseer (Brahman) insults the chief queen: 'Hey, chief queen, hey, chief queen, your mother and father climb to the top of a tree....' She has as her attendants a hundred daughters of kings; they insult the overseer in return: 'Hey, overseer, hey, overseer, your mother and your father play in the top of a tree....' Then the cantor (Udgatri) insults the king's favourite wife: 'Hey, favourite, hey, favourite wife, raise her up erect....' She has as her attendants a hundred royal women; they insult the cantor in return: 'Hey, cantor, hey, cantor, raise him *up erect....' Then the invoker (Hotri) insults the rejected wife: 'Hey, rejected wife, hey, rejected wife, when inside her tight crack....' She has as her attendants a hundred daughters of bards and village headmen; they insult the invoker in return: 'Hey, invoker, hey, invoker, when the gods see that miserable penis....'*

Then the carver (Kshatri) insults the fourth wife: 'Hey, fourth wife, hey, fourth wife, when the deer eats the barley, (the farmer) does not hope to nourish the animal....' She has as her attendants a hundred daughters of carvers and charioteers; they insult the carver in return: 'Hey, carver, hey, carver, when the deer eats the barley, (the farmer) does not hope to nourish the animal....'

These insulting speeches are for all kinds of attainment, for through the horse sacrifice all desires are achieved. Thinking, 'With all kinds of speech we will achieve all kinds of desires', they make the chief queen get up. Then the women walk back the way they came, and the others utter at the end a sweet-smelling verse, the verse that begins, 'I praise Dadhikravan.'. For the life-span and the gods go out of those who speak impure speech in the sacrifice. Thus they purify their speech to keep the gods from going out of the sacrifice."—Satapatha Brahmana

Lord Rama's Mom snf Co-moms Participate in the Queen-horse Sexual Ritual of the Asvamedha in the Valmiki Ramayana.

To ensure the birth of sons, King Dasaratha conducted both the *asvamedha* and the *putrakamesti yajnas.* The following quote from the *Valmiki Ramayana* details the first of the two sacrifices that King Dasaratha conducted—the *asvamedha yajna*, in particular the queen-horse sexual portion of the sacrifice. Although all three of King Dasaratha's wives were united with the carcass of the horse, Rama's mom Kausalya was the one who had the honour of spending a whole night with the dead animal's genitals plugged in her vagina:

"The prescribed victims—snakes, birds, the horse, and aquatic animals—were bound at the place of immolation; each was dedicated to a specific divinity as is set forth in the ritual texts. The priests then bound them all to the posts in the manner set forth in the ritual texts. Three hundred beasts in addition to Dasaratha's jewel of a horse were bound there to the sacrificial posts. Kausalya walked reverently all around the horse and then with the greatest joy cut it with three knives. Her mind unwavering in her desire for righteousness, Kausalya passed one night with the horse.

The priests—the hotr, the adhvaryu, and the udgatr—saw to it that the second and the juniormost of the king's wives, as well as his chief queen, were united with the horse. Then the officiating priest, who was extremely adept and held his senses in check, removed the fat of the horse and cooked it in the manner prescribed in the ritual texts. At the proper time and in accordance with the ritual prescriptions, the lord of men then sniffed the fragrance of the smoking fat, thereby freeing himself from sin. Then, acting in unison, the sixteen brahman officiating priests threw the limbs of the horse into the fire, in accordance with the ritual injunctions. In other sacrifices, the oblation is offered upon branches of the plaksa tree, but in the Horse Sacrifice alone the apportionment of the victim is made on a bed of reeds. The Horse Sacrifice is known as the Three-Day Rite; for both the kalpasutra and the brahmanas refer to the Horse Sacrifice as a rite lasting for three days."—Ramayana

Yajna, Mahayajna, Asvamedha Yajna: In ancient times, simple yajnas used to play an important role in inner refinement and self-purification. The mahayajnas used to be performed to purify the social life. But, when the need for complete renovation of the nation (Rashtra) and that of the environment was felt, there was a tradition of Asvamedha yajnas at the universal level. Thus, the yajnas have been classified into three categories; viz, yajna, mahayajna and Asvamedha yajna. The magnitude of their results also increases in the same order.

The importance of yajna has been described in detail in Srimad Bhagwat Purana. Several such events have been described in this scripture, which acquaint us fully with the enormous power of yajna. According to this Purana, the universe was created with the help of yajna. This phenomenon has been described as follows.

In an answer to a query, Brahmaji describes the form of yajna as follows-

"Yadasya nabhyam .... caturhortram ca sattam"
—Bhagwat, Skandha 2, Addhyaya 6, slokas 22,23,24.

Meaning: "When I was born from the navel of the all-pervading Brahma, I did not see any articles for oblation except the body of the Purush (the male God). Therefore, I created the animals, vegetables, Kusa (a sacred grass), the sacred land where gods can perform yajna and the time, which is full of virtues (meaning the time in which the virtues are worshipped). Then I created all the ingredients of yajna, herbs, milk fats, sweetmeats, metals like gold, clay (earth), water, four Vedas (Rig, Yaju, Sama and Atharva), four Brahmans, and such procedures too by which the yajna may be performed."

There is description in the Brahma Purana (Purva Bhag, Addhyaya 1, sloka 5,6,7) that in the beginning of the Kalpa, a very sacred mahayajna was performed for one thousand years. The organizer of this mahayajna was Brahmaji himself accompanied by His wife Ila. The role of Shamitraka was performed by intelligent and radiant Mrityudev himself.

The king Daksha felt very sorry when his yajna was spoiled by her daughter Sati by her self-immolation. After begging pardon from Shiva, he organized Visad yajna as atonement for his sin. Its description is found in slokas 16 to 18 of seventh chapter in the fourth Skandha of Bhagwat; as follows:

Thus Daksha got his sin pardoned, and after consulting Brahmaji, he expanded the work of yajna, beautifully, by taking into account all the aspects, e.g. upadhyaya, ritvija, *agni* for yajna, etc. A Purodasa (an oblation made of ground rice and offered in kapalas or vessels) of three kapalas was offered to Lord Vishnu. In order to complete the yajna, offerings were given to virtuous Brahmans to purify the chief stalwarts. When the Adhwaryu took the Havi in his hand and meditated on God after performing havan with pure intelligence along with the Yajman, he sighted the Virat Purush (Lord Vishnu)".

Rishabhdev is considered the incarnation of God. This country has been named as Bharatvarsha in the memory of his son Bharat. The latter made this country a sacred land through the performance of mahayajnas.

Wherever the mahayajnas were performed, Tirthas (holy places) were established. After removing the suffix 'pra' from 'Prayag', what remains is the word 'yag', (which means yajna). This place has become Tartharaj (the king of Tirthas) because a large number of yajnas have been performed there. The Dasasvamedha Ghat (a bathing place on the bank of the river Ganga) in Kashi (Varanasi) is a proof of the fact that ten major yajnas had been performed there. This is why so much holiness has been attributed to this place. It is mentioned in part 4 of Skand Purana that the king of Kashi, Divodas performed yajan of the Lord Mahayagyeshwar in Kashi city by ten Asvamedha yajnas. From that day, that place became famous as Dasasvamedha Tirtha. Previously, it was known as Rudrasarovar.

The sages asked reverend Sootaji about the place, time, type etc of the first mahayajna. Whatever Sootaji said, in an answer to this question, is described in the second chapter in the first part of "Vayu Purana", as follows:

"The creator in the primordial state (i.e. before the actual creation of this universe), performed the sacred yajna for thousands of years with an aim to create this world. In this mahayajna, indeed Tapa (penance) was Yajman and Brahmaji Himself was Brahma of the yajna. In this long and grand yajna of great souls, the 'Nemi' (wheel) of Dharma revolved so much that it shattered and hence that area which was worshipped by the sages and saints, was named as Naimisharanya.

The fourth sloka in the first chapter in first skandha of Bhagwat says-

Naimishe ninishiksetre rshayah saunkadayah

Satra swargaya lokaya sahastra samamasat

***Meaning*:** Once upon a time, 88000 sages including Shaunak performed a 10,000 years long mahayajna in the sacred area of Naimisharanya, with a desire to achieve Heaven. It is the sacred effect of these yajnas that this area is supposed to be sacred even today. A description is found about Ayodhya-that this city was the capital of Suryavanshi (descendants of Sun) king Vaivashwat Manu, who established himself as a universal monarch. He used to indulge himself always in Mahayajnas and Dana (donations). That is why in his reign no one suffered from the pangs of death, disease and old age, in the city of Ayodhya.

The rewards of Asvamedha yajna are far more purifying. In the medieval period, Asvamedha was thought to be the war for the expansion of the empire, whereas it used to be a special mahayajna performed for the benefit of the society and the nation, in the earlier ages.

The pages of Vedas, Upanishads, Darsans and Puranas are filled with the description of the importance of these Asvamedha yajnas. In ancient times, they were performed to achieve ecological balance, to seek the grace of God and to unite the nation. The writer of a scripture says that one gets the same sacred reward by participating in Asvamedha yajna as that achieved by visiting the holy place Gaya, taking a holy dip in rivers Ganga and Yamuna and performing one crore oblations (-Matsya Purana).

Ima nu kam bhuvana sishadhamendrasca visve ca devah

Adityairindrah sagano marudbhirasmabhyam bheshaja karat

Yajnam ca nastanvam ca prajam cadityairindrah-Sahasishadhati
-Yajurveda 25-46

Meaning: Certainly, the whole world gets joy (by performing Asvamedha yajna). Indra and all the Gods alongwith their Ganas (attendants), accompanied by twelve Adityas and forty nine Marutas make the herbs beneficial. Majestic Indrayajna (for ecological balance) surcharges the bodies of the performers and their children with superior virtues. —Mahidhar Bhashya

Sarvan ha vai kaman apnoti

Yo Asvamedhen yajate
-Shatpatha13/4/1/1

Meaning: Those who perform Asvamedha yajna, all their desires are fulfilled.

Yajnenasvamedhenayuh kalpatam ....

One's life span is increased by performing Asvamedha yajna.
—Mahidhar Bhashya 22-23

Oh dear! The sacred reward of participating in that Asvamedha yajna is matchless, in which the body of Nakul (a mongoose) became golden after it rolled its body in the water left over after eating by ritvijas (priests) who came to conduct the Asvamedha yajna there. —Mahabharata

Rashtram va AsvamedhahViryam va asvah —Satapatha Brahmana 13/1/6

The aim of Asvamedha is to increase the power and strength of the habitants of the nation, and the nations at large.

The king Vasu performed the Asvamedha. Vrahaspati Upadhyay was its Hota. The three sons of Prajapati, the superior sages Kapil, Katha, Taittari, Kanva, etc were its rtvikas. This sacred yajna was completed without hurting anyone. "Na tatra pasu ghatoabhuta"-(meaning) no animal was sacrificed therein.

—Mahabharata santiparva (3/336)

The following description is found in chapter 14 of fourth Skandha of Bhagwat Mahapurana. The king Vena had forbidden the performance of yajna etc in his kingdom. He said-"All the gods reside in the king and hence the people should praise and worship me only". In reply to this the sages tried to convince the king Vena thus –

"Oh king! The entire universe and the gods reside in the yajna. The priests perform yajan of the God who is full of Vedas (knowledge), wealth and devotion, through unique yajnas performed by different methods for your benefit and the prosperity of the people. You are in a position to help in such yajnas. Oh brave man if the people in your kingdom perform yajna, all the gods, who are indeed the different forms of Sri Narayana, will get satisfied and will grant the desired result to all. Therefore, you should not disregard these yajnas".

When he did not agree even after much persuasion and still remained adamant in his opposition to yajna, the sages cursed him so that king Vena died. After that, his arms were churned which gave birth to king Prithu.

"Adhadiksat raja tu hayamedha satena sah

Brahmavartta manahksetre yatra praci saraswati"

Meaning: After that Prithu promised to organize one hundred Asvamedha yajnas. These yajnas were performed where the river Saraswati flows towards the west and which is the area of Brahma and Manu, normally called Brahmavarta.

It is a sad story that in the medieval period confusion was created about animal sacrifice in these yajnas; partly due to the foreign invasions and partly due to the gradual decline of the true vedic culture. In this context, Pandit Beniramji in his hook "Yagya mimansa" and reverend Satavalekarji have given the correct clarification. The learned Satvalekarji, in his book, writes:

"The gods of upright thinking and the demon animals of evil tendencies, both exist in the human body. They are shapeless in the human body, but when the evil tendencies, assume the form they become the animals of the visible world.

That is to say-"It is the evil motives that condemn the human soul to slide back to sub-human (animal) forms. The arrogance results in the shape of hawk. The vulture is the representative of greed. The cunningness leads to birth as a dog. The ignorant souls have to go in the form of owl or donkey. When the animal-like tendencies become universal and assume the powerful shape as that of a horse, the Asvamedha yajnas are organized. The mode of sacrificing these animal-like tendencies is called Asvamedha".

The references, about the purity of preparation of Asvamedha yajna that are available in the ancient scriptures also do not enjoin the killing of any creature in these yajnas.

The Hindu Dharma Kosha States: "Three Ishtis (worships) of *Savita* (the Sun) used to be performed daily in the morning, afternoon and evening from the day the horse of Asvamedha used to be sent for global conquest. ***Savita*** used to be worshipped by the name of Satya-prasava in the morning, by the name of Prasavita in the afternoon and by the name of Asavita in the evening. This fact has been described in Ashwalayan shroutsutra (10/6/8), Latyayan shroutsutra (9/9/10) and Katyayan shroutsutra (20/2/6). "This means that Gayatri used to be worshipped for the entire year, following which Asvamedha yajna used to be performed for three days.

Gandharvo asya rasanam gribhanat Suradaswam vasvo niratashta.

-Rigveda 1/163/2

-Vasus have created the horse of yajna through the Sun. (It is, therefore, necessary to worship Sun (Gayatri) for the success of Asvamedha).

It is in this form that one should participate in the Asvamedha yajnas and attain peace and happiness in one's life.

Dasaratha's Desire for a Child

Ramacandra appeared in the Iksvaku dynasty. He is known as Iksvaku Kuladhana. Kula means "dynasty" and dhana means "property" or "valuable jewel." So he is the jewel of the Iksvaku dynasty. Dasaratha was known as such because he could fight in ten directions simultaneously.

Dasaratha was such a great fighter that sometimes Indra would summon for him when there was a fight with the demons. So

Dasaratha would go to the heavenly planets and fight with the demons. And these demons were so expert with maya, they would create darkness, expand into various forms etc. So Dasaratha would fight in ten directions, and when you looked at his ratha, his chariot, it would look as though there were ten kings and ten chariots fighting simultaneously. Dasa means "ten" and ratha means "chariot". That is how he got the name Dasaratha. So Dasaratha was famous for fighting for demigods and righteous kings. And he married Kausalya. From Kausalya, only one daughter was born. She was named Shanti, or "peace." But Dasaratha had no peace, because he only had one daughter, and that daughter would only get married and go to another dynasty. The Vedic system is that when a woman marries, she belongs to the husband's gotra or family line. So if Shanti married to another dynasty, she would belong to it. What about the Iksvaku dynasty?

Dasaratha was so worried. Then he married Sumitra. At least Kausalya had a daughter, but Sumitra had no child. Then Dasaratha was getting old. He gave up the idea of producing dynasties. As he was getting older he saw that some less powerful kings were doing small yajnas, so he did big yajnas. They were trying to get their name known, because once Dasaratha died Kosala would be broken. The kingdom of Kosala started all the way from what they now call the Dalai lama's line. From up in the north, in Tibet, all the way down to the river Godavari in Andhra Pradesh. So this was Kosala, practically it was the whole of India, not the democratic India but the Vedic India. So he was very worried that this kingdom will be broken to pieces and some small-timers will become emperors. Then Vasistha advised him to go to Kaikeya. This kingdom was right on the border of Afghanistan. They now call it the Sind region. Kaikeyi was the only daughter of the king of Kaikeya. The king's name was also Kaikeya. And when Dasaratha came for marriage negotiation, Kaikeya told him, "You have two queens, and they both have no children. Now you will marry my daughter, but what will happen to her if the other wives have children?"

Dasaratha replied, "I don't think they will have children because they have had none up to now. I am also getting old. They're not going to get any child. Only Kaikeyi will get a child."

So Kaikeya said, "That's all right, but you must give this in writing." There is a system in the Ksatriya marriage known as kanya-sulka. Sulka means "will". When you accept a virgin in marriage, you must give in writing what properties she will enjoy as your wife if you are a ksatriya. This is kanya-sulka, the "will of dowry." So Dasaratha wrote kanya-sulka. He said, "Whoever is born to Kaikeyi will enjoy my kingdom, even if my other wives produce children later." This kanya-sulka was known to three people. Of course, now we all know it, but at that time only three people knew it. Vasistha knew it, Dasaratha knew it, and Kaikeya knew it. It was kept a secret, because otherwise they would blame Dasaratha, "What is this? He is giving the kingdom to a younger woman." So this kanya-sulka was kept secret.

But at the time of the marriage, due to great attachment, Kaikeya told his daughter this secret, that whoever is your son will rule this kingdom. Kaikeyi kept this at heart. Once Vasistha advised Dasaratha to perform asvamedha-yajna. He was telling him, "If you perform asvamedha-yajna, then all the demigods will personally come to accept the oblations." There are two kinds of offering oblations to the yajna. One is that Agni will take the oblations and offer it to the different destinations. Another is that the devas will personally come in the sacrificial arena. They will stand in the sky holding their hands open, and when you offer in their name in the fire then the harvest will get up from the fire and go into their hands. And they will eat it right there in front of everyone,. These types of sacrifices are considered first-class, because the devas have come in person. So Dasaratha should perform asvamedha, and all the devas will come. And then Dasaratha will tell them, "You have your kingdom only because of my fighting. So why don't you continue my dynasty and give me blessings that I can get some son?" That was the plan. There was a big arrangement for asvamedha-yajna, and wherever Dasaratha's horse went, no-one objected.

Asvamedha-yajna means that you have to select a horse with certain lakshanaṣ or qualities. The ears have to be a certain way, the nose a certain way. There has to be a black part behind the tail. The hooves have to be a certain shape, 35 degrees bent. There is a whole description in karma-khanda. So you have to find out that horse, and after finding it you have to tie a golden leaf on his head. There it will be written, "This horse belongs to King Dasaratha. He will perform asvamedha-yajna, so everyone should donate liberally. And whoever stops this horse will have to meet the army of King Dasaratha." So this horse will go around the whole world, and if any king dares to stop the horse there will be one army which is following about 100 metres behind the horse.

They will have to meet that army. This army would consist of the best fighters in the army, all the generals, and if one can defeat that then more army would be sent. In this way the challenger would have to fight and prove that he is the emperor. So asvamedha-yajna was already started, and then when the yajna was going on, Sumantra (the minister of Dasaratha) came to Dasaratha and said, "I remember one incident when Sanat-kumara came to our assembly, when you were a prince." At that time Dasaratha was not married, and Sanat-kumara was visiting Dasaratha's father, Aja. Sanat-kumara made some predictions. "Maharaja Dasaratha will become very famous throughout the three worlds, and he will perform a putra-kamesti yajna, a sacrifice for getting a son. So in this sacrifice, the yajna-purusha, the personification of fire, will come there and give him some sweet rice. And out of this sweet rice Dasaratha will get the Supreme Lord as his sons." This was predicted by Sanat-kumara.

At that time Dasaratha was just an unmarried prince, a brahmacari. So Sumantra was a very old man and he suddenly remembered this. He came to Dasaratha and said, "You are doing asvamedha for getting a son, but Sanat-kumara told you that you should do putra-kamesti." So then there was confusion over which yajna should be performed. In Treta-yuga everything was yajna. For material benefits, for spiritual realization, for anything tretayam yajato makhaih. Makha means "yajna". Now Dasaratha got confused. So he went to Vasistha's house and prostrated himself before him. "Guru maharaja, we have spent 60% of the treasury, and now we come to know that this is not the proper yajna, that there is another yajna. How am I supposed to do this?" So then Vasistha said, "Oh yes, I remember too now. Sanat-kumara said this.

It is not a very expensive yajna, but the purohit, the priest who performs the yajna must be a very special person. That is the difficulty. That person must have not seen a woman until the time of his marriage. He should not have even known what a woman is. Such a great personality must perform the yajna. Then only can the putra-kamesti be performed with the purnahoti and we will get a son." Then Dasaratha said, "You must tell me where this person is." Vasistha was a walking encyclopedia, because he had been there three lifetimes with the same remembrance. There is no-one in this world who knows better than Vasistha. So Vasistha said, "Yes, there is a person like that."

Dasaratha said, "Who is this person? He has never seen a woman or known what a woman is until marriage? At least he must have known about his mother! What kind of a person is he, that he has never heard of a woman yet he has taken birth?"

THE UNIVERSE AS A SACRIFICIAL HORSE

The commencement of the Brihadaranyaka Upanishad is a description of a symbolic placement of the parts of the individual in the cosmic quarters, with the spiritual intention of an undivided meditation, where the subject commingles with the object. The peculiar technique, adopted here in this Upanishad, is ritualistic as it is characteristic of the Brahmanas in the Vedas, and this technique is supposed to be adopted in the case of every individual character in its correlation with the universe. Here the individual concerned is the horse of the Asvamedha Sacrifice, which is the object of consecration and while, exoterically considered, it is one of the items in the Asvamedha Yajna, and it becomes a part of an external act, in the Upanishad it becomes a piece of contemplation, which is the avowed purpose of the Upanishad-to convert every act into a mode of contemplation, to transform every object into the Universal Subject. This is the aim of the Upanishad finally; and for this purpose various methods are prescribed. One method is, here, in this Brihadaranyaka Upanishad, at its beginning, the transformation of the ritual technique into an inward contemplation of the Spirit.

1. aum. usa va asvasya medhyasya sirah, suryas caksuh, vatah pranah, vyattam agnir vaisvanarah; samvatsara

atmasvasya medhyasya, dyauh pristham, antariksam udaram, prithivi pajasyam, disah parsve, avantaradisah parsavah, ritavongani, masas cardhamasas ca parvani, ahoratrani pratisthah, naksatrany asthini, nabho mamsani; uvadhyam sikatah, sindhavo gudah, yakric ca klomanas ca parvatah, osadhayas ca vanaspatayas ca lomani, udyan purvardhah nimlocan jaghanardhah, yad vijrimbhate tad vidyotate, yad vidhunute tat stanayati, yan mehati tad varsati; vag evasya vak.

Verses with Diacritical Marks

This is the first Mantra which is written in prose, the style of the Brahmana portion of the Vedas. Usa va asvasya medhyasya sirah: The dawn is the head of this sacred horse. The idea is that every part of the essential item in the sacrifice is to be identified, correspondingly, part by part, with the sections of the universe outside. In worship, especially that performed in temples, we have also a similar technique adopted, which is known as the Nyasa method-the placement. Nyasa means placement. The parts of the body of the worshipper are correspondingly placed in the parts of the body of the deity, so that the distinction between the worshipper and the deity is abolished. The two become one. Such a Nyasa is done here. The head of the sacrificial horse must be contemplated as the dawn. Here, the dawn does not necessarily mean a particular time of the eve of the rise of the sun at any particular place, but the eastern part, mostly conceivable by the mind, as the world, as it can be visualised by us to the extent possible. Now, if it is not possible to conceive it in this manner, it can be taken literally as the eastern part of the world where we are living. The dawn is the head of the consecrated horse. The dawn, the beginning of the day, is the head, because the head is the beginning of the body. That is the similarity. The day begins with the dawn, and the body begins with the head. This is the similarity conceived here.

The eyes may be compared to the sun. The similarity is very obvious, because the sun is the eye of the day through which perception is made possible; and the eyes, of course, in the body, are the means of every kind of visual perception.

The Cosmic Wind, the Air that pervades, is the Prana within. We should identify the Prana within the horse with the Air that is outside, because the two are essentially the same, one working in the world outside and another working within the body of the individual, here, the horse.

The mouth is the Agni Vaisvanara. In some Upanishads, the Aitareya particularly, we have another cosmological description where we are told that from the Cosmic Virat, Fire broke out through the mouth. And the organ of speech is supposed to be presided over, in every case, by the principle of Fire. So the mouth of the individual horse, here, may be identified with the cosmic fire which is Vaisvanara. Vaisvanara is a word which has two or three meanings. It is a fire principle which is hiddenly present in all things, the principle of fire which manifests itself as the visible fire outside, which, again, is sometimes identified with the Cosmic Being. Vaisva-Nara means the Cosmic-Man, and the derivative of this word is Vaisvanara. The Vaisvanara is the Cosmic Person who represents the energy of all things, manifested outwardly as the fire principle, energy secondarily manifest, again, as the power of speech. And so, the mouth is to be identified with the Vaisvanara, the principle of Divine Fire.

The body is the entire process of the year. The Time process is the body, because the body has many limbs, many parts; and likewise, time can be segmented into parts-past, present, future; and if it is concretised further, it becomes capable of division into years, months, days, nights, etc. The comparison is that, as the time has divisible parts, so the body also has divisible parts. The two are identified.

The Sky is the back, as it were. The comparison is that it is on the top, above the body.

The Atmosphere is the belly, because it is hollow, as it were.

The Earth is the hoofs, on which the animal is placed.

The sides are the quarters of the heavens.

The sides of the body, consisting of the bones, may be compared to the intermediary quarters, which are between the main quarters.

The seasons are the limbs of the body. Even as the Samvatsara, or the year, is constituted of various seasons, the body is constituted of various limbs. The divisions of the year, namely the month, the half-month, the bright half and the dark half of the month, etc., are the parts of the entire physical body, just as the year may be supposed to be placed on the parts consisting of the months, days, etc. The day and night are the essence of the calculation of Time, and, therefore, the year may be supposed to be rooted in the calculation or conception of day and night. Thus is also the body rooted, or placed, or supported by the feet. So, the day and night are said to be the feet of the horse.

The constellations in the sky may be compared to the whitish bones which are spread out, as it were, in all parts of the body. The clouds are the flesh of the whole body. The sand that you can see anywhere, physically, in the world, may be compared to the half-digested food that is in a seed condition in the stomach.

The rivers are the veins and the arteries. The spleen and the liver are the mountains, as it were, which are something like an elevation in the body within. The trees and the plants and the shrubs may be compared to the hairs of the body.

The sun, rising, is the earlier, fore part of the body. The hind part of the body may be compared to the sun that is about to set. The horse's yawning is something like the lightening. The shaking of the members of the body is like the thunder in the rainy season. Its making water is like the rainfall. The sound that it makes, neighing, is the principle of speech.

This description of the Cosmos as Horse is entirely symbolic, and highly complicated to conceive, because the purpose of the Upanishad is to bring out the psychological element that is present in the comparison that is made between the physical counterparts of the body of the horse, and the body of the universe outside. The difference between the horse conceived here, or to make a wider comparison, the case of any individual, for the matter of that, the distinction between the body of an individual, whether of an animal or a human being, and the world outside, is psychological. If it were not psychological and is really physical, an identification would be impossible. That one person is different from another person, is a psychological division. It is not physical. We have had occasion to discuss this subject earlier in some of our discourses.

I shall give you a small example of how physical division does not exist. It is only imaginary. The bodies of people are constituted of the five elements-earth, water, fire, air and ether. Your body, my body and everybody's body is constituted of only these things, nothing else-earth, water, fire, air, ether. If the body of one individual, 'A', is substantially the same as the body of another individual, 'B', because of its being formed of the same five elements, what is the reason for the distinction or the difference that we make between one body and another body? It is that which exists between the two bodies. The space is the cause. But space is a part of the very constitution of the body itself. So, how does this become an element of distinction? That which we regard as spatial, and, perhaps, the only reason for the distinction that we usually make between one body and another, is an element essentially present in the constitution of the body itself. So to say that space is the distinctive mark of division between one body and another is logically not tenable. It is a peculiar thinking of the minds of people that makes it impossible for them to feel the coextensive nature of bodies, as if they are connected at the bottom, like the waters of the ocean. Inasmuch as physical distinctions are not tenable ultimately, the distinctions are to be regarded as purely mental, or psychological; and therefore, a mental act can abolish the mental distinction that has been thus created.

The entire psychology of meditation is nothing but a setting right of errors in thought; and the details of these methods we shall be considering as we proceed further. So, to come to the point, this distinction between the individual unit and the Universal Substance is to be abolished for the purpose of the removal of the sorrow of the individual. Meditation is the technique of the removal of sorrow in the sense that sorrow is caused by the segregation of the individual from the world outside. For this purpose, one enters into the technique of meditation. Now, here, the context being sacrifice, we are given a method which is ritualistic in its nature, and thus the ritualistic horse of the Asvamedha Sacrifice becomes an object of contemplation, literally, liturgically as an animal in the sacrifice, but psychologically and spiritually, as an element like any other element in creation as a whole. The subject is continued in the next Mantra.

2. ahar va asvam purastan mahima nvajayata. tasya purve samudre yonih, ratrir enam pascan mahima nvajayata, tasyapare samudre yonih, etau va asvam mahimanav abhitah sambabhuvatuh hayo bhutva devan avahat, vaji gandharvan, arvasuran, asvo manusyan; samudra evasya bandhuh, samudro yonih.

Again, this is a ritualistic peculiarity of the Brahmana, concerned with the Asvamedha Sacrifice. Mahima is a term used to designate certain sacrificial vessels, gold and silver, placed in the performance of the sacrifice. The daytime may be compared, says the Upanishad, to the golden cup that is placed in the front of the horse. The eastern ocean, by which what is intended is the farthest eastern limit of the conceivable world, is the base. The world ends with the ocean. That is how we have to think, because we cannot think more than that. What can a child think? If you ask a baby to think of the world, it will think only up to the ocean. Beyond that, no thought is possible. But this is only a beginning of the method of extending the thought to further and further limits, until we reach the limit of the psychological horizon. The idea is that the eastern ocean is to be regarded as the limit, the farthest possible for the mind in contemplating the horizon of the universe. That is the limit of the horse.

Similarly, the rear part may be compared to the night, and the western ocean, which is the other side of conceivable limit. Thus, the horse is enveloped, encircled by the ritualistic elements, which means to say, in this process of contemplation, the parts of the world are contemplated as associated with the world which is, here, the object of contemplation. Just as the parts in a sacrifice are associated with the element in the sacrifice which is the horse, the parts of the world or the universe are to be conceived as associated with it as parts are associated with the whole. Here is a very difficult passage whose meaning is very obscure. But evidently what its meaning is, is this, that there is a gradual ascent and descent of the degree in the concept of the horse, or rather, the concept of the universe. When you think of the universe as an object of contemplation, you think of it in various degrees-the gross, the subtle and the causal. And the commentators, especially Acharya shankara, and others, tell us that the horse mentioned here is the Prajapati, or the Creator of the cosmos. It is not merely the animal in the sacrifice. That is how we have to think in meditation. So, as there is a descent from the causal condition to the subtle condition, and from the subtle to the gross, and from the gross to the variegated forms of manifestation in this world, so also is the horse to be contemplated in the various aspects of its functions, and the functions are mentioned here in respect of the ritual of the Asvamedha Sacrifice.

When the horse becomes the vehicle of the celestials, it is called 'Hayo'. When it becomes the vehicle of Gandharvas, demi-gods, above the earth, it is called 'Vaji', a peculiar name ascribed to the horse. When it becomes the vehicle of the demons, it becomes 'Arva'. It becomes the ordinary horse, Asva, when it becomes the vehicle of human beings. The substance of all these things is the ocean. Here, the great commentator, Acharya shankara, tells us the ocean means the Cosmic Soul. It does not mean the ocean which is water.

The Universal Soul is the basis of the world, as the horse is the basis of the entire sacrifice. It is the substratum; and every activity-name, form, action-is something like a wave in the ocean. But the wave is the ocean. The wave is in the ocean, or on the ocean, as you may think of it. Likewise, all actions, name and form, rise and subside within the bosom of the universal Soul, so that you may say, just as waves are the ocean, actions are the Universal Soul. So the universe is the ocean, or rather, the Universal Soul is the ocean. That is the deepest and the nearest associate. The greatest friend of man is God. That is what is intended here. And He is the support, ultimate resort and refuge-Samudra evasya bandhuh, samudro yonih

YAGNA, DANA AND GOTRA

Every society has passed through a tribal stage at some time or the other. Some societies are still in the tribal stage for instance the Australian aborigines, and the Red Indians living in the preserves or nearer home in India the Nagas and Bhils, etc.,. This stage is normally characterized by a collective way of living where property is under common ownership of the tribes the institution of monogamous family has not yet been accepted and where livelihood depends on tending of cattle, collection of wild fruits and roots and shifting, subsistence agriculture.

THE TRIBAL WAY OF LIFE WAS OF COLLECTIVE ACTIVITY

This Collective way of life is conducive to the birth of many of the folklore and rituals of later stages of development when the tribal way of life is no more. The origins of these folklore and rituals is normally lost and hence they are looked upon as timeless and having divine sanction. The main reason for their origin being lost is the absence of a written language during the tribal stage when most of the folklore is born. Due to the absence of a written language, ideas had to be passed on from generation to generation by means of oral narration. Although the origin of most rituals is lost to us, the nature of the rituals that we perform today is at times eloquent about their origins.

A HARD LOOK AT OUR RITUALS CAN BRING OUT MANY OF THEIR LOST ORIGINS

A hard look at these rituals can bring out many of their lost origins. The practice of oral transmission of knowledge due to the absence of a literary medium itself becomes a tradition in some cases. In India our traditions of smriti (remembrance) and Shurti (listening) and sloka pathan (oral narration) are instances of this. Even during our prayers and sacrificial invocations (Yagna) we rarely see the officiating priests reading out the prayer (slokas and Mantras). These are generally recited or chanted. In this chapter we take up a set of traditions which we observe in today's society and try to reconstruct the social ethos in which they could have originated. The issues we take up are the ritual of fire sacrifice (Yagna) our traditional practice of charity Dana), the concept of Gotra which is a consideration while arranging marriages, the institution of monogamous marriage (Dwanda-Vivaha) and the worship of the Mother Goddess.

YAGNA AS A SACRIFICE

Yagna is a term we normally hear in today's society. It is popularly understood as a fire sacrifice involving the offering of grains, clarified butter, sandalwood etc, to a fire. This fire is ignited in a special fireplace called the Kund, which literally means a "Pot". Yagna is normally performed with the objective of ushering in prosperity or to avoid disaster. For performing a Yagna a minimum number of five priests are required although many more priests may participate. A **Yagna** is normally accompanied by mass feeding of people, the food being distributed as Prasad (i.e food which has been sanctified by offering it to the Gods). Rituals similar to yagna are performed during marriage, thread ceremony, vaastu shanti (opening ceremony for a house), etc. when a homa or sacred fire is ignited in a kund. It is widely known that Yagna is a very old tradition in the Hindu religion and it is looked upon as a Vedic ritual. In Vedic literature there are innumerable descriptions of a Yagnas being performed. The origin of the Yagna though lost in history, the rituals associated with it today throw light as to its nature.

YAGNA CENTRES AROUND A FIREPLACE

Yagna as a ritual centres around a fireplace. Thus, it obviously must have come into being after fire was domesticated. Even the oldest of the Vedas, the Rigveda describes a society where man had no fire, no protection against wild beasts, uncertainty of prey and hence the spectre of being perished. This environment is poetically expressed in Vedic literature.

Prajapati, the creator suffered abortion in the act of creation and was threatened with extinction. But the world was saved when he was given milk and roasted meat. Praiapati, symbolizes the Aryan man in his most primitive stage, who to the Aryans became a personification of their existence, the memory of which was kept alive by Prajapati being deified in the hymns and songs that constitute the Rigveda.

THE FABLISED RECOLLECTION OF THE DISCOVERY OF FIRE

This fableised recollection also narrates the discovery of making fire and the art of domesticating animals. Agni-fire has been referred to as an eater of dead flesh (Kravyad). Fire also served as a formidable weapon against wild animals and other tribes. It also helped during the hunt for capturing prey and as a shield against the oppressive cold winters of the higher latitudes. Society obtained a respite from the threat of extinction and was lifted above the margin of sustenance.

SATRA-THE COLLECTIVE LABOUR

However man individually was powerless in the fight; against nature, hence whatever was collected or hunted had to be done collectively in large groups (Gana). Thus the auxiliary practices of distribution and consumption were also performed collectively. The absence of the institution of the monogamous marriage and family life as we know it today was another factor that ensured collectivity in all facets of life. The collective labour that was undertaken by Vedic Aryans was termed Satra which means a session, implying collectivity. Thus there was no question of division of society into Varnas and Jatis, so prominent in later Hindu society.

THE FIREPLACE WAS THE NUCLEUS OF THE TRIBAL SOCIETY

But the domestication of fire provided a gravitating nucleus for the collective life of the tribe (Gana). As to what the tribal Aryans did around this central fireplace can be guessed from the original Yagna rituals which today are kept alive in the Yagnas as performed by Sadhus (i.e. ascetics and hermits).

THE YAGNA RITUAL RE-CREATES ALL ASPECTS OF PRIMITIVE TRIBAL COLLECTIVE LIFE

Contemporary writer describes this Yagna ritual as follows: " The Yagna ritual "... " is a process in which almost all primitive social life has to be recreated. You have to produce fire by friction of two pieces of wood, to build a cottage where no iron is used but only specific wood and grass, to milk cows, make curds, pound corn with stone (not even a stone mill), boil and cook it,..." This description brings out the fine semblance between the original Yagna ritual and the function of cooking for a tribal household. In the public Yagnas, like the Rajasuya and Ashwamedha Yagna that were sponsored in later ages by kings, many alterations and refinements were introduced but the original primitive features stuck fast. These royal Yagnas involved the coming together of innumerable Brahmins, the consigning to the central fire, generous quantities of sandalwood, camphor, ghee (clarified butter), grains, and even sacrificial animals and birds. All this corresponds to the central fireplace theory as the origin of the Yagna.

BEFORE ITS DOMESTICATION FIRE WAS AN OBJECT OF AWE AND FEAR

Fire had, before its domestication been observed by cavemen and savages only as a formidable destructive medium in the gigantic forest fires, volcanic eruptions etc. Hence it had always been looked upon with fear and awe. But after its domestication, fire spelt prosperity for the nomadic people. Hence it could easily become an object of worship. When the nomadic Aryans had progressed towards settled civilized life the fireplace no longer remained the gravitating nucleus of their daily life. But their social memory continued to be ruled by the past reality.

THIS LINGERING SOCIAL MEMORY PERPETUATED THE PRACTICE OF HAVING THE CENTRAL FIRE AS THE YAGNA

This lingering social memory perpetuated the practice of having the central fire, which in the changed circumstances became a ritualised form of worship. The recollection of the extinct past fermented ideas that invocation of the fire would again spell wealth and prosperity as it had after its domestication. In the Yagna ritual of later days up to our own age, the hymns sung in the Vedic days are recited, the collective social life is reconstructed in a ritualised rnanner with the fond hope that all this would spell prosperity for the performers of the Yagna. This is one instance of a past being kept alive in later ages by crystallizing it into a ritual.

DANA AND DAKSHINA

At some time or the other during our lives we observe the practices of dana and dakshina. Dana is the traditional Indian form of charity. We are told that giving away of dana secures divine blessings for the giver. As such dana can be given to anybody but the emphasis has always been on giving dana to Brahmins. Hindu tradition has never extolled Dana to Kshatriyas, Vaishyas or Shudras. Since ancient times kings and noblemen have organised mass feeding ceremonies, distribution of grain and utilities as dana. Such giving away of wealth without expecting anything in return except blessings, was termed Dana. On any occasions like marriage, thread ceremony, opening ceremony, rites at death etc., we ask a Brahmin priest to officiate over the ceremony and in return for his services we offer him grain, cloth, gold and nowadays even cash. This offering is termed dakshina.

DANA AND DAKSHINA ARE GIVEN IN CASH AND KIND, BUT NEVER AS FREE PHYSICAL LABOUR

Traditionally dakshina was given, and had the nature of a payment in kind for services rendered by a priest. But nowadays with this offering being made also in terms of cash its nature as a payment becomes clear. When it is given in cash, it is in the denomination of eleven, twenty-one, fifty-one, one hundred and one-etc Although has the nature of a voluntary payment it is not looked upon as such and is considered to be an offering to an officiating prbst. In spite of the fine difference between the terms dana and dakshina, these terms are used interchangeably with the same connotation. But the common element in both dana and dakshina is that they are payments in cash or kind articles of use, such as, cloth, grain, utensils etc. Dana and dakshina are never offered in terms of physical labour in the form of social work. This is where they are different from the Christian concept of charity which involves social work and provision of social services. The custom of dana has always been part of Indian society and like Yagna, its origins seem to be in the collective hunting and common sharing way of life of life of the Vedic period.

THE HAVANA-A METHOD OF DISTRIBUTION OF THE COMMON TRIBAL WEALTH

The Rigveda mentions the incendiary wars that the different nomadic tribes fought in their search for better pastures and hunting grounds. The way of life both during peacetime and war was based on collective activity. In the tribal way of life even during peacetime the share (Havi) of every member of the tribe was distributed in a function called the Havana. Whatever was gathered, hunted or cooked was shared among all members of the tribe. The same principle was applied to the distribution of the booty of war. Articles that were plundered after a successful military campaign such as weapons, clothing and other articles of personal consumption were distributed amongst members. This distribution which was carried out in festive atmosphere after a successful campaign is perhaps the progenitor of our custom of offering dana especially on festival days and other auspicious occasions like the crowning of a king, royal birthdays, etc.

DANA ORIGINALLY CONNOTED DISTRIBUTION NOT CHARITY

The term dana is used in Vedic literature to describe the act of distributing such wealth among members of a tribe. The original connotation of the word dana was thus not just to give but to distribute. And in the tribal way of life this distribution did not have the nature of one person giving away his wealth to another but as distribution among members of a tribe (Gana) the captured property that was under common ownership of the tribe as a whole, but for its consumption it had to be allotted to individual members. That dana connoted only the distribution of proceeds of war is corroborated by the fact that it was not part of daily life and was held on select occasions that called for festivities. The practice of offering of dana especially on festive occasions survived the passing away of the tribal way of life of collective activity and common sharing.

But with the passage of time, the tribal way of life broke up and so did the institution of common property. With the division of labour according to different specialised occupations, war became a profession of a select body of men who constituted the army, the commander of which was the king. In India those of the warrior profession were known as Kshatriyas or Rajanyas and their chieftain was the Rajan.

The proceeds of war and later on the proceeds of tributes and taxes came into the hands of the warriors and the king. These proceeds were no longer looked upon as common property to which every member of society had an equal claim. It now came to be looked upon as Rajasva, literally meaning that which belongs to the king (Raja = king, sva = own or self).

But the practice of distributing wealth accumulated in the royal treasury and in the smaller private hoards of noblemen-warriors, among the kingdom's of populace continued. Religious festivals and public events such as coronation were occasions for distributing wealth and this distribution was looked upon as dana. This practice was normally respected but it was not a compulsory or obligatory requirement. If the king followed it he was looked upon as virtuous if not then he was an evil king.

DANA BECAME A TRANSFER OF WEALTH FROM THE NOBILITY TO THE CLERGY

But there was no formal law that made it imperative for the king and noblemen to observe this custom. Dana, thus acquired a voluntary character which was looked upon as an act of piety. With the passage of time Dana came to be bestowed mainly upon the clergy which in India was the Brahmin caste.

Dana which under the tribal set up was an instrument for equi-distribution of wealth became one of discriminatory enrichment of a section of the society. This was so as the practice of Dana gradually came to acquire the nature of transfer of wealth from the nobility to the clergy. The clergy by virtue of the psychological hold exercised on all sections of society enforced this transfer though not always successfully.

There did exist some justification for this transfer as it was normally the clergy which was a repository of knowledge as under the caste system only it had the right to acquire education. It was mainly the king and the nobility who could sustain the practice of dana although the trading community (Vaishyas) also joined their ranks of donees, when mercantile activity favoured them with disposable surplus wealth. In the later ages the observance of dana was ensured by fostering ideas that giving of dana results in Punya (God's blessings). Hence, it was the holy duty of everybody to offer dana this was especially so for the King and the nobility to give dana.

2

THE HINDU FESTIVALS

MAKAR SANKARANTI

The great diversity of Indian religious beliefs is projected through the various festivals that are celebrated in our country. They arise from the innate desire of man to seek diversion from humdrum activities and they help in symbolising, reflecting and enriching social life in a specific cultural setting.

The festival of Makar Sankrant traditionally coincides with the beginning of the Sun's northward journey (the *UTTARAYAN*) when it enters the sign of Makar (the *CAPRICORN*). It falls on the 14th of January every year according to the Solar Calendar. This day has a very special significance because the day and night on Makar Sankrant are of exactly of equal hours. This day is celebrated as a festival right from the times of the Aryans and is looked upon as the most auspicious day by the Hindus.

The evidence of this festival being lucky is found in our great epic Mahabharat wherein it is told that the great warrior-hero, Bhishma Pitamaha even after being wounded and lying on the bed of arrows, lingered on till Uttarayan set in, to breathe his last. It is believed that the person who dies on this auspicious day of Sankrant escapes the cycle of birth and re-birth and that his soul mingles with the Almighty.

This festival is celebrated differently in different parts of the country yet the use of til that is sesame is found everywhere. Til or sesame seed contain lot of oil and they therefore have a quality of softness in them. Therefore, firstly the use of til in sweets is good for health and secondly being soft their exchange means exchange of love and tender feelings.

In Maharashtra on the Sankranti day people exchange multi-coloured tilguds made from til (sesame seeds) and sugar and til-laddus made from til and jaggery. Til-polis are offered for lunch and these are specialities of Maharashtra. Maharashtrian women are proud of their excellence in preparing these delicacies. While exchanging tilguls as tokens of goodwill people greet each other saying - "til-gul ghya, god bola" meaning "accept these tilguls and speak sweet words". The underying thought in the exchange of tilguls is to forget the past ill-feelings and hostilities and resolve to speak sweetly and remain friends. This is a special day for the women in Maharashtra when married women are invited for a get-together called "Haldi-Kumkoo" and given gifts of any utensil, which the woman of the house purchases on that day.

In Gujarat Sankrant is observed more or less in the same manner as in Maharashtra but with a difference that in Gujarat there is a custom of giving gifts to relatives. The elders in the family give gifts to the younger members of the family. The Gujarati Pundits on this auspicious day grant scholarships to students for higher studies in astrology and philosophy. This festival thus help the maintenance of social relationships within the family, caste and community.

In Punjab where December and January are the coldest months of the year, huge bonfires are lit on the eve of Sankrant and which is celebrated as *"LOHARI"*. Sweets, sugarcane and rice are thrown in the bonfires, around which friends and relatives gather together. The following day, which is Sankrant is celebrated as *MAGHI.* The Punjabi's dance their famous Bhangra dance till they get exhausted. Then they sit down and eat the samptions food that is specially prepared for the occasion.

In Bundelkhand and Madhya Pradesh this festival of Sankrant is known by the name *"SUKARAT"* or *"SAKARAT"* and is celebrated with great pomp merriment accompanied by lot of sweets.

In South Sankrant is known by the name of *"PONGAL"*, which takes its name from the surging of rice boiled in a pot of milk, and this festival has more significance than even Diwali. It is very popular particularly amongst farmers. Rice and pulses cooked together in ghee and milk is offered to the family deity after the ritual worship. In essence in the South this Sankrant is a "Puja" (worship) for the Sun God.

In Uttar Pradesh, Sankrant is called *"KICHERI"*. Having bath on this day is regarded as most important. A mass of humanity can be seen bathing in the Sangam at Prayagraj where the rivers Ganga, Jamuna and Saraswathi flow together. At the confluence of these holy rivers every year Kumbh Mela is held for full one month.

In Bengal every year a Mela is held at Ganga Sagar where the river Ganga is believed to have dived into the nether region and vivified the ashes of the sixty thousand ancestors of King Bhagirath. This mela is attended by a large number of pilgrims from East India.

The tribals in our country start their New Year from the day of Sankrant by lighting bonfires, dancing and eating their particular dishes sitting together. The Bhuya tribals of Orissa have their Maghyatra in which small home-made articles are put for sale.

There is also a fair in the Western Ghats at a place called Shabari Mala, where the temple of the Community Goddess is decorated with dazzling lights. The Goddess is worshipped by touchables and untouchables both and the "bhog" to the Goddess is cooked in the touchables and untouchables both. These tribals participate in the Mela and enjoy all together as if they belong to one single family. May be therefore, the experts pine that this festival of Makar Sankrant comes to us from those olden times when the caste system did not exist in India as it emphasises or communal harmony.

Thus we see that this festival occupies a significant place in the cultural history of our country and symbolises the victory of ORDER over CHAOS and of Love over Hate.

These are specially prepared for the Sankrant festival because a mixture of til (sesame) and jaggery contribute to the health if eaten during cold season.

Sankranti means to go from one place to another place (to change direction). It also means one meets another. The time when the sun changes direction from one constellation (of the zodiac) to another is known as Sankranti.

Transition of the Sun from Sagittarius to Capricorn during the winter solstice in the northern hemisphere (Uttarayana) is known as Makar Sankranti.

Solar Year – Importance of the Sun: There are 12 signs of the zodiac. There are 12 Sankrantis as well. They are given names according to the position of the sun in relation to the signs of the zodiac. Each of the 12 Sankrantis has its relevant importance but two of these are most prominent.

These two are *Mesh* Sankranti and *Makar* Sankranti (Aries and Capricorn).The solar year commences when the sun is in Aries (the first sign of the zodiac). From the point of view of mathematical calculations, the solar year is more scientific than the lunar year. One lunar year has 354 days only and lunar days (or nights) increase or decrease according to the phases of the moon. Compare this to the solar year which has 365 ¼ days and remains the same. Many astrological books are based upon solar calculations. The sun is the most important and the most prominent of our stars and the undisputed lord of our planetary system. The sun always comes first. First day of the week commences with Sunday (Ravi).

Science attaches great importance to the sun. The sun is the inexhaustible storehouse and the source of light and energy. Without sunlight creatures and vegetation would cease to exist. People will lose their life sustaining vitality. Lack of nourishing substances would lead to the end of creation. This is why the sun's existence, movements and positions in the cosmos are so important and that is why the sun earns our respect, admiration and reverence.

The solar year commences when the sun is in Aries (the first sign of the zodiac). During this auspicious period, great deal of merits are acquired by performing Havan (Yajna or Sacred Fire ceremony), Japa (repetition of Mantra or God's name), Shraddha, Charity etc. Householders top up their grain jars and families start wedding preparations for their sons and daughters of marriageable age.

The second Sankranti of great importance is Makar. Transition of the Sun from Sagittarius to Capricorn during the winter solstice in the northern hemisphere (Uttarayana) is known as Makar sankranti. The sun and journeys northward. The days are gradually lengthening in the northern hemisphere.

Makar Sankranti is also known as KHICHADI (Indian dish made from rice and lentils) Sankranti because on this day the injunction to eat Khichadi, is generally observed by people. Seasonal crops become available. Ghee, and spices are used for making tasty nourishing Khichadi. Winter loosens its grip on shiver producing cold, admitting springtime that brings with it the chance for all round health improvement.

In addition to Khichadi, great importance is attached to the use of TIL (Sesame seeds) during Makar Sankranti. Therefore, this Sankranti is also called TIL Sankranti. People make Laddoos (round balls) from Til. Til oil is used for massaging.

Six types of usage of Til are described. Til is used for Bathing, for Massaging, for Havan (sacred fire ceremony), Tarpan with Til (oblations of water with Til), Til used as food, and Til is donated in charity.

It is said that Til emanates from Vishnu's body and that the above described usage wash away all kinds of sins. Sankranti period is held to be very auspicious and any good deeds during this time will produce merits. Gifts of clothing, blankets etc., on this day are productive of merits in both this life and in the next lifo.

Makar Sankranti is also celebrated with great enthusiasm as the Kite flying day.

At Sankranti time great importance is attached to Ganga snaan (bathing with waters of the river Ganges) and Surya Puja (worshipping the sun). Bathing, worshipping gods, Havan, Japa, Fasting and Charity; each of these are extremely holy deeds.

From Makar Sankranti onwards when the sun is travelling northwards, innumerable auspicious things start happening. Climate and atmosphere improve. Children born during this period are naturally progressive, well mannered, pleasant and of noble disposition. The Bhagavad Gita mentions the importance of the northern path of the sun at the time of death. This was the reason why Grandsire Bhishma, who was wounded in battle and in semi conscious state, while lying on the bed of arrows, chose to wait it out, awaiting the northward path of the sun, before choosing to die.

All such special reasons make the northward journey of the sun sacred and auspicious at Makar Sankranti.

This is the day when the sun begins its northward journey. It usually falls in the middle of January. For the people of the northern hemisphere, the northward path of the sun marks the period when the sun is getting closer and closer to them, when the days are getting longer, and it is becoming warmer and warmer.

To Hindus, the sun stands for knowledge, spiritual light and wisdom. Makara Shankranti signifies that we should turn away from the darkness of delusion in which we live, and begin to joyously let the light within us shine brighter and brighter. We should gradually begin to grow in purity, wisdom, and knowledge, even as the sun does from this day.

In fact, the sun itself stands for all the ideals of the Pongal festival. Its message is that of light, unity, equality and true selflessness. These are the ideals of Karma Yoga. Hence, the sun is the greatest Karma Yogi. Does it ask any reward for all that it gives to us? If it stops shedding its light, we are doomed to death. If we learn this one lesson from the sun, our lives will shine with divine lustre like that of the sun.

Makara Shankranti is called Pongal by the Tamilians, from whom it ushers in the New Year. The day begins with Surya Pongal or sun worship. The newly harvested corn is then cooked for the first time.

Joyous festivities mark the celebration in every home. Servants, farmers and the poor are fed and clothed, and given presents of money. On the next day, the cow, which is regarded as the symbol of the Holy Mother, is worshipped. Birds and animals are also fed. In this manner the devotee's heart gradually expands during the course of the celebrations. Love extends from the household to servants, the poor, the cow and all other living creatures. During this holy festival we learn to feel our oneness with all creation;

we learn to be unselfish and to tread the path of love, purity and forgiveness. We learn that our real wealth is the goodwill and friendship of those around us, the land on which our food grows, and the animals that help to make our work lighter.

Makar Sankranti marks the commencement of the sun's journey to the Northern Hemisphere (*Makara raasi*), signifying the onset of *Uttarayana Punyakalam*, and is a day of celebration all over the country. The day begins with people taking holy dips in the waters and worshipping the Sun.

Traditionally, this period is considered an auspicious time and the veteran Bhishma of Mahabharata chose to die during this period. Bhishma fell to the arrows of Arjuna. With his boon to choose the time of his death, he waited on a bed of arrows to depart from this world only during this period. It is believed that those who die in this period have no rebirth.

For the people in the Indo Gangetic plain, the day begins with taking dips in the Ganga and offering water to the Sun God. The dip is said to purify the self and bestow *punya*. Special *puja* is offered as a thanksgiving for good harvest. According to folklore, girls who take the holy dip get handsome husbands and boys get beautiful brides.

In Maharashtra, when two persons greet each other on this festive day, they exchange a few grains of multi-coloured sugar and fried *til* mixed with molasses and say *"til gud ghya, god god bolu"* (henceforth, let there be only friendship and good thoughts between us).

In Gujarat, the *pandits* consider Sankranti an auspicious day to grant scholarships and certificates of merit to students who have successfully completed their studies in philosophy. In a Hindu household, new utensils are purchased and used for the first time. Brightly coloured kites dot the skies on this day.

In Karnataka, men, women and children attired in colourful tunics visit friends and relatives and exchange pieces of sugarcane, a mixture of fried *til*, molasses, pieces of dry coconut, peanuts and fried gram. The significance of this exchange is that sweetness should prevail in all the dealings. As part of the festival, cows and bulls are given a wash and the horns are painted with bright colours and decorated with garland, and are taken in a procession in the village to the accompaniment of pipes and drums. In the night a bonfire is lit and the animals are made to jump over the fire.

It is a big event for the Tamils and the people of Andhra Pradesh. The Telugus like to call it *'Pedda Panduga'*, meaning big festival. The whole event lasts for four days, the first day *Bhogi*, the second day *Sankranti*, the third day *Kanuma* and the fourth day, *Mukkanuma*. One month preceding Sankranti is called *Dhanurmasam* and is also an auspicious period. People wake up early, take bath and go around the streets singing devotional songs. Houses are whitewashed and farmers clean their warehouses. Colourful *rangoli (muggulu)* are drawn in the front yards of every house during this month. These artistic floral designs are drawn on the floor with rice flour or fine powder from limestone. These patterns are decorated with marigold placed on cow dung balls. Colourfully dressed young girls go round them singing songs.

To know the other fabulous festivals of India better you may visit the following link:

According to the lunar calendar, the sun moves from the Tropic of Cancer to the Tropic of Capricorn, or from Dakshinayana to Uttarayana, in the month of Poush in mid-January.

This end of the winter solstice also coincides with the harvest season and cessation of the northeast monsoon in South India. The movement of the earth from one zodiac sign into another is called Sankranti, and is celebrated as Makar, or Uttarayana, Sankranti, or Lohri, in the North, and as Pongal in the South.

The word Pongal, in both Telugu and Tamil, signifies the boiling over of the rice in the cooking pot. Though little is known about the origin of Pongal, it is probably a Dravidian harvest festival that has survived for millennia. The Sankranti season ends with Ratha Saptami, the seventh day of the bright half of Magha, when the sun and his golden chariot are honoured. Pongal is a three-day festival. On the first day, Bhogi Pongal, celebrations are confined to the house. Evil spirits are driven out of the home and burned in bonfires, and the house is whitewashed.

The second day, Surya Pongal, honours the Sun god. Members of the family wear new clothes and cook - on a new stove and in new pots - a dish with the newly harvested rice, jaggery and moong dal. Sugarcane stalks characterise this festival, as do til, and sweets made from jaggery and peanuts. The third day is Maattu Pongal, honouring cattle. Cows and bullocks are washed, decorated, and worshipped for their role in ensuring a good harvest.

Punjab celebrates Lohri by feasting on sweets made of jaggery, peanuts and sesame seeds, and making a symbolic bonfire of the departing winter.

In the days leading up to Lohri, children visit homes of neighbours, sing traditional Lohri songs, and ask for coins and sweets in return. While being Indian in spirit, this custom is similar to the tradition of singing Christmas carols.

In Gujarat and other western states, people observe Uttarayana, when the winds change, by flying kites. The winter sky bursts into colour with thousands of paper kites. The festivities conclude with a winter feast.

In Maharashtra, people dress in new clothes and distribute sesame sweets. New brides are welcomed into the family with sugar ornaments and a turmeric-and-vermilion ceremony. In rural Maharashtra, feasts of the new harvest mark the festival.

Assam celebrates the paddy harvest in winter with Magha or Bhogali Bihu. Pavilions with thatched roofs come up in the villages and there is feasting in the night. The pavilions are set afire in the morning. The festivities continue for a week.

At Ganga Sagar, where the Ganga enters the sea, a grand fair is held.

The festival is also called Til Sankranti or Kichri Sankranti, after its main ingredient or preparation.

In Thanjavur, Madurai, and Thiruchirapalli, in Tamil Nadu, Pongal is marked by jallikattu, or bull fights. A money bag is tied to the horns of a bull, and the man who succeeds in tethering the beast to the tree gets the money and a prize.

PONGAL

Pongal is the first festival beginning off each new year in the Indian state of Tamil Nadu. As the dates for this festival are calculated by the solar calander (ie. Western), the dates of January 13-16 never change. Each day of this festival has a special significance, however, it is celebrated more grandly in the villages, while the city folk mainly celebrate on the second day only.

The first day of the festival is called *Bhogi*. On Bhogi all people clean out their homes from top to bottom, and collect all unwanted goods. In the evening, people will light bonfires and burn what can be burnt. In the village where I celebrated Pongal, the people lived in mud huts with thatched roves. The porches of these homes was fully covered by the thatch material, but somewhat elevated from the ground. This part of the home was taken apart and reconstructed on this day along with the front section of the walkway in front of their home. Both the porch and ground in front of their home was solid mud which had dried. So, to undo this, they put in water to soften it, and dug it out and rebuilt it. After rebuilding it, they took cow dung and added water to make a paste and spread this mixture evenly over the new fixtures to coat and sanitize them. This mixture was also spread on the floor of the hut, on which we slept at night. As they don't have beds, we slept on the floor of the mud hut with a mat between our bodies and the floor. Although, the mixture had been spread on the floor, it did not at all smell fowl in any way. In addition, the family I stayed with installed a new ceiling fan for Pongal.

The second day of the festival, Surya Pongal, is the day on which the celebrations actually begins, is the first day of the Tamil month Thai. On this day, Surya, the sun God is worshipped and women will wake early on this day to create elaborate kolum on the grounds in front of their doorway or home. Kolums are created with colored rice flour placed on the ground carefully by using one's hand. The picture shown to the right shows the beginnings of this. The women in the picture took several hours to finish that kolum. All people will wear their new dresses and use the new utensils or household items which replace the ones discarded the previous day. On this day the new rice is collected and cooked in pots until they over flow. It is this overflowing which means

Pongal. This overflowing of rice is a joyous occasion, and the children and adults as well will shout out 'Pongal-o Pongal!' Children will dance and make music to the tune of these words. As far as I know, the words have no real meaning but an expression of happiness that the new harvest is here and we should enjoy it! The rice is cooked and prepared as a dish called Pongal, which is rice with dhal and sugar.

This Pongalvariety is called *venpongal,* ven meaning white. Another variety is also prepared with dhal and jaggery (sweet), called *chakrai pongal,* chakrai meaning sweet. To accompany the venpongal, people eat brinjal (eggplant) sambar (stew), vadai, idli, and spicy accompaniments. This is one of my favorite meals!!

The third day is called *Mattu Pongal,* maatu meaning cattle. This day is devoted to paying homage to cattle. Cows and Bulls are decorated with paint and bells and people pray to them. In fact, in my Pongal experience, the cattle were decorated with bells on their neck, and kum placed on their head, and we (My friend, her family and I.) paid respect to them by bending down, like praying in temple, and touching their feet and foreheads, followed by an aarthi (showing fire to the object of praise) and offering the cattle prasadam (food offering, in this case, Pongal). In some villages in south India, there are bull fights of varying types. These are not so common as they once were, I understand.

The fourth day is termed as Kaanum Pongal. On this day, people travel to see other family members. As in the family I stayed, we traveled to another village to meet her family there. On this day, the younger members of the family pay homage to the elders, and the elders thank them by giving token money (like Rs. 10 or US 25 cents).

Another thing many do is leave food out on banana leaves for birds to take. I don't remember having done this, but I do know many South Indian people will take the first bit of rice cooked in any given day and set it outside for the crows to take, so this is not necessarily a habit only for Pongal. Some also go to temple, as shown in the photo. The photo is taken from the top of the staircase we climbed to get in the temple.

The great diversity of Indian religious beliefs and the varied cultured traditions of the different states are very interesting and this is seen in the festival of Pongal.

"May the pot of prosperity boil over

May the Pongal that we cook,

the fragrance of turmeric

the taste of sugarcane, ginger and honey

Bring the joy of Pongal into our homes

May the blessings of the Sun God flood our lives.

With many other verses like this the people of Tamil Nadu greet the great festival of Pongal celebrated all over the South as Makar Sankranti, in Tamil Nadu it has an additional significance as Pongal welcomes the occasion of the incoming harvest.

The Puranas, usually prolific in legends connected with festivals, have little to say about this Pongal festival. It is in all probability a Dravidian harvest festival that has survived the preponderant influence of the Indo-Aryan religion in the South.

There is a beautiful Tamil composition of the ancient Sangam period which was known for the ancient Tamil Academics. This charming composition describes the joy of a love-born young woman on the return of her husband from the battlefield. Her happiness is likened to the month before Pongal. When, with the end of rains, the "kaya" flowers blossom, the tender 'Konrai' flowers shower their golden polen on the ground, the white "kandal" flowers blossom, the tender 'Konrai' plant is in full bloom and with receding clouds the female and male deer are making love in the fields. This poem describes the mood of anticipation and excitement of the people in Tamil Nadu which gets its main rains from the north-eastern monsoon in October and November and the harvest is gathered in the period just preceding this Pongal festival.

This festival of Pongal falls in the month of January after the winter solstice and as such this Pongal festival marks the favourable course of the Sun. It is a three-day festival and the fourth day is a day for outdoors and excursions.

Pongal is a festival when god is praised with a simple faith and sincerity. Old vices are all washed out and all that is good is welcomed in this New year. This festival is of all living things, of man, his beast and his crop and of the birds that fly in the sky making man look up to the heaven in joy and thankfulness to God for everything that He gives to man specially peace and happiness and the feeling of brotherhood.

The astronomical significance of the festival is that it marks the beginning of Uttarayana, the Sun's movement northward for a six month period. In Hinduism, Uttarayana is considered auspicious, as opposed to Dakshinaayana, or the southern movement of the sun. All important events are scheduled during this period. Makara Sankranti refers to the event of the Sun entering the zodiac sign of Makara or Capricorn.

VASANT PANCHAMI

Vasant Panchami is the festival dedicated to Saraswati, the goddess of learning. (Deepavali is dedicated to Lakshmi, goddess of wealth, and Navaratri Durga is dedicated primarily to Kali, goddess of strength, might and power.)

Magh Sud 5 (5th day of the bright fortnight of the lunar month of Magh) is the day of Vasant Panchami. Hindus all over the world celebrate this festival with great enthusiasm. This Panchami is also known as Saraswati Day. It is believed that this day is Saraswati's birthday. Hindu temples are full of activities on this day.

Yellow colour is given special importance on this day. On Vasant Panchami, Saraswati is dressed in yellow garments and worshipped (with Puja, Havan etc.). Men and women try to wear yellow clothes on this day. Sweetmeats of yellowish hues are exchanged with relations and friends.

Some people feed Brahmanas on this day. Pitri-Tarpan (ancestor worship) is done on this day. The god of love (Kamdev) is also worshipped on this day.

Children are taught their first words on this day (as an auspicious beginning to learning). Schools, colleges etc., (places of learning) organise special worship of Saraswati. Pandit Madan

Mohan Malviya laid the foundations of Kashi Hindu Vishwa Vidyalaya on Vasant Panchami. This has become a world famous top class academic institution. Hinduism has taken into account special significance of seasons and interwoven that with religious festivals e.g., Makar Sankranti, Vasant Panchami. People generally feel inclined to worship the presiding deity of the family (Ishta Devata or Devi) according to the individual's faith and desires. Also, people generally tend to accumulate wealth and power. During the Kala Yuga (present age), the pursuit of money (wealth, power, name and fame) is everything to most people. Money is accorded god-like status.

But men of principle (men who can discriminate) worship goddess Saraswati for spiritual enlightenment. In their opinion, there can be no comparison between the king and the learned (spiritually advanced). The king is honoured within his kingdom, whereas the learned is respected (or worshipped) everywhere. Saintly people and people inclined towards spiritual progress attach great importance to the worship of goddess Saraswati.

The vehicle assigned to each of the three goddesses also symbolically represent their special powers. The white swan of Saraswati is symbolising Sattwa Guna (purity and discrimination). The owl of Lakshmi and the lion or tiger of Durga symbolise the other two gunas (Rajas and Tamas).

The first faint signals of the forthcoming festival of Holi manifest at Vasant Panchami. Seasons undergo change. The coming of springtime is heralded. Trees are displaying new shoots. New life is evident in the woods and fields. Nature decorates Mango trees with new blossoms. Wheat and other crops enliven with evidence of new life.

Vasant Panchami is a festival full of religious, seasonal and social significance and is celebrated by Hindus all over the world with verve and new sense of optimism.

Vasant means, "the spring season". This is the great spring festival, falling on the fifth day of the month of Magh, the first day of spring.

On this day everyone wears a yellow cloth. It represents the ripening of the spring crops. Even the food is coloured yellow by using saffron. Spiritually, the yellow colour is a sign of prosperity; it is the colour of love.

On this day we offer special worship to the sun god, to Mother Ganga (the deity of the sacred river Ganges), and Mother Earth. They provide us the means of acquiring food and all that we need to keep alive. We express our gratitude to them by worshipping them. Hindus are ever mindful of the debt they owe to all nature. Worship of nature is extremely important to them.

Basant Panchami heralds the beginning of spring. Cool lingering breeze replaces the cold harsh winter and there is a touch of rejuvenation and joy in the air. The buds of leaves and flowers come into full bloom. Girls in different shades of yellow dresses enhance the beauty of nature on the day of Basant Panchami. Kite flying, a popular sport in India, is associated with the Basant Panchami day. It is a day for the students – no studies, only merry making.

Basant means spring and Panchami is the fifth day of the fortnight of waxing moon (*Shukla Paksha*) in the month of January-February of English calendar (*Magh*). This year (2001), the Basant Panchami falls on the 29th of January.

The day of Basant Panchami is dedicated to Goddess Sarasvati. It is not a national holiday in India but the schools are closed and the students participate in decoration and arrangement of the worship place. A few weeks before the celebration, schools become active in organizing various annual competitions of music, debate, sports and other activities. Prizes are distributed on the day of Basant Panchami. Many schools organize cultural activities in the evening of the Saraswati Puja day when parents and other community members attend the functions to encourage the children.

Sarasvati is the goddess of learning. Sarasvati bestows the greatest wealth to humanity, the wealth of knowledge. In the Vedas the prayer for Sarasvati depicts her as a white lady in white dress bedecked with white flowers and white pearls, sitting on a white lotus, which is blooming in a wide stretch of water. She holds Veena, a string-instrument, like Sitar, for playing music. The prayer finally concludes, "Oh Mother Sarasvati remove the darkness (ignorance) of my mind and bless me with the eternal knowledge."

The Vedas describe Sarasvati as a water deity, goddess of a river of the same name. According to popular belief Sarasvati, originating from the Himalayas, flowed southeast, ultimately meeting the Ganges at Prayag, near the confluence of Yamuna. Hence the place is called *Triveni*. In due time this course of water petered away.

The mythological history of Sarasvati associates her with the holy rituals performed on the banks of the river Sarasvati. She is worshipped as a goddess of speech, attributed to the formation of Vach (words), invention of Sanskrit language and composition of hymns.

In the United States, the Bengali community observes Basant Panchami in the form of community worship of goddess Sarasvati. It is usually organized on the following weekend. Conservative Indians, however, prefer to celebrate it on the day of Panchami. The commue cultural activities and the participation of kids is encouraged.

Vasant Panchami heralds the advent of spring. This festival that marks the first day of spring. Vasanta means the spring. The fields are mustard yellow with the ripening of crops. Yellow is of auspicious colour - a colour of sprituality. Vasant Panchami falls on the fifth day, of Magh (January-February) Shukla or the bright of lunar.

Saraswati is the consort of Lord Brahma and is the Goddess of Wisdom and Knowledge. She is the personification of knowledge - arts, science, crafts. She represents Shakti, creativity and inspiration and presents herself when the weather is complacement and Nature is in its full grandeur. It is a season of inspiration and passion.

On Vasant Panchami, Saraswati is worshipped and in Bengal it is called the Saraswati Puja. They worship her with flowers, specially with basaka (justicia gendarussa), and decorations are made chiefly with 'Ganda' (marigold_, the yellow coloured flower to represent the season - Vasanta. All ladies attire themselves in yellow and worship her. She is generally represented sitting cross-legged on a lotus or a water-lilly holding Vina. Her vehicle is swan in Bengal and peacock in some regions.

Goddess Saraswati being the embodiment of intellect and wisdom is depicted as pure white in colouris knowledge is in itself the antithesis of the darkness of ignorance. The Padmapurana describes Goddess Saraswati being seated on a white Lotus clad in a spotless white apparel with a necklace of white beads, decked with white flowers and holding the Vina. She is sometimes described to have four hands holding Vina, aksamala (rosary) and Pushtaka (book). Saraswati is extolled by the Gandharvas, worshipped by both Devas and Asuras and adored by Munis and Rishis. She is the embodiment of universal knowledge. It seems, Goddess Saraswati has been compared by Sir William Jones to the unarmed Minerva, the Goddess of Wisdom of the Greeks and Romans. Raraswati is also compared to their nine Muses.

Saraswati literally means 'the flowing one'. In Rigveda it is said she represents a river and the deity presiding over it. In the later mythology, Saraswati was identified with Vach or Speech. The 'flowing one' in allegorical sense may mean speech also; perfect speech which denotes intelligence. On this Vasant Panchami day, Brahma is said to have created Saraswati and infused speech into her and bestowed the Vina in her hands. She was thus named as 'Veena Vandini (Vina player) and 'Vani Dayyani recipient of speech). As the spouse of Brahma and the goddess of wisdom and eloquence, She is known by various names such as Vinapani (due to holding the Vina), Sharada (giver of essence), Vagisvari (mistress of speech), Brahmi (wife of Brahma), Mahavidya (knowledge supreme) and so on.

In the Maratha countries, Goddess Saraswati is sometimes called the wife of Ganesh and sometimes his attendant. At the name-giving ceremony in marriage, if a man's name, for instance, is Ganesha, his wife is named Saraswati, just as a Ramachandra's wife is named Sita, or a Krishna's wife is named, after his spouse Rukmini.

Vasant Panchami is also known as Shri Panchami. As Saraswati Puja, it is observed religiously almost in all parts of India expecially in Bengal. Goddess Saraswati being pure and white and representing learning, no animal sacrifice is made to her. Idols of Saraswati are brought and worshipped.

Floral offerings are made in a big scale. Books, articles, instruments of music and arts are placed before her. In the evening after the Puja is over, the idol is immersed in the sea with serenity unlike other major festivals. In all educational institutions of music, arts and science, Saraswati Puja is observed with great reverence. Legend has it that on this day Lord Shiva burnt the God of Love, Cupid of Kamadev. Lord Shiva was lost in Samadhi and to break his Samadhi into impassion him to beget a son powerful enough to kill the demon Tarakasur, Gods send Cupid the God of Love. Cupid or Kamadev discharges an arrow at Lord Shiva from behind a tree. But, Shiva gets terribly angry and reduces Cupid or Kamadev to ashes with his third eye. The Festival of Vasant Panchami is observed on a grand scale in Punjab and the North when the mustard crop is ripe. They cook yellow rice and also wear yellow garments. Saraswati Puja is also performed during the Navaratri or Dussehra.

Hinduism is a way of life rather than a religion, demure to the special significance of seasons in our lives through religious festivals. Vasant Panchami is one of them. Vasant Panchami is referred to as the spring festival, and signifies the beginning of Vasant Ritu (spring season). Magh Sud 5 (5th day of the bright fortnight of the lunar month of Magh) is the day of Vasant Panchami. It is also called as Shree Panchami and Saraswati Puja is also celebrated on the same day.

On this day Goddess Saraswati is worshipped as the Goddess of Learning, the deity of Gayatri, the fountain of fine arts and science, and the symbol of supreme vedantic knowledge. Religious paintings depict each of these goddess alighted on a vehicle that symbolizes their special power. The white swan of Saraswati symbolizing Satwa Guna (purity and discrimination), the lotus of Lakshmi the Rajas Guna and the tiger of Durga the Tamas Guna. Saraswati is shown possessing four hands and plays "Veena", an Indian string musical instrument. Vasant Panchami is also known as Saraswati Day and commemorates the birth of goddess Saraswati. Hindu temples throng with people and are abuzz with prayers and rituals. The name itself signifies the festival BASANT means SPRING and PANCHAMI means FIFTH i.e. The fifth day of Spring. It Falls on Panchami of the Sukal Paksh (Waxing moon) in the month of February/March.

Vasant Panchami heralds the spring season. It is one of the first festivals of the year and is celebrated all over India. It is hence celebrated with gaiety and festivity to mark the end of the winter. The festive colour yellow, symbolic of spring, plays an important part of this day. People wear yellow clothes, offer yellow flowers in worship and put a yellow, turmeric tilak on their forehead. They visit temples and offer prayers to various gods. At home, kesar halva, also yellow in colour, is prepared. On Vasant Panchami, people also worship Saraswati. In fact, in Bengal the day is more popularly known as Saraswati Puja. No authentic explanation exists as to why this day has been chosen for Saraswati. Some believed it to be the birthday of Saraswati. Others believe that on this day the goddess came down to earth, along with Durga to drive away the ignorance that Mahishasura was nurturing within him. In a wider sense though, this is the end of winter, symbolic of darkness and ignorance and the beginning of spring, symbolic of knowledge. By making Saraswati, the goddess of learning and wisdom, (the consort of Brahma, the creator) the progenitors apparently sought to link creation or origin with learning and knowledge.

MAHA-SHIVRATRI

Maha Shivratri is celebrated throughout the country; it is particularly popular in Uttar Pradesh. Maha Shivratri falls on the 13th (or 14th) day of the dark half of 'Phalgun' (February-March). The name means "the night of Shiva". The ceremonies take place chiefly at night. This is a festival observed in honour of Lord Shiva and it is believed that on this day Lord Shiva was married to Parvati. On this festival people worship 'Shiva - the Destroyer'. This night marks the night when Lord Shiva danced the 'Tandav'. In Andhra Pradesh, pilgrims throng the Sri Kalahasteshwara Temple at Kalahasti and the Bharamarambha Malikarjunaswamy Temple at Srisailam. About *The Lord Shiva* - the word meaning auspicious - is one of the Hindu Trinity, comprising of Lord

Brahma, the creator, Lord Vishnu, the preserver and Lord Shiva or Mahesh, the Destroyer and Re-Producer of life. Shiva is known by many names like "Shankar", "Mahesh", "Bholenath", "Neelakanth", "Shambhu Kailasheshwar", "Umanath", "Nataraj" and others.

For few people, Shiva is "Paramatman", "Brahman", the Absolute, but many more prefer to see Shiva as a personal God given to compassion for his worshippers, and the dispenser of both spiritual and material blessings. Related to the Absolute concept is Shiva as "Yoganath" meaning the Lord of Yoga, wherein he becomes teacher, path and goal. As such he is the "Adi Guru" or the Highest Guru of 'Sannyasins' who have renounced the world to attain the Absolute. He is the most sought-after deity amongst the Hindus and they pray to him as the god of immense large-heartedness who they believe grants all their wishes. Around him are weaved many interesting stories that reveal His magnanimous heart. Not only this, but these stories and legends also enrich the Indian culture and art. Time is invisible and formless.

Therefore Mahakal Shiva, as per the Vedas, manifested himself as "LINGUM" to make mankind aware of the presence of Eternal Time. That day when Shiva manifested himself in the form of "Lingum" was the fourth day of the dark night in the month of 'Magha' i.e. February-March. Maha Shivratri continues to be celebrated forever and ever. The Story Of King Chitrabhanu In the Shanti Parva of the Mahabharata, Bhishma, whilst resting on the bed of arrows and discoursing on Dharma, refers to the observance of Maha Shivaratri by King Chitrabhanu. The story goes as follows - Once upon a time King Chitrabhanu of the Ikshvaku dynasty, who ruled over the whole of Jambudvipa, was observing a fast with his wife, it being the day of Maha Shivaratri. The sage Ashtavakra came on a visit to the court of the king. The sag asked the king the purpose of his observing the past. King Chitrabhanu explained that he had the gift of remembering the incidents of his previous birth. The king said to the sage that in his previous he was a hunter in Varanasi and his name was Suswara. His only livelihood was to kill and sell birds and animals. One day while roaming through forests in search of animals he was overtaken by the darkness of night. Unable to return home, he climbed a tree for shelter. It happened to be a Bael tree. He had shot a deer that day but had no time to take it home. So he bundled it up and tied it to a branch on the tree. As hunger and thirst tormented him, he was kept awake throughout the night. He shed profuse tears when he thought of his poor wife and children who were starving and anxiously waiting for his return. To pass away the time that night he engaged himself in plucking the Bael leaves and dropping them down onto the ground.

The next day he returned home and sold the deer and then bought some food for himself and his family. The moment he was about to break his fast a stranger came to him, begging for food. He served the food first to stranger and then had his own. At the time of his death, he saw two messengers of Lord Shiva. They were sent down to conduct his soul to the abode of Lord Shiva. He learnt then for the first time of the great merit he had earned by the unconscious worship of Lord Shiva during the night of Shivaratri.

The messengers told him that there was a Lingam at the bottom of the tree. The leaves I dropped fell on the Lingam. His tears, which had shed out of pure sorrow for his family, fell onto the Lingam and washed it and he had fasted all day and all night. Thus, he unconsciously worshiped the Lord. As the conclusion of the tale the King said that he lived in the abode of the Lord and enjoyed divine bliss for long ages and now he has reborn as Chitrabhanu. People observe a strict fast on this day. Some devotees do not even take a drop of water and they keep vigil all night. The Shiva Lingam is worshipped throughout the night by washing it every three hours with milk, curd, honey, rose water, etc., whilst the chanting of the Mantra "Om Namah Shivaya" continues. Offerings of Bael leaves are made to the Lingam as Bael leaves are considered very sacred and it is said that Goddess Lakshmi resides in them. Hymns in praise of Lord Shiva, such as the "Shiva Mahimna Stotra" of Pushpadanta or Ravana's "Shiva Tandava Stotra" are sung with great fervor and devotion. People repeat the 'Panchakshara' Mantra, "Om Namah Shivaya". He, who utters the names of Shiva during Shivratri, with perfect devotion and concentration, is freed from all sins. He reaches the abode of Shiva and lives there happily. He is liberated from the wheel of births and deaths. Many pilgrims dock to the places where there are Shiva temples.

On the day of Shivratri, the lingam is bathed with the five sacred offerings of a cow, called the panchagavya - milk, sour milk, urine, butter and dung. Thereafter the five foods of immortality - milk, clarified butter, curd, honey and sugar - are placed before the lingam. Dhatura and jati, though poisonous fruits, are believed to be sacred to Shiva and thus offered at his temple. Eleven is considered to be the sacred number of the Lord. Devotees keep a fast (vrat) on Shivratri and observe strict rules, for vardan (boon). Special celebration are held at important Shiva temples at Chidambaram, Kalahasi Khajuraho and Varanasi. Worship of Shiva is to release the worship perform the cycle of birth and rebirth. In Kashmir, the festival is held for 15 days; the thirteenth day is observed as Hearth, a day of fast followed by a family feast.

During the samudra manthan by the gods and demons, haalaa-hala, a poison came out of the ocean. It was so toxic, that it effects would have wiped out the entire creation. At this juncture, as per the advice of Vishnu, gods approached Mahadev and prayed him to protect life by consuming this poison. Pleased with their prayers, out of compassion for living beings, Lord Shiva drank this poison and held it in his throat by binding it with a snake. The throat became blue due to the poison (Thus Lord Shiva is also know as Neelakantha) and Shiva remained unharmed. The doctors advised gods to keep Lord Shiva awake during the night as part of the therapy. To amuse Shiva and to keep him awake, the gods took turn performing various dances and playing music. A vigil was thus kept by the gods in contemplation of Shiva. As the day broke out, Shiva, pleased with their devotion blessed them all. Since then, on this day and night - devotees fast, keep vigil, sing glories of Lord and meditate.

After creation was complete, Parvati asked Shiva of which rituals pleased him the most. The Lord replied that the 14th night of the new moon, during the month of Phalgun, is my most favourite day. It is known as Shivaratri. Parvati repeated these words to her friends, from whom the word spread over all creation.

Once upon a time, a hunter worshipped Lord Shiva unknowingly on Shivaratri. He did this by dropping bheel leaves on a shiva linga at the base of a bheel tree from its branches where he was hiding and fasting all night. For this he was forgiven of all his sins. This forms the basis behind the offerings of bheel to the Lord on Shivaratri.

In the Shanti Parva of the Mahabharata, Bhishma, whilst resting on the bed of arrows and discoursing on Dharma, refers to the observance of Maha Shivaratri by King Chitrabhanu. The story goes as follows:

Once upon a time King Chitrabhanu of the Ikshvaku dynasty, who ruled over the whole of Jambudvipa, was observing a fast with his wife, it being the day of Maha Shivaratri. The sage Ashtavakra came on a visit to the court of the king.

The sage asked the king the purpose of his observing the past. King Chitrabhanu explained that he had the gift of remembering the incidents of his previous birth.

The king said to the sage that in his previous he was a hunter in Varanasi and his name was Suswara. His only livelihood was to kill and sell birds and animals. One day while roaming through forests in search of animals he was overtaken by the darkness of night. Unable to return home, he climbed a tree for shelter. It happened to be a Bael tree. He had shot a deer that day but had no time to take it home. So he bundled it up and tied it to a branch on the tree. As hunger and thirst tormented him, he was kept awake throughout the night. He shed profuse tears when he thought of his poor wife and children who were starving and anxiously waiting for his return. To pass away the time that night he engaged himself in plucking the Bael leaves and dropping them down onto the ground.

The next day he returned home and sold the deer and then bought some food for himself and his family. The moment he was about to break his fast a stranger came to him, begging for food. He served the food first to stranger and then had his own.

At the time of his death, he saw two messengers of Lord Shiva. They were sent down to conduct his soul to the abode of Lord Shiva. He learnt then for the first time of the great merit he had earned by the unconscious worship of Lord Shiva during the night of Shivaratri. The messengers told him that there was a Lingam at the bottom of the tree. The leaves he dropped fell on the Lingam. His tears, which had shed out of pure sorrow for his family, fell onto the Lingam and washed it and he had fasted all day and all night. Thus, he unconsciously worshiped the Lord.

As the conclusion of the tale the King said that he lived in the abode of the Lord and enjoyed divine bliss for long ages and now he has reborn as Chitrabhanu.

Maha Shivratri, the night of the worship of Shiva, occurs on the 14th night of the new moon during the dark half of the month of Phalguna (Feb / March) when Hindus offer special prayer to the lord of destruction.

Here're Three Reasons to Celebrate Shivratri:

1. The absolute formless God, Sadashiv appeared in the form of "Lingodbhav Moorti" exactly at midnight on Maha Shivratri. That is why all Shiv devotees keep vigil during the night of Shivratri and do "Shivlingam abhishekham" (coronation of the phallic idol) at midnight.
2. Lord Shiva was married to Devi Parvati on Shivratri. Remember Shiva minus Parvati is pure Nirgun Brahman. With his illusive power, (Maya, Parvati) He becomes the "Sagun Brahman" for the purpose of the pious devotion of his devotees.
3. It is also believed that on Shivratri, Lord Shiva became Neelkantham by swallowing the deadly poison that came up from the ocean during the churning of "Kshir Sagar". The poison was so deadly that even a drop in His stomach, which represents the universe, would have annihilated the entire world. Hence, He held it in His neck, which turned blue due to the effect of poison. Shivratri is therefore also a day of thanksgiving to the Lord for protecting us from annihilation.

The 14th shloka of *Shivmahimna Stotra* says: "O three eyed Lord, when the poison came up through the churning of the Ocean by the gods and demons, they were all aghast with fear as if the untimely end of all creation was imminent. In your kindness, you drank all the poison that still makes your throat blue. O Lord, even this blue mark does but increase your glory. What is apparently a blemish becomes an ornament in one intent on ridding the world of fear.

Kashmiri Pandits used to clebrate Shivratri festival over a period of 23 days. First six days (hurye okdoh to hurye shayam) were devoted to cleaning of the house and buying puja articles. Next 2-3 days were the days for devotional prayers. Dyara daham was designated for giving presents to married daughters and newly weds. Gadkah and Vager bah were special days for the worship of Bhairavas. Herath truvah is the day for Shiva worship. Herath Kharch (gift of money) is given by the eldest person to all members of the family on the following day. Herath truvah is the day for lord Shiva's worship. On Doon mavas, the prasad of walnuts and rice cakes (tomala-chuut) are distributed, in past, this often continued until Tila ashtami. The latter day also marks the end of winter, and is celebrated by burning kangris and singing the chorus of ja-tun-]tn'. On the social side, there used to be great joy all around. People wore new and their nicest clothes, and families would sit together and enjoy the game with sea shells.

Since a number of us have migrated to far off places, all over the world, it is rather difficult to perform the Vatak-puja in the traditional way. However, we need to maintain the spirit of this, the most important festival of ours. Jotshi Prem Nath Shastriji has recently produced an audio tape for a relatively simple Vatak-puja together with a Mahimna Stotram. Offering and eating meat and fish on Shivratri is strictly a Kashmiri Pandit ritual, probably to please 'Bhairavas'. However, there were people like Gurtus and Razdans, who observed strict vegetarinism during the Shivratri festival. Most of us have given up the tradition of offering and eating meat on Shivratri day.

One other practice was the celebration of salam on the day following Shivratri. Muslim neighbors and friends used to visit us and wish happy Shivratri. People would also invite their relatives and friends for a sumptous dinner. Since for us the significance of this day is gone, we can either do away with it or at least call it by a different name. Bhagwan Shiva is portrayed with ash on his forehead, and devotees of Lord Shiva frequently apply sacred ash to various parts of their body. This symbolizes two things. Everything that today has a form on the Earth once was ash in the ground and again will be reduced to nothing but ash. Therefore, the ash serves to remind us that all that we are, all that we do, all that we earn and acquire will only be reduced to ash one day, and therefore we should live our lives dedicated to God and dedicated to serving humanity, rather than to the accumulation of temporary possessions and comfort. When we apply the sacred ash or see it, we are reminded "Ah yes, it is only by the grace of Lord Shiva that I am still here today, and that I have not yet been turned to ash. It is His grace that my home, my family and my possessions are still with me and that they have not become ash. Therefore, I should remember Him, pray to Him and devote myself to Him."

The stories and the messages of Bhagwan Shiva are innumerable; however, one of the most important is the story of how He – for the sake of humanity – swallowed the poison which emerged from the ocean.

The story says that the devas and their brothers, the demons, were churning the ocean in search of the pot of the nectar of immortality. However, after a great deal of effort, what emerged was not nectar, but poison!! This happens frequently in life as well. When we embark upon a divine plan or when we undertake a noble challenge, frequently before the success comes, before our effort bears fruit, we face failure or condemnation or seemingly insurmountable hurdles. Yet, we must never give up.

The devas and demons knew that in order to continue churning, and ultimately to unearth the Divine nectar, they could not simply toss the poison aside. Someone had to drink it. But, naturally, no one was willing to drink the poison. Everyone had some excuse for why he or she was too valuable to be sacrificed. Finally, Bhagwan Shiva came forward, very calmly and with serene poise. He said "I will drink the poison if it will preserve peace in the family and enable my brothers and sisters to attain the nectar of immortality." After drinking the poison, and thereby enabling the churning to continue, Bhagwan Shiva held the poison in his throat – hence the name Neelkanth which means Blue Throat – and sat peacefully in meditation for eternity.

In our lives, in our families, so much poison emerges – between parents and children, between husband and wife, between in-laws. We wait and wait for the divine nectar to emerge, but it seems that only poison comes. So many times people come to me, complaining, "But why should I always be the one to compromise? Why should I always be the one to sacrifice? Why should I always say I'm sorry? It's not fair!"

The night of Shivratri is especially auspicious for winning this same battle within ourselves – the battle between good and evil, between right and wrong, between poison and nectar, between death and immortality. Let us use our puja, our prayers, our meditations on this night to pray for divine intervention so that within ourselves the good might vanquish the evil, the nectar within us might emerge, rather than poison, and that we too may be carried from death to immortality.

Maha Shivratri, as the name suggests, is in the honour of Lord Shiva, the third lord of the Trinity (Bramha— the creator, Vishnu— the preserver and Shiva– the destroyer).

As the legend goes, once Lord Vishnu and Lord Bramha argued over each other's prowess. However, Lord Shiva challenged both of them. He appeared as a flaming linga and challenged the duo to measure the gigantic linga (phallic symbol of Lord Shiva). Lord Bramha, who took the form of a swan, and Lord Vishnu who became a boar and went to Netherland, were both unable to measure the Shivlinga. Then Lord Shiva came out of the linga and declared himself the most powerful. Maha Shivratri therefore means the grand night of Shiva. The devotees of Shiva fast during this day and pray to the lord throughout the night. This legend goes to prove the supremacy of Mahadev over other Hindu Gods.

Lord Shiva's first wife was Sati. Sati's father, King Daksha, opposed her marriage with Shiva. At a yagnya (holy sacrifice) the king ignored Shiva's presence and thereby insulted the latter publicly. Sati was so angered by this that she jumped into the sacrificial fire and ended her life. Lord Shiva unleashed his fury at the death of his wife by performing the violent dance, Taandav. He wiped out Daksha's kingdom, undertook rigorous penance and retired to the Himalayas. The Gods, who feared that the severity of Shiva's penance might bring an end to the world, revived Sati in the new avatar of Parvati. Shiva-Parvati married and this reunion is celebrated on Maha Shivratri.

Lord Shiva is offered special food, made from fruits of the season, root vegetables and coconuts, during ritual worship. The Shivling (phallic symbol of the Lord) is bathed with the panchagavya (five sacred offerings of a cow including milk, sour milk, urine, butter and dung). Thereafter, milk, butter, curd, sugar and honey, (believed to be the foods granting immortality), are offered. Dhatura and jati, though poisonous fruits, are sacred to Shiva and therefore placed in front of him.

Unmarried girls are supposed to perform the Maha Shivratri pooja with great faith. They pray to the lord for eligible husbands. Moreover, married women pray to Lord Shiva for marital bliss and a long prosperous married life

Legend has it that one night Lord Shiva's devotee, a hunter, lost his way in the forest. As he was wandering in the night, he heard a tiger growl. The frightened man scurried up the nearest tree that was a Bel tree. He spent the night up there, out of the reach of tigers. To keep himself awake, he kept plucking and dropping Bel leaves while chanting the name of Lord Shiva. The next morning, when the devotee climbed down, he had unknowingly dropped thousands of leaves on a Shiva linga. The night-long worship pleased Lord Shiva who saved the hunter from the clutches of a tiger. This legend is recited on every Maha Shivratri.

HOLI

The festival of Holi is celebrated on the day after the full moon in early March every year. Originally a festival to celebrate good harvests and fertility of the land, Holi is now a symbolic commemoration of a legend from Hindu Mythology. The story centres around an arrogant king who resents his son Prahlada worshipping Lord Vishnu. He attempts to kill his son but fails each time. Finally, the king's sister Holika who is said to be immune to burning, sits with the boy in a huge fire. However, the prince Prahlada emerges unscathed, while his aunt burns to death. Holi commemorates this event from mythology, and huge bonfires are burnt on the eve of Holi as its symbolic representation.

This exuberant festival is also associated with the immortal love of Krishna and Radha, and hence, Holi is spread over 16 days in Vrindavan as well as Mathura - the two cities with which Lord Krishna shared a deep affiliation. Apart from the usual fun with coloured powder and water, Holi is marked by vibrant processions which are accompanied by folk songs, dances and a general sense of abandoned vitality.

Today Holi is an excuse for Indians to shed inhibitions and caste differences for a day of spring fever and Big Fun. Teenagers spend the day flirting and misbehaving in the streets, adults extend the hand of peace, and everyone chases everyone else around, throwing brightly colored powder (gulal) and water over each other.

The festival's preamble begins on the night of the full moon. Bonfires are lit on street corners to cleanse the air of evil spirits and bad vibes, and to symbolize the destruction of the wicked Holika, for whom the festival was named. The following morning, the streets fill with people running, shouting, giggling and splashing. Marijuana-based bhang and thandai add to the uninhibited atmosphere.

Promptly at noon, the craziness comes to an end and everyone heads to either the river or the bathtub, then inside to relax the day away and partake of candies. In the afternoon an exhausted and contented silence falls over India. Although Holi is observed all over the north, it's celebrated with special joy and zest at Mathura, Vrindavan, Nandgaon, and Barsnar. These towns once housed the divine Krishna.

Each area celebrates Holi differently; the Bhil tribesmen of western Madhya Pradesh, who've retained many of their pre-

Hindu customs, celebrate Holi in a unique way. In rural Maharashtra State, where the festival is known as *Rangapanchami* it is celebrated with dancing and singing. In the towns of Rajasthan— especially Jaisalmer — the music's great, and clouds of pink, green, and turquoise powder fill the air. The grounds of Jaisalmer's Mandir Palace are turned into chaos, with dances, folk songs, and colored-powder confusion.

Holi or Holika, also called holikotsava, is an extremely popular festival observed throughout the country (India). It is especially marked by unmixed gaiety and frolics and is common to all sections of the people.

This festival is very ancient. Known originally as *'Holika'* it has been mentioned in very early religious works such as Jaimini's Purvamimamsa-sutras and Kathaka-grhya-sutras. It must have therefore existed several centuries before Christ. It was at first actually a special rite performed by married women for the happiness and well-being of their families and the full moon (Raka) was the deity worshipped by them.

There are two ways of reckoning a lunar month: *Purnimanta* and *Amanta*. In the former, the first day starts after the full moon; and in the latter, after the new moon. Though the latter reckoning is more common now, the former was very much in vogue in the earlier days. According to this purnimanta reckoning, Phalguna purnima was the last day of the year and the new year heralding the Vasanta-ritu (with spring starting from next day). Thus the full moon festival of Holika gradually became a festival of merrymaking, announcing the commencement of the spring season. This perhaps explains the other names of this festival: Vasanta-Mahotsava and Kama-Mahotsava.

According to the stories in the Puranas and various local legends, this day is important for three reasons.

- It was on this day that Lord Siva opened his third eye and reduced Kamadeva (the god of love, Cupid or Eros) to ashes.
- It was on this day that Holika, the sister of the demon king Hiranyakasyapu, who tried to kill the child devotee Prahlad by taking him on her lap and sitting on a pyre of wood

which was set ablaze. Holika was burnt to ashes while Prahlad remained unscathed!

- It was again on this day that an ogress called Dhundhi, who was troubling the children in the kingdom of Prthu (or Raghu) was made to run away for life, by the shouts and pranks of the mischievous boys. Though she had secured several boons that made her almost invincible, this - noise, shouts, abuses and pranks of boys - was a chink in her armour due to a curse of Lord Siva. The day itself came to be called 'Adada' or 'Holika' since then.

There are practically no religious observances for this day like fasting or worship. Generally a log of wood will be kept in a prominent public place on the Vasantapanchami day (Magha Sukla Panchami), almost 40 days before the Holi Festival. An image of Holika with child Prahlada in her lap is also kept on the log. Holika's image is made of combustible materials whereas Prahlada's image is made of non-combustible ones. People go on throwing twigs of trees and any combustible material they can spare, on to that log which gradually grows into a sizable heap. On the night of Phalguna Purnima, it is set alight in a simple ceremony with the Raksoghna Mantras of the Rgveda (4.4.1-15; 10.87.1-25 and so on) being sometimes chanted to ward off all evil spirits. (Coconuts and coins are thrown into this bonfire).The next morning the ashes from the bonfire are collected as prasad (consecrated material) and smeared on the limbs of the body. Singed coconuts, if any are also collected and eaten.

In some houses the image of Kamadeva is kept in the yard and a simple worship is offered. A mixture of mango blossoms and sandalwood paste is partaken as the prasad.

The day- Phalgun krsna pratipad - is observed as a day of revelry especially by throwing on one another gulal or coloured water or perfumed coloured powder. Throwing of mud or earth dust was prevalent in the earlier days also, but among the low culture groups.

Instead of the gay and frenzied celebrations that are witnessed elsewhere in the country, Bengal observes this festival in a quiet and dignified manner as Dolapurnima or Dolayatra (the festival of the swing). The festival, said to have been initiated by the king

Indradyumna in Vrndavana, is spread over 3 or 5 days, starting from the sukla Chaturdasi of Phalguna. A celebration in honour of Agni and worship of Govinda (Krsna) in image on a swing are the important features. The fire kindled on the first day is to be preserved till the last day. The swing is to be rocked 21 times at the end of the festival.

The day is also celebrated as the birthday of Sri Krsna Chaitanya (A.D. 1486-1533), mostly in Bengal, as also in Puri (Orissa), Mathura and Vrndavan (in Uttar Pradesh).

Holi or *Phagwah* (Bhojpuri), is an annual and popular Hindu spring festival. It takes place over two days in the latter part of March or early April. As per the Hindu calendar, it falls on the Phalgun Purnima (or Pooranmashi, Full Moon). It is also called the Festival of Colours.

On the first day, a bonfire is lit at night to signify burning Holika. On the second day, known as *Dhulandi,* people go around until afternoon throwing coloured powder and water at each other, although the powder stings the eyes. A special drink called 'thandai' or bhang is also consumed sometimes, which actually contains small amounts of marijuana (*Cannabis sativa*). People invite each other to their houses for feasts and celebrations later in the evening. *Rangapanchami* occurs a few days later on a Panchami (fifth day of the full moon), marking the end of festivities involving colours.

This festival occurs at the onset of spring. This period, during which the weather changes, is prone to cause viral fever and cold. Thus, the playful throwing of the coloured powders has a medicinal significance as the coloured powders are made of Neem, Kumkum, Haldi, Bilva, and other medicinal herbs prescribed by Âyurvedic doctors.

Amongst India's innumerable festivals, Holi ranks as the most colourful. It celebrates the arrival of spring and death of demoness Holika, it is a celebration of joy and hope. Holi provides a refreshing respite from the mundane norms as people from all walks of life enjoy themselves. In a tight knit community, it also provided a good excuse for letting off some steam and settling old scores, without causing physical injury.

Holi continues to be celebrated with great vigour through out India. Countless Hindi films have brought the vibrant colours of the festival to the screen. Indians all over the world eagerly await the Festival of Colours, as bonfires are lit to banish the cold dark nights of winter and usher in warmer spring. Dhuleti, day after Holi, is the actual festival of colours, when everything in sight is covered in a riot of colours.

Twin towns of Nandagow (where Lord Krishna grew up) and Barsana (where Shri Radha grew up), near Mathura, are the epicentre of the celebrations. Lord Krishna, while growing up in Vraj, popularised the festival with his ingenious pranks. Gopies of Vraj responded with equal enthusiasm and the festivities have continued ever since. Role reversal, feminism etc. are accepted customs for the duration of the festival! Men and women of Vraj clash in a colourful display of battle of the sexes.

Celebrations start a week earlier than rest of India. Men of Nandagow raid Barsana with hopes of raising their flag over Shri Radhikaji's temple. They receive a thunderous welcome as the women of Barsana greet them with long wooden sticks. The men are soundly beaten as they attempt to rush through town to reach the relative safety of Shri Radhikaji's temple. Men are well padded as they are not allowed to retaliate. In this mock battle the men try their best not to be captured. Unlucky captives can be forcefully lead away, thrashed and dressed in female attire before being made to dance!!

Rush through Barsana is far more lethal than running with the bulls in Spain, at least you don't have to marry them one day! Famous poets like Surdas, Nand-das, Kumbhan-das and others, have written beautifully as to how Lord Krishna was similarly received and forced to wear a sari, forced to wear makeup and made to dance before being released by the gopies of Vraj.

The next day, men of Barsana reciprocate by invading Nandagow. Clouds of pink and white powder mark the frenzy of activity taking place in it's narrow streets. A naturally occurring orange-red dye, Kesudo, is used to drench all participants. Today, the women of Nadagow beat the invaders from Barsana. It is a colourful site. In the interest of tourisum and safety, the state tourist board has set up excellent vantage points for the public. A large open ground, on the outskirts of the town is specially set aside for the most magnificent display of the festivities.

The next day, the temples in Vrindavan celebrate the festival with great guesto. The renowned temple of Bakai-Bihari, the beloved lord of the 15th century saint Haridas, is at the centre of the festivities. Clouds of pink and white descend upon the pilgrims, as the Lord of Vrindavan plays Holi with all his beloved visitors.

The festival moves on to other parts of Vraj. Soon enough, it is Dhulati and entire India celebrates the joys of spring as the "festival of colour".

Gulal-Kund in Vraj is a beautiful little lake, set in a delightful groves near the mountain Goverdhan, in the Mathura district. Here the festival is commemorated on a more regular basis. Pilgrims who visit the holy land of Vraj, can see the reenactments of Holi throughout the year at this lake. Local boys, acting in the Krishna-Lila drama troupes reenact the scenes of holi for the pilgrims.

Royal courts all over North India refined the festival in to an art form of its own. Rajput warriors of the Rajasthani courts used to show off their equestrian skills during the festival. Rajput men would ride their steeds through the white and pink clouds of colour, throwing colour powders on each other. Even the members of the royal families were not immune from being drenched by colour. The entire court would be drenched in saffron water and an orange-red dye of the "kasuda" flowers.

Pushti-Marga temples, spread throughout North and Western States of India, celebrate the festival in a way reminiscent of rajput courts.

The Deity, and the laity, are liberally sprinkled with perfumes, saffron water, kesudo, and covered in sandalwood aswell as the white and pink powder, abil and gulal. Joyous celebration is accompanied by classical music, poetry and folk songs appropriate for the occasion. Deity's white clothes' are soon transformed into a mass of colour as gold and silver syringes spray colourful water on all participants.

The celebrations officially usher in the pleasant season of love, spring. In the Pushti-Marga temples, the festivities last for almost a month. Beginning on the day of Vasant-Panchami, the festivals last till the day after Holi. This helps prolong the season of joy.

The weather is most pleasant and the spring flowers are in full bloom.

Skies are clear, days are warm and nights are pleasantly cool.

What more could you ask for,

except to be covered in the "ranga" (colour) of your beloved!

After *dakshayAga,* shakti took the form of the daughter of the mountain king *himavAn* called *Arvati.* From the early childhood she was devoted to Lord shiva and started penance for getting married to the God Shiva. Lord Shiva was however staying as *dakshinamurthi* making the sages *sanaka, sanandana, sanatana, sanatkumara* realize the Ultimate Truth.

In the meanwhile the celestials were put to deep hardship by the demons lead by *sUrapadma, simhamukha and tharaka*. This was a curse on them for attending the dakshayaga. Surapadma had the boon that none other than the son who is the power of shiva could kill him. As Lord shiva was teaching the path of Bliss to the sages and Parvati doing penance, the celestials were desparate for the solution which is the son of Lord Shiva. Out of the desperation, they lost the sense of what they were doing and sent forcibly the *kama* (cupid) to induce lust in God for Arvati.

Kama, whose arrows never failed elsewhere, was sure that he was getting into trouble. However out of pressure from the celestials (devas) he went to the abode of Lord Shiva and shot an arrow that would kindle lust on the God. kama has been vested with the power by Lord Shiva to induce lust in all creatures - lives in order to maintain the reproduction as a system, so he was successful.

Will that logic work on the One Who is beyond all these principles, the One Who has no pleasure out of external things? The arrow of kama failed to induce lust in God. As the Lord opened slightly the third-eye, kama who shot the arrow was burnt down to a heap of ash. Unperturbed the Lord continued the explanation to the sages!

This incident of burning off kama is called *kamadahana* or Holi. The posture of God burning kAma is called *kama dahana murthi* and is one of the 25 *mAhEshvara murthis*.

As the lust was won over by the Eternal Bliss of Lord Shiva the kamadahana or Holi festival is celebrated as an event associating with the Bliss of God. The Holi bonfire is in commemoration of this event. The ash of kama's body settled over the Lord shiva. (The kama dahana murthi dhyana shloa states, *bhasma uddhulita vigraham*). So following kamadahana during Holi, people put the powders on themselves and others remembering this victory over lust. To this day, people offer sandalwood paste to Kamadeva to relieve from his stinging burns and mango blossoms that he loved on Holi.

The celebration of Holi is very ancient in its origin. And by its very origin, it celebrates an ultimate triumph of the 'good' over the 'evil'. While, a feast of colors associated with the Holi, is the face of this celebration, the original reason of celebrating Holi, lies in its soul. And this gives us the 'why' of this ancient festival.

Literally "Holi" signifies "burning" in Indian language. But, how it came to be associated with 'burning', is a story. The reference is found only in ancinet Indian mythology. And It is the legend of Hiranyakashipu, to whom the celebration of Holi is associated.

Way back in the pre-Christian era, there lived a demon king named Hiranyakashipu in ancient India. He wanted to avenge the death of his younger brother. The brother, also a demon, had been killed by Lord Vishnu, one of the supreme trio, monitoring the life and death in the universe, (according to the Hindu belief). To take on Vishnu, the tyrant king wanted to become the king of the heaven, earth and the underworld. He performed severe penance and prayer for many years to gain enough power. Finally he was granted a boon. Powered by the boon, Hiranyakshipu thought he had become invincible. Arrogant, he ordered all in his kingdom to worship him, instead of God. The demon king, however, had a very young son, named Prahalad.

He was an ardent devotee of Vishnu. Despite his father's order, Prahalad continued to pray to Vishnu. So the demon king wanted to kill his son. He asked the favor of his sister Holika who, because of a boon, was immune to fire. They planned that Prahalad would be burned to death. A pyre was lit up and Holika sat on it, clutching Prahalad. Yet, at the end Prahalad emerged unscathed by the fire, And Holika, the demon, was burned to ashes. The earnest devotion and complete submission to Lord Vishnu saved young Prahlad. Thus was the triumph of Prahlad, the representative of good spirits. And the defeat of Holika, the representative of evil. Later, even the demon king Hiranyakashipu was killed by Lord Vishnu. But that is quite a different story. It is from Holika, that the Holi originated.

This legend is relived even today on the Holi-eve when the pyre is relit in the form of bonfires. Even today, people celebrate this occasion. Huge bonfires are lit up every year on the eve of the full moon night of the Holi to burn the spirit of the evils. Hence the story associated with the soul of the celebration.

According to the Hindu belief, Krishna was a reincarnation of lord Vishnu himself.

It was Krishna, or, Krishn, the king of the ancient city of Dwarka, who popularised the tradition of Holi. The origin of the colorful and frolicking tone of Holi lies in the boyhood of Krishna. It all came up as part of his pranks, he used to play with his boyhood mates of Gokul and Vrindavan. Situated in north India, these are the places where he spent his childhood.

It was at this time of year, Krishna used to play pranks by drenching the village girls, with water and colors. At first it offended the girls. But they were so fond of this mischievous boy that soon their anger melted away.

For other boys to join in, making it a popular sport in the village. Later, as Krishna grew up, the play assumed a new dimension. It added more colors to Krishna's legendary love life. The legend of Krishna's courtship with Radha, and playing pranks with the 'Gopi's. The girls in the 'dairy' village of Gokul were mostly milkmaids, and, hence locally known as the Gopis. The same tradition has transpired through the ages, turning it into a community festival of the masses. As time kept flowing, the culture spread roots to other regions of the country. The Holi play of Krishna is documented in hundreds of ancient paintings, murals, sculptures and scriptures found across the subcontinent.

The purana continues that later the celestials realized their foolishness in trying to alter the course of God by force and smartness. They begged to God for pardon and pleaded to revive kAma. They further begged that the Lord accept Arvati as the consort and put an end to their sufferings from the demons. The highly benevalent Lord accepted their prayers and married Arvati. On the day of wedding revived kama but made him invisible except for the eyes of his wife rati, making him *ananga*. This day of Arvati parameshvara wedding is the *kalyana vratam* also known as *panguni uttaram* kamadahana festival is celebrated in the month of *masi* (mid Feb to mid Mar) on the full moon day.

Holi is spread out over two days (it used to be five, and in some places it is longer). The entire holiday is associated with a *loosening of social restrictions* normally associated with caste, sex, status and age. Holi thus bridges social gaps and brings people together: employees and employers, men and women, rich and poor, young and old. Holi is also characterized by the *loosening of social norms* governing polite behavior and the resulting general atmosphere of licentious merrymaking and ribald language and behavior. A common saying heard during Holi is *bura na mano, Holi hai* ("don't feel offended, it's Holi").

On the evening of the first day of Holi, a *public bonfire* is held, commemorating the burning of Holika. Traditionally, Hindu boys spend the weeks prior to Holi combing the neighborhood for any waste wood they can find for the bonfire. The fire is lit sometime between 10 PM and midnight (at the rising of the moon), not generally in an orderly fashion. Everyone gathers in the street for the event, and the air rings with shouts, catcalls, curses and general mayhem.

The central ritual of Holi is the throwing and applying of *colored water and powders* on friends and family, which gives the holiday its common name "Festival of Colors." This ritual is said to be based on the above story of Krishna and Radha as well as on Krishna's playful splashing of the maids with water, but most of all it celebrates the coming of spring with all its beautiful colors and vibrant life.

In Bengal, Holi features the *Dolayatra* (Swing Festival), in which images of the gods are placed on specially decorated platforms and devotees take turns swinging them. In the meantime, women dance around and sing special songs as men spray colored water at them.

Holi - Legends and Myths: Interesting legends of Holi that are most commonly cited revolve around the soul bond of Lord Krishna and Radha, Prahlad, the child-devotee of Lord Vishnu, Kamdeva, the Indian Cupid-God and Dhundhi, the immortal ogress. All these legends focus on different aspects of Holi that can be attributed to them. The romantic fervor of Holi festival is derived from the love pranks of Radha and Krishna while the story of Kamdeva gives a clue to celebrate this festival to welcome the Spring. The story of Prahlad encompasses the religious nature of the festival and the origin of Holi while the tale of Dhundhi gives a reason to use rude words and play pranks to the young boys of the village.

There was a mighty demon king named Hirnakashyipu who had won all the three worlds of heaven, earth and hell and had thus, become very proud. He assumed that he could defeat even Lord Vishnu with his valor. He went to the extent that he had enforced a law that everybody would worship him instead of gods and deities. However, his little son Prahlad refused to accept his commands and continued to worship Lord Vishnu with complete devotion. Infuriated by this defiance of his son, he ordered his soldiers to throw him down a hill. Praying fervently and having full faith in Lord Vishnu, Prahlad did not retract from his word. True to his faith, Lord Vishnu rescued him at the last moment.

Flustered by this news, Hirnakashyipu invoked the help of his sister Holika, who had a boon that she could walk through the fire unharmed to do away with his son. The wicked aunt agreed to the evil desires of his brother and entered the fire with her nephew Prahlad. However, the brother and sister had forgot that Holika could only enter the fire alone or she would perish. Thus, blessed by Lord Vishnu, the child Prahlad remained unharmed but Holika got burnt and died instantly. Holi is thus celebrated to commemorate the death of the evil aunt, after whom the festival is named, and the new life granted to Prahlad for his devotion and faith. To this day, cow dung is hurled into the fire and obscenities are shouted at the Holi fire at some places to insult Holika.

Invincible Dhundhi: During the reign of Prithu, there was a terrible ogress called Dhundhi, who loved to devour innocent children. She had performed severe penances and had won several boons from the deities that made her almost invincible. However, due to a curse of Lord Shiva, she was not so immune to the pranks and abuses of young boys as she was to weapons and arrows. One day, the courageous boys of the village decided to get rid of her forever and chase her away from the village forever. They got intoxicated on bhaang and drunk and then followed Dhundhi to the limits of the village, beating drums, making loud noise, shouting obscenities and hurling insults at her and continued doing this until she left the village for good. This is the reason that even today young boys are allowed to indulge themselves in rowdiness, using rude words and intoxication on Holi.

Love Play of Radha Krishna: Lord Krishna has often been portrayed as a naughty prankster in his childhood and a lover-boy in his youth. His beloved Radha and the cowherd girls 'Gopis' in general loved him even more for his pranks and eve teasing. The Holi of Braj is famous all over India for its intimate connection with the divine deities and their love plays. It is said that when Krishna was a young boy, he asked the reason for his dark color while Radha was so fair. His mother Yashoda playfully suggested that he should smear color on Radha's face too and change her complexion to any color he wanted. Captivated by the idea, Krishna proceeded to do so and thus, introduced the play of colors on Holi. Even today, Holi is one of the most important festival of Braj, where the men of Nandgaon and women of Barsana play 'latthmar Holi' in the remembrance of the playful throw of colors by Krishna on 'Gopis' and their resistance. The trace of eroticism and romance pervades Holi as depicted in the love plays of Krishna and Radha. In Mathura, Vrindavan, Gokul and Barsana, Holi is a two-week long festival featuring play of colors, folk songs called 'Hori', folk dances such as Raas-Lila, staging the various aspects of Radha and Krishna's love. The world's balance soon crumbled in his absence and Sati took rebirth as Goddess Parvati to try and win Lord Shiva's heart and wake him up from his trance. She tried all ways to get the attention of Shiva. When she had exhausted all her feminine ways, she invoked the help of Kamadava, the Indian cupid-god, who agreed to help her in the cause of the world despite the risks involved. He shot his love-arrow on Shiva's heart. Disturbed in his trance, Lord Shiva opened his third eye that fired anger and instantly incinerated Kamadeva. It is said that it was on the day of Holi that Kamadeva had sacrificed himself for the good of all beings. Later, when Lord Shiva realized his mistake, he granted Kamadeva immortality in invisible form. To this day, people offer sandalwood paste to Kamadeva to relieve from his stinging burns and mango blossoms that he loved on Holi.

Sacrifice of Kamadeva: According to Hindu mythology, the world is looked after the Trinity of Gods - Lord Brahma, the creator; Lord Vishnu, the nurturer; and Lord Shiva, the destroyer. According to a legend, Goddess Sati, the daughter of Daksha Prajapati, one of the first sons of Lord Brahma, married Lord Shiva against the wishes of her father. Thus, Daksha did not invite her and her husband to a grand yagya arranged by him. When Sati came to know about the event in her father's house, she thought it to be a slip of mind and proceeded to participate in the event despite the warnings of her husband. But once she reached there, she realized her fault and was infuriated by the insult of her husband. As a penance for her disobedience, she entered the fire. When Lord Shiva came to know of her sudden demise, he was furious. Even after he controlled his anger, he started a severe meditation and renounced all work.

Holi or Holikotsava is a festival that occurs around March and is celebrated over two days. On the evening of the first day bonfires are lit, normally in a public place. On the second day people throw coloured powder and water at each other. The first day is Holi proper, the second day is called Dhuleti or Rangapanchami (Ranga-colour, Panchami=fifth day). Rangapanchami was originally the fifth day as the festival was earlier spread over five days and so it was called Rangapanchami because in earlier times it was celebrated till the fifth day of the fortnight.

Holi Centers Around a Bonfire: Holi is one of the few festivals that has yet to acquire the character of being a religious and private festival along with being a public occasion for rejoicing which all festivals are. Holi is almost totally a public festival and as such there is hardly any Holi celebrations inside private homes in the sense in which is understood. Holi is not only a purely public festival in the manner of its celebration but also in the manner in which people prepare for it.

Weeks before the arrival of Holi, gangs comb the neighborhood and collect all waste-wood, old wooden furniture etc. which they can lay their hands upon. After weeks of preparation judiciously combined with activities that come close to pillaging, assorted pieces of wood are piled up to be lit on the evening of the festival day. (These days with Cable TV, the interest of the boys in urban India seems to be waning in the pre-Holi preparations).

Sexual License during Holi: The lighting takes place late in the night between 10 P.M. and 12 P.M. Very rarely is this ceremony conducted in an orderly manner. Except when the ceremony is taking place in a temple, gesticulation, howling, catcalls and trading of abuses is a part of Holi. All this is obviously reminiscent of attitudes originating in a backward cultural environment. But even against this background, the aspect that stands out is the sexual license that the mobs exercise. A display of loose morals, a morbid rejoicing with contempt for all laws and norms of behaviour that are considered civilized by present-day standards - what does this reflect?

How is it that even those sections of society that are educated and cultured allow themselves to bo carried away by the wild outburst associated with this festival? Why is it that this has been the nature of Holi for centuries together?

These questions sound quite provocative to an average Indian mind. To answer them we need to look beyond what is visible and evident as there is more to it than meets the eye during Holi celebrations. As already mentioned, Holi does not have much of a private or individual character, it is almost entirely a public festival. But does it at least have any religious significance? A hard look proves otherwise. Holi is not dedicated to any deity from the Hindu pantheon, as are other festivals like, Mahashivaratri, Ramanavami, Krishnastami, etc. And although mythology does involve Shiva and Madana (the God of love) with Holi, the religious significance is not immanent as in the case of other festivals. It is for this reason that very few religious rites are associated with Holi and almost none of them are generally observed.

Festivals displaying features similar to Holi can be found in many modern societies. Carnival and Guy Fawkes Day are two instances. The Guy Fawkes Day which is observed in Britain on the 5th of November commemorates the discovery of Gunpowder and is celebrated with fireworks and bonfires.

The Carnival which is another instance of a similar festival is celebrated in Portugal and Spain. Carnival is an occasion for revelry. Carnival that is celebrated before the beginning of Lent - the beginning of the austerity period that goes up to Good Friday and Easter. The term carnival being close to terms like carnal (meaning sensual or bodily), carnage, carnivore, carnivorous is itself quite suggestive of the origin of carnival in a less civilized environment. Recently in India the Roman Catholic Church of Goa has refused to extend religious sanction to carnival, but this has not succeeded in abating the tide of public enthusiasm. This is one instance of how a popular festival which owes it origin to a life-style (existing or extinct) can continue in face of withdrawal of religious sanction.. The on-goings during Holi celebrations closely resemble life in a nomadic tribal society especially in the wintry regions. The festival revolves around a bonfire. It is observed in the winter. These two aspects are eloquent as to the festival's social origin. Fire, we know was one of the earliest tool used to ward off the freezing cold of the long winters in the northern hemisphere. Even today among the poorest sections of society, the lighting of fire made of waste-wood is the cheapest and affordable form of keeping oneself warm during the long wintry nights.

Although no offence is meant, we cannot help saying that the tradition of mobocracy and sexual license reflects in a telling manner an attitude typical of tribal people living in a harsh environment in a society where the institution of monogamous marriage had not developed fully.

But such elements in a festival are not specific to India. Festivals displaying features similar to Holi can be found in many modern societies. Carnival and Guy Fawkes Day are two instances. The Guy Fawkes Day which is observed in Britain on the 5th of November commemorates the discovery of Gunpowder and is celebrated with fireworks and bonfires.

The Carnival which is another instance of a similar festival is celebrated in Portugal and Spain. Carnival is an occasion for revelry. Carnival that is celebrated before the beginning of Lent - the beginning of the austerity period that goes up to Good Friday and Easter. The term carnival being close to terms like carnal (meaning sensual or bodily), carnage, carnivore, carnivorous is itself quite suggestive of the origin of carnival in a less civilized environment. Recently in India the Roman Catholic Church of Goa has refused to extend religious sanction to carnival, but this has not succeeded in abating the tide of public enthusiasm. This is one instance of how a popular festival which owes it origin to a life-style (existing or extinct) can continue in face of withdrawal of religious sanction.

The Burning of Kama Deva Madana: For that matter, a formal religious sanction does exist in the case of most festivals. For instance, it is said that Holi commemorates an event in lord Shiva's life. In mythology Shiva is portrayed as having a meditative but violent temperament. For hours together he is said to meditate in his icy abode atop mount Kailas in the Himalayas. Solitude and serenity are essential for him. Looking at Shiva's abnormal trait, Madana, the God of love decided to see for himself if Shiva was, in fact, above normal passions. To do this he took on the form of a beautiful nymph and tried to disturb Shiva's meditation by singing and dancing in front of him. Unfortunately for Madana, he succeeded in disturbing Shiva's meditation, and when Shiva opened his eyes and recognised the beautiful nymph as Madana in disguise, he was furious. In a fit of rage he opened his third eye located on his forehead, that could emit fire and reduced the guileful Madana to ashes. Holi we are told is observed in memory of this event.

Holi: The Lordly Way: But the most famous Holi has to be that of Barsana, (a small town in the Northern Indian state of Uttar Pradesh) the house of adolescent Krishna's love, Radha. Romance is not quite what comes to mind when you see men from Nandgaon (Krishna's home) being beaten up with sticks from Radha's village, after they have been provoked by the colorful language.

Celebrations start a week earlier than the rest of India. Men of Nandagaon raid Barsana with hopes of raising their flag over Shri Radhikaji's temple. They receive a thunderous welcome as the village women greet them with long wooden sticks. The men are soundly beaten as they attempt to rush through the town and reach the relative safety of Shri Radhikaji's temple. Men are well padded with foam, since they are not allowed to retaliate. In this mock battle, the men try their best not to be captured. Unlucky captives can be forcefully lead away, thrashed and dressed in female attire before being made to dance!

Poets like Surdas, Nand-das, Kumbhan-das and others have recounted tales of Krishna being captured and forced to wear a sari, makeup and then dance before being released by the gopis of Vraj.

The next day, men of Barsana reciprocate by invading Nandagaon. Clouds of pink and white powder mark the frenzy of activity taking place in its narrow streets. The women of Nadagaon beat the invaders from Barsana. There are even vantage points for tourists who choose to look on. A large open ground, on the outskirts of the town, is specially set aside for the most magnificent display of the festivities.

The next day, the temples in Vrindavan (close to Mathura) celebrate the festival. The temple of Bakai-Bihari, the beloved lord of the 15th century saint Haridas, is at the center of the festivities. Clouds of pink and white descend upon the pilgrims, as the Lord of Vrindavan plays Holi with all his visitors.

The festival moves on to other parts of Vraj. Gulal-Kund in Vraj is a beautiful little lake, set in delightful groves near the mountain Goverdhan, in the Mathura district. Here, the festival is commemorated on a more regular basis. Pilgrims, who visit the Holy Land of Vraj, can see the reenactments of Holi throughout the year. Local boys, acting in the Krishna-Lila drama troupes, reenact the scenes of Holi for the pilgrims. The next day onwards it's business as usual in both God's houses and men's. And spring can be a hard taskmaster. One returns to the business of living with fun to last a year.

Holi festival of India. The *Holi Festival* is known as the "Festival of Color" and is a celebration of Lord Krishna and God's Creations. The colorful festival of *Holi,* literally means 'burning', is celebrated on the full moon day in the month of Phalguna and heralds the onset of spring season. *Holi* is the time when people from all castes and social strata come together forgetting all past differences and grievances.

Originally the festival was primarily for the Shudras who were otherwise not allowed to participate in festivals. This is specially significant in the rural areas where in many places, there still exists a clear demarcation between each caste and community.

In ancient India too, this festival was celebrated as a day when people forgot caste and gender differences and were allowed many liberties, otherwise forbidden. In fact Holi bears close resemblance to the important ancient festival called Vasantotsava.

In Bengal, Holi is called Dol Yatra, or the swing festival. Idols of Radha and Krishna are placed on swings and devotees take turns to swing them. Women dance around the swing and sing devotional songs, as men spray colored water at them. In Manipur too, Holi is extremely interesting. It is a six-day festival here, commencing on the full moon day of Phalguna. The traditional and centuries-old Yaosang festival of Manipur amalgamated with Holi in the18th century with the introduction of Vaishnavism. The entire theme of the festival is woven into the worship of Krishna and Chaitanya Mahaprabhu, also known as Lord Gauranga.

Thabal Chongba, a popular Manipuri folk dance, is associated with this festival. The literal meaning of Thabal is 'moonlight' and Chongba means 'dance', thus 'dancing in the moonlight'. Traditionally conservative Manipuri parents did not allow their daughters to go out and meet any young men without their consent. Thabal Chongba therefore provided the only chance for girls to meet and talk to the boys. In earlier times, this dance was performed in the moonlight accompanied by folk songs. The only musical instrument used was a dholakor drum. It is performed in every locality on all the six days of the festival. Instead of a fire, a hut is built and then set ablaze. The next day, boys go in groups to play gulal with the girls. And in return for playing with them, the girls extract money from the boys.

Another significant feature of the festival in Manipur is the groups of devotees from different areas who gather at the Shree Govindaji Temple in Imphal. Dressed in the traditional white and yellow turbans, they sing songs in praise of Krishna and Chaitanya Mahaprabhu, play gulal and dance in front of the temple. On Halangkar, the last day of the festival, hundreds of devotees gather at the temple as usual and march together towards the Vijay Govindaji Temple about 3 km west of Imphal where various cultural activities are performed. This brings to an end the Yaosang festival

Holi or Holika: Holi or Holika, also called holikotsava, is an extremely popular festival observed throughout the country (India). It is especially marked by unmixed gaiety and frolics and is common to all sections of the people.

This festival is very ancient. Known originally as 'Holika' it has been mentioned in very early religious works such as Jaimini's Purvamimamsa-sutras and Kathaka-grhya-sutras. It must have therefore existed several centuries before Christ. It was at first actually a special rite performed by married women for the happiness and well-being of their families and the full moon (Raka) was the deity worshipped by them.

There are two ways of reckoning a lunar month: purnimanta and amanta. In the former, the first day starts after the full moon; and in the latter, after the new moon. Though the latter reckoning is more common now, the former was very much in vogue in the earlier days. According to this purnimanta reckoning, Phalguna purnima was the last day of the year and the new year heralding the Vasanta-rtu (with spring starting from next day). Thus the full moon festival of Holika gradually became a festival of merrymaking, announcing the commencement of the spring season. This perhaps explains the other names of this festival: Vasanta-Mahotsava and Kama-Mahotsava.

According to the stories in the Puranas and various local legends, this day is important for three reasons:

1. It was on this day that Lord Siva opened his third eye and reduced Kamadeva (the god of love, Cupid or Eros) to ashes.
2. It was on this day that Holika, the sister of the demon king Hiranyakasyapu, who tried to kill the child devotee Prahlad by taking him on her lap and sitting on a pyre of wood which was set ablaze. Holika was burnt to ashes while Prahlad remained unscathed!
3. It was again on this day that an ogress called Dhundhi, who was troubling the children in the kingdom of Prthu (or Raghu) was made to run away for life, by the shouts and pranks of the mischievous boys. Though she had secured several boons that made her almost invincible, this – noise, shouts, abuses and pranks of boys – was a chink in her armour due to a curse of Lord Siva. The day itself came to be called 'Adada' or 'Holika' since then.

Festivals like Holi have their own spiritual value. Apart from the various amusements, they create faith in God if properly observed. Hindu festivals always have a spiritual significance. They wean man away from sensual pleasures and take him gradually to the spiritual path and divine communion. People perform *havan* and offer to the gods the new grains that are harvested.

On such holy occasions there should be worship of God, Satsangs, and Kirtan of the Lord's Names, not merely the sprinkling of coloured water and lighting of bonfires. These functions are to be considered most sacred and spent in devotional prayers, visiting holy places, bathing in sacred waters, and Satsang with great souls. Abundant charity should be done to the poor. Then only can Holi be said to have been properly celebrated. Devotees of the Lord should remember His delightful pastimes on such happy occasions.

All great Hindu festivals have religious, social and hygienic elements in them. Holi is no exception. Every season has a festival of its own. Holi is the great spring festival of India. Being an agricultural country, India's two big festivals come during the harvest time when the barns and granaries of our farmers are full and they have reason to enjoy the fruits of their hard labour. The harvest season is a festive season all over the world.

Man wants relaxation and change after hard work. He needs to be cheered when he is depressed on account of work and anxieties. Festivals like Holi supply him with the real food and tonic to restore his cheer and peace of mind.

The religious element in the Holi festival consists of worship of Sri Krishna. In some places it is also called the Dol Yatra. The word *dol* literally means "a swing". An image of Sri Krishna as a babe is placed in a little swing-cradle and decorated with flowers and painted with coloured powders. The pure, innocent frolics of little Krishna with the merry milkmaids—the Gopis of Brindavan—are commemorated. Devotees chant the Name of Sri Krishna and sing Holi-songs relating to the frolics of little Krishna with the Gopis.

The social element during Holi is the uniting or "embracing" of the great and the small, of the rich and the poor. It is also the uniting of equals. The festival teaches us to "let the dead bury the dead". We should forget the outgoing year's ill-feelings and begin the new year with feelings of love, sympathy, co-operation and equality with all. We should try to feel this oneness or unity with the Self also.

Holi also means "sacrifice". Burn all the impurities of the mind, such as egoism, vanity and lust, through the fire of devotion and knowledge. Ignite cosmic love, mercy, generosity, selflessness, truthfulness and purity through the fire of Yogic practice. This is the real spirit of Holi. Rise from the mire of stupidity and absurdity and dive deep into the ocean of divinity.

The call of Holi is to always keep ablaze the light of God-love shining in your heart. Inner illumination is the real Holi. The spring season is the manifestation of the Lord, according to the *Bhagavad Gita*. Holi is said there to be His heart.

If you're in any of the northern states of India around the time of the full moon in late February/early March be prepared to come under heavy fire from hordes of dye-totin' revellers. The festival of Holi is a riotious celebration of the coming of spring and, in that infectious flowers-are-a'bloomin' and sun-is-a'shinin' kind of way, sweeps everything before it.

More than any other festival, Holi brings out the flagrant, gaudy India - the land of hennaed hands, maharanis and silk saris, tikas and bindis, sparkling bangles, fluttering prayer flags, burnished temples, and bejewelled mausoleums.

There are several different myths surrounding the festival of Holi - the version you get depends on where you are. Down in the southern regions, particularly around Kerala, legend has it that Kamdev-the-love-God, forgetting all those boyhood admonitions about not pointing sharp missiles at people ('it's all fun and games until someone gets their eye poked out'), aimed an arrow at Lord Shiv's third eye.

For this silly adolescent act he was not just grounded but, hyper-punitively, burnt to the ground. His wife pleaded for his return, a wish that was only half-granted when Lord Shiv sent him back but sent him back ever-'anang' (without human form). Hence the lamentations sung during Holi.

Another more lurid and gothic story has she-demons suckling children to death and attempting to take the life of Krishna in the same manner. The fires on the eve of Holi somehow represent the death of the she-devil, Putana, and the triumph of spring life over deathly winter. Then there's the Hiranyakashyap-Prahlad myth, a kind of Luke Skywalker-Darth Vader Yoda-less tale of fathers and sons, good and evil, and the triumph of abstract faith over physical limitations.

In this version Holika, the sister of Hiranyakashyap, was sent to kill Prahlad, the good son, who refused the blandishments of the Dark Side by continuing to worship Lord Vishnu over his father who had installed himself as a god. For this sin, Holika carried him into a crematorium, but she was hoisted on her own petard when she was burnt by the very fires that were meant for Prahlad. Holika's firey nature is remembered in the bonfires that are burnt each Holi eve.

While the legend has all the elements of a classic tragedy, the festival itself is a day of uninhibited exuberance and joy, fuelled by spring's arrival and the timely consumption of marijuana-based bhang and thandai. Gangs of revellers roam the streets armed with packets of gulal (dye) and coloured water bombs and, from early in the day, it's on for young and old. The coloured wars rage all morning but promptly at midday a general cease-fire is observed and the streets turn eerily quiet as people flock to bathtubs and rivers for a hose down. The afternoon is spent eating candy and reliving the glories of battle. Originally the colours were extracted from a flower that blossoms only during the festival but these days ammunition is usually bought at the local markets. The row upon row of luscious gulal- mountains of tumeric yellow, saffron orange, indigo blue, deep turquoise and the entire spectrum in between - will have you itching to join in.

Tourists and foreigners should be warned that they are not immune to the kamikaze water-bomb raids and there's not much point in getting upset over being the target. Better to drag out an old wash-n-wear from the back pack or something that could do with a bit of a dye-job, get your own gulal ammunition and fight fire with fire.

Mardi Gras: Usually associated with half-nude debauchery and flammable rum drinks, Mardi Gras gets a bad—if not completely undeserved—rap. Despite its *Girls Gone Wild* reputation, it's more than simple "boobs for beads" transactions; if that's your goal, head for Bourbon Street with the out-of-towners. Locals congregate in neighborhood bars on hidden side streets and along the parade routes on Uptown stretches of St. Charles Avenue. Fat Tuesday itself always falls on the day before Lent—late February or early March—though the Mardi Gras *season* starts on January 6, the 12th night of Christmas. But the carnival spirit never quite leaves the city, so for an off-season view of the celebration, ride the Canal Street Ferry for a short ride across the Mississippi to nearby Algiers. Blaine Kern's Mardi Gras World offers daily tours of its working studios, where artists sculpt floats for next year's parades. The tour also includes time to roam the warehouses, where larger-than-life visages of Louis Armstrong sit next to 15-foot papier-mache bullfrogs

Mardi Gras Carnival: It occurs on three days in February or early March. Meant to be a feasting-drinking-merrymaking orgy just before the 40 days of Lent. It is Goa's most famous festival and has been celebrated since the 18th century. Huge parades through the cities are organised with bands, floats and dances and balls in the evenings. The final day concludes with the famous red-and-black dance held by the Clube Nacional in Panjim. The origins of carnival are apparently the hedonistic feasts of ancient Rome and Greece. It made its appearance in the Spanish and Portuguese colonies, where it metamorphosed into the very Latin singing-dancing-drinking bouts. The carnival is presided over by King Momo, who on the opening day orders his subjects to party. Hotel bookings must be done in advance for carnival as the festival attracts thousands of tourists.

RAM NAVAMI

The birthday of Lord Rama, the celebrated hero of the famous epic, 'Ramayana', is enthusiastically celebrated all over India. Lord Vishnu is worshipped in his human incarnation as Rama, the divine ruler of Ayodhya.

Celebrations begin with a prayer to the Sun early in the morning. At midday, when Lord Rama is supposed to have been born, a special prayer is performed. Temples of Rama are decorated, religious discourses are held and the Ramayana is recited for ten days. People sing devotional songs in praise of Rama and rock, images of him in a cradle to celebrate his birth. Rathyatras or chariot processions of Rama, his wife Seeta, brother Lakshmana and devotee Hanuman are held from many temples. The chariot is accompanied by several devotees dressed up in ancient costumes as Rama's soldiers. The procession is a gusty affair with the participants shouting praises echoing the happy days of Rama's reign. People gather in thousands on the banks of the sacred river Sarayu for a dip. Some observe a strict fast on this day.

Ayodhya is the focus of great celebrations. Devotees throng the temples of Ayodhya and Pondicherry, two places closely connected with the events of the Ramayana to participate in Ramnavami festivities.

Ramanavami celebrates the birth of Rama or Ramachandra. On the ninth day of the first fortnight of Chaitra the birth of Rama is commemorated. The story of Rama was first written by

Vaalmeeki in about the 4th century B.C. Rama is supposed to have lived during the 8th or 7th century B.C. The epic known as the Ramayana. In some parts of India, it is a nine-day festival, coinciding with the Vasanta Navaratri.

The public worship starts with morning ablutions, chanting Vedic mantras dedicated to Vishnu, and offering flowers and fruit to the god. People keep a fast throughout the day, breaking it only at midnight with fruit. In some parts of India, especially Bihar and Uttar Pradesh, public gatherings called satsangs are organised to commemorate the birth of Rama. Excerpts from the Ramacharitamanas, extolling the glory of Rama, are recited. People of all castes and creeds participate in these gatherings to listen to the stories and their explanations offered by the learned.

Rama's Birth: The country of Kosal was situated on the banks of the river Sharayu. Ayodhya was the capital founded by the king rishi Manu. During the reign of king Dasarath, Ayodhya reached a period of great prosperity. But Dasarath faced a big problem: he had no children. Therefore he decided to perform a sacrifice known as "ashvamedh", or horse-sacrifice. Elaborate and difficult rituals had to be observed. A very holy man, rishi Rishyashring, was chosen to conduct the sacrifice with the utmost accuracy. The performance of this sacrifice was a great event in Ayodhya. At the end Rishyashring recited a mantra and made an offering to the fire. Then the gods, gandharvas, siddhas, and rishis present arid began to pray to Brahma.

At that time Ravan, king of Lanka, was terrorizing the people, and all were longing for liberation from his menace. Ravan had acquired great power because he had obtained from god Brahma the boon that he would never die at the hands of gods, or gandharvas, or yakshas (demigods) or demons. As he was not afraid of men he did not care to include men in the list of his potential slayers. So Brahmadev declared that Ravan would die at the hands of a man. Then the gods went to Vishnu with the request, "Dasarath is a glorious king. Please, take birth in the wombs of his three queens in four different degrees of your divinity."

When Dasarath's sacrifice came to an end a shining figure appeared over the sacrificial kund, and offered the king a divine beverage called "payasam" to be given to his queens Kausalya, Kaikayi, and Sumitra. In due time Kausalya gave birth to Rama, Kaikayi to Bharat and Sumitra to Laxman and Shatrugna. Rama was born at noon of the bright ninth day of Chaitra. He was believed to be the embodiment of half degree of Vishnu's divinity, (ardha ounsh).

Four storeys - even the original Ravana may not have been so tall. But this is the Kali Yuga, when evil is supposed to assume an even more terrifying form. Ravana has his moments of glory, and that too, on Rama Navami, the birthday of Rama.

The effigy of the ten-headed Ravana swaggers through the town, wearing a gaudy crown and exaggerated moustache, with shouting hordes following. But once Ravana reaches the open ground that is his final destination, he is suddenly deserted by most of his "followers" - because the noble Rama has made his appearance.

In the end, righteousness does triumph, even in Kali Yuga. Rama engages him in battle, and finally pierces him with a potent arrow. And the huge effigy of Ravana, filled to bursting with firecrackers, is set alight, and explodes into a thousand bits amid loud cheers from the crowd and shouts of Jai Shri Ram. This ritual is an important part of the Rama Navami celebrations in most parts of North India.

Rama Navami falls on the ninth day of the shukla paksha, or bright phase of the moon, in the lunar month of Chaitra (April-May). The first day of Chaitra , or Ugadi, also marks the beginning of the Indian year.

Rama is one of the ten avatars of Lord Vishnu, and one of the two most popular, along with Krishna. Consequently, Rama Navami is widely celebrated, though not on the scale of festivals like Diwali or Dussehra.

According to legend, Rama was born at noon. Rama is the epitome of perfection, the uttama purusha, fulfilling all his duties towards both family and subjects.

Rama was the first of the four sons of King Dasharatha of Ayodhya. When it was time for Rama to be made crown-prince, his stepmother, Kaikeyi, got Dasharatha to send him to the forest for 14 years. His wife Sita and his brother Lakshmana also accompanied him. In the forest, Sita was kidnapped by Ravana, the demon king of Lanka. Rama, together with Hanuman and the monkey army, built a bridge to Lanka, killed Ravana, and brought Sita back.

It is believed that listening to the story of Rama cleanses the soul. Meditating on the noble Rama and chanting his name is believed to ease the pains of life and lead one to moksha, or liberation. It is also common practice to chant the name of Rama while rocking babies to sleep. Though Rama Navami is a major festival for Vaishnavites, it is widely celebrated by worshippers of Shiva, too.

It is considered auspicious to undertake a fast on the day in the name of Rama. The more devout fast for nine days, from Ugadi to Rama Navami. The objective of the fast is not to ask for special favours of the deity but to seek perfection as a human being. Devotees perform elaborate pujas and chant the name of Rama. Temples of Rama have special services and bhajan sessions through the day.

One significant and popular element of the celebration is the Ramayana parayana, a discourse on the Ramayana, by a pundit or a professional story-teller. It usually lasts nine days, beginning on Ugadi and ending on Rama Navami. A skilled story-teller who can liven up the event by weaving in contemporary events attracts massive crowds.

Since Rama is also one of the most sung-about deities in Indian classical music and literature, week-long (and sometimes, month-long) musical programmes are organised.

Sacred places associated with Rama, like Ayodhya, Ujjain and Rameshwaram, draw tens of thousands of devotees. In Rameshwaram, thousands take a ritual bath in the sea before worshipping at the Ramanathaswamy temple.

Many places in North India host fairs in connection with the festival, culminating in spectacular fireworks on Rama Navami.

On the auspicious Ramnavami day take a firm resolve that you will repeat Ram-Nam with every breath and that you will endeavour to lead a righteous life.

Ramnavami is one of the most important festivals of the Vaishnava sect of the Hindus. However, even those who adore Lord Shiva celebrate the occasion. Some observe a strict fast on the day. Temples are decorated and the image of Lord Rama is richly adorned. The holy Ramayana is read in the temples. At Ayodhya, the birthplace of Sri Rama, a big fair is held on this day.

In South India the Sri Ramnavami Utsavam is celebrated for nine days with great fervour and devotion.

At the Sivananda Ashram, Rishikesh, Ramnavami is celebrated for nine days as follows:

1. Spiritual seekers do as much Japa as possible. The sacred Mantras Om Sri Ramaya Namah or Om Sri Ram Jai Ram Jai Jai Ram are chanted.
2. Devotees read the whole of the Ramayana, either the Sanskrit version of Sage Valmiki or the Hindi version of Saint Tulsidas, during these nine days.

Those who cannot recite the entire epic may read this single verse which contains in a nutshell the story of the Ramayana: "Formerly, Sri Rama went to the forests, where Rishis did penance, and killed the illusive deer. Sita was carried away and Jatayu was killed. Rama met Sugriva, killed Vali and crossed the ocean. The city of Lanka was burnt by Hanuman. The demons, Ravana and Kumbhakarna, were then killed. Thus is recited the holy Ramayana".

3. Devotees greet one another with "Sri Ram" or "Jai Ram-ji-ki".
4. Those who have adopted Lord Rama as their favourite Deity observe a fast, taking only milk and fruit for all the nine days. Some fast only on the Ramnavami day itself
5. On the final or Ramnavami day, there is a grand worship of Lord Rama in the gorgeously decorated temple. All the Vedic rituals including Laksharchana are performed.
6. A havan is also performed.
7. From four in the morning to late at night, there is Ram and Ram alone everywhere!
8. Leaflets, booklets and books relating to Lord Rama are distributed.

9. Special meetings are held in the evening at which discourses on the life and teachings of the Lord are delivered.
10. Earnest seekers take resolves to accelerate their spiritual progress.

O beloved seekers! Time is fleeting. Know the value of time. Time is most precious. Utilise every second profitably. Do not procrastinate. Abandon all idle gossiping. Forget the past. Live every moment of your life for the realisation of the divine ideal and goal. Unfold your latent faculties. Grow, evolve and become a superhuman or a dynamic Yogi. Struggle hard and reach the goal of life.

May you all attain the final beatitude of life through intense devotion towards Lord Rama! May you live immersed in the ecstasy of divine love! May Sri Rama who is as effulgent as a million suns and who is adored by the gods and devotees, protect you all! May the blessings of Lord Ramabe upon you all!

Wherever four Hindus live, Rama and Sita will be there" so said Swami Vivekananda, one of the foremost harbingers of modern national renaissance of Bharat. The reverse also is equally true- wherever Rama and Sita live, the people there will remain and live as Hindus. Every hill and rivulet of Bharat bears the imprint of the holy feet of Rama and Sita. Sri Rama reigns supreme to this day in the hearts of our people, cutting across all barriers of province, language, caste or sect. Even the tribes living in isolated valleys and jungles have names like Mitti-Ram and Patthar-Ram. In some other tribes, every name carries the proud suffix of Ram, such as Lutthu Ram, Jagadev Ram, etc. In many northern parts of Bharat mutual greetings take the form of *Jay Ramjee Ki.* Sri Rama has become so much identified with all the good and great and virile qualities of heroic manhood that expressions such as *'Us me Ram nahi hai'* (there is no Rama in him) - meaning that a person has lost all manliness and worth - have become common usage. And when a Hindu quits the world stage, he is bid God-speed in his onward journey [with *Ramanama satya hai* or *Raghupati Raghava raja Ram, patita paavana Sita Ram*. In fact, the latter couplet has become the nation's *bhajan* par excellence.Sri Rama's story, Ramayana, has been sung and resung in all the languages and dialects of Bharat. The tradition of writing epics centering round the saga of Rama's achievements started by Valmiki and Samskrit was continued by Tulsidas in Hindi, by Kamban in Tamil, by Ramanujan in Malayalam, by Krittivasa in Bengali and Madhav Kambali in Assamia and in fact, in almost every Bharatiya language. The tradition is being continued up to the present day.

The *Ramayana Darshanam* of K.V. Puttappa, the national literary award of Bharat by the Jnana Peeth. The enchanting Geet Ramayana composed in Marathi by G.D. Madgulkar and set to tune by Sudhir Phadke is now thrilling the hearts of millions in Maharashtra.This festival celebrates the birth of Lord Ram or Ramachandra and is an occasion for great rejoicing especially for the Vaishnav's. The holy books and ancient texts believe that one should fast on this day, and anyone who does not will go to the worst hell. It is also said that Rama fulfills the wishes of all those who pray to him on this day. On this day, temples are decorated and the image of Lord Ram is richly adorned. Traditional worship begins with chanting Vedic mantras dedicated to Vishnu, and offering flowers and fruit to the god. Satsangs (public gatherings) are organized to commemorate the birth of Lord Ram. Excerpts from the "Ramacharitamanas", praising Lord Ram, are recited. People of all castes and creeds participate in these gatherings to listen to the stories and their explanations offered by the learned. Lord Ram's devotees, fast for nine days with fruit and milk, whilst some fast on the ninth day only.

Rama was the Lord Hari Himself incarnate on earth for the destruction of Ravana. He was well accomplished, beautiful and endowed with royal marks. His glory and prowess were unlimited. He was peerless on earth. He was free from malice. He was gentle. He was the protector of all His people. He always addressed them in gentle words. He never used any harsh words even when somebody provoked Him. He held sway over the whole world.

Let Sri Rama be your ideal. Ideals are remembered and adored for the purpose of adopting them in your own life. The Ramnavmi celebration or the Vasanta Navaratri every year is an opportune period for us to saturate ourselves with the spirit of Lord Rama. We love and adore our ideals because we express thereby our yearning to unite with them. In our worship of God it is implied that we should be virtuous, good and perfect even as God is. Hence the wise instruction: "One should become divine in order to be able to worship God". One cannot be a real worshipper of Lord Rama unless one makes an honest attempt to grow in the virtues that the Lord represents. On the other hand, worship of Lord Rama is itself the surest means to develop such virtues.

One who approaches Sri Rama with love and devotion becomes large-hearted, pure in spirit good-natured and dispassionate in thought word and deed. A true devotee of Lord Rama is His representative, with His power and His knowledge.

Lord Rama was the prince of the Ikshvaku race. He was virtuous and of manly strength. He was the Lord of the mind and the senses. Brave and valiant. He was yet gentle and modest He was a sage in counsel, kind and sweet in speech, and most courteous and handsome in appearance. He was the master of all the divine weapons, and a great warrior. Ever devoted to the god and prosperity of His kingdom and His subjects, He was a defender of the weak and the protector of the righteous. Endowed with numerous wondrous powers of the mind, He was well versed in all sciences-in military science as well as the science of the Self.

Deep and unfathomed like the ocean, firm and steadfast like the Himalayan mountains, valiant like Lord Vishnu, He was the joy of Kaushalya. Though fierce like fire on the battlefield, He was calm like the cool breeze of the Mandara Hills, Patient like Mother Earth, bounteous like the god of wealth and righteous like the lord of justice himself. In the pains and the griefs of His people, His heart swiftly sympathized with the sufferers. In the festive scenes which held them in joy, He like a father, shared their joys. By His honour and heroism, as well as by His gentleness and low for His subjects, He greatly endeared Himself to the hearts of His people. Such a great person was the Lord Rama!

Lord Rama was the best of men with a sterling character. He was the very image of love. He was an ideal son, an ideal brother, an ideal husband, an ideal friend and an ideal king. He can be taken to embody all the highest ideals of man. He led the ideal life of a householder to teach the tenets of righteousness to humanity. He ruled His people so well that it came to be known as Ram-Rajya, which meant the rule of righteousness, the rule which bestows happiness and prosperity on all.

The noblest lesson embodied in the Ramayana is the supreme importance of righteousness in the life of every human being. Righteousness is the spiritual spark of life. Cultivation of righteousness is the process of unfoldment of the latent divinity in man. The glorious incarnation of the Supreme Being in the form of Lord Rama has exemplified the path of righteousness. Let mankind follow His footsteps and practise the ideals cherished by Him, for it is only thus that there can be everlasting peace, prosperity and welfare in this world.

If we wanted to build a great temple, we would want the finest materials, expert architecture and skilled craftsmen. But all that will be of little use unless we build our temple on a solid foundation. And so too it is with our lives. We are meant to be living temples of the indwelling Spirit. Through various spiritual practices we are meant to build a beautiful temple. But unless there is a solid foundation, sooner or later the temple will collapse.

In the Vedic way of life, the temple is built through yoga, and the supreme exemplar of yoga is Lord Krishna. But the foundation of the temple of our life—the irreplaceable necessity—is *dharma*. And today is the special worship of the *avatar* of *dharma*, Lord Rama. But *dharma* is far more than ethical behaviour; *dharma* is the expression of God in manifestation. Therefore, *dharma* is not only the foundation of our spiritual life, it is actually the essence of the edifice as well.

The only purpose of our birth is to express God on earth, and that is what *dharma* is. Therefore, our worship today omits no aspect of our spiritual life from the bottom to the highest point of the superstructure. It represents a dedication to be a perfect vehicle of the Lord. May we worship in that spirit, and may our lives be an expression of that worship.

As further worship on this auspicious Rama Navami day, The Divine Life Society of Maryland has organized a 4th Global International 24 hour Non-stop Japa Yajna of the Sacred Mrityunjaya Mantra. Divine Life devotees from around the world will repeat this sacred Mantra, which most appropriately this time will be offered for world peace and the spiritual upliftment of all mankind. May God and Gurudev bless us all in the celebration this morning as well as our participation in this worldwide Japa Yajna.

His name conjures up a long and incessant cultural history of our country. The renowned masterwork of Valmiki's Ramayana describes the birth in the following manner: *(Following the end of six seasons and the completion of the twelfth month (by the Hindu calendar) On* the ninth day of the month of *Chaitra*, under the star *Punarvasu*, with the sun, mars, Jupiter, Saturn and Venus in Aries, Capricorn, Libra, Cancer and Pisces. When the moon with Jupiter entered Cancer of the Zodiac, Kaushalya gave birth to great Ram with mighty arms and lotus shaped eyes. The preparations start early in the morning and the people take bath in the holy water and also keep a fast until 12 in the noon, when the *avatar* is thought to have taken place The ritualistic puja is done in the morning. *Tulsidas* says that placing Lord Rama's name on the tip of the tongue ensures enlightenment. Ram Navami is also celebrated as the Vasanta Navaratri festival with the celebration starting from the first lunar day of the bright half of the month of *Chaithra*.

Swami Vivekananda said, "Rama, the ancient idol of the heroic ages, the embodiment of truth, of morality, the ideal son, the ideal husband, and above all, the ideal king, this Rama has been presented before us by the great sage Valmiki. No language can be purer, none chaster, none more beautiful, and at the same time simpler, than the language in which the great poet has depicted the life of Rama."

Tulsidasji (The Author of the *Ram-Charit-Manas* - Ramayan), tells us that Shri Ram was born on this day. He goes on to state that he who sings Shri Ram's praise on this day, has all the pilgrimage Centres come to his door-step.

Navami Means the Number 9: Shri Ram is connected with the number 9. The No. 9 is the Highest number. After the number 9, comes the 0. In order to truly worship Shri Ram either become complete like the number 9, or empty like the 0. In order to be a completely full Spiritual Human being, do the following:

1. Keep good company
2. Sing the Lord's praises
3. Listen to the Almighty's 'Katha' (scriptural narrations)
4. Have faith in God

In order to become 0, or 'Shunya' remove the following:-

1. Ego
2. Doubt
3. Desires

The Tarak Mantra "Shree Ram Jayaram Jaya Jaya Ram" is enchanted in its Bhajan form by the devotees throughout 9 days and on the concluding day Ramnavami is celebrated with pomp, fervour and enthusiasm. The celebration attracts devotees from all over the country who crave to have the glimpse of Lord Shree Ram in the cradle. Thousands of devotees join the Santharpana being arranged by the Shree Ram Mandir Math Committee. This holy celebration begins from Samvatsara Pratipada Day and concludes with Avabhrata (Ranga Panchami / Okkuli) the day following Ramjannmsotsav.

On this day, temples are decorated and the image of Lord Ram is richly adorned. Traditional worship begins with chanting Vedic mantras dedicated to Vishnu, and offering flowers and fruit to the god. Satsangs (public gatherings) are organized to commemorate the birth of Lord Ram. Excerpts from the "Ramacharitamanas", praising Lord Ram, are recited. People of all castes and creeds participate in these gatherings to listen to the stories and their explanations offered by the learned. Lord Ram's devotees, fast for nine days with fruit and milk, whilst some fast on the ninth day only.

Sri Ram is the seventh incarnation of Lord Vishnu and Ramnavami is dedicated to the memory of Lord Rama. It occurs on the ninth day (navami) of the bright fortnight of the Hindu month of Chaitra. The festival commemorates the birth of Rama who is remembered for his preperous and righteous reign.

This is an occasion for great rejoicing especially for the Vaishnavas who celebrate it with due solemnity all over the country.

The ancient texts lays tress on fasting on this day, and it is believed that anyone who does not fast will go to the worst hell. It is also said that Rama fulfills the wishes of all those who pray to him on this day.

The public worship starts with morning ablutions, chanting Vedic mantras dedicated to Vishnu, and offering flowers and fruit to the god. People keep a fast throughout the day, breaking it only at midnight with fruit. In some parts of India, public gatherings called satsangs are organised to commemorate the birth of Rama.

Excerpts from the Ramacharitamanas, extolling the glory of Rama, are recited. People of all castes and creeds participate in these gatherings to listen to the stories and their explanations offered by the learned. Ramanavami brings together people of different castes.

Ayodhya is the focus of great celebrations. A huge fair is organized for two days. Ratha yatras or 'chariot processions' of Rama and his wife Sita, brother Lakshmana and devotee Hanuman, are taken out from many temples. Hanuman is worshipped for his unflinching devotion to Rama, and his worship forms an important part of the Ramanavami celebrations.

Personality of Sri Rama: Sri Rama has become so much identified with all the good, great and virile qualities of heroic manhood that expressions such as 'Us me Ram nahi hai' (there is no Rama in him) - meaning that a person has lost all manliness and worth - have become common usage. And when a Hindu quits the world stage, he is bid God-speed in his onward journey [with Ramanama satya hai or Raghupati Raghava raja Ram, patita paavana Sita Ram. In fact, the latter couplet has become the nation's bhajan par excellence.

The story of Rama is not that of a single towering personality dwarfing all others. The other characters like Sita, Lakshmana, Bharata and Hanuman too shine in their own greatness. All of them are so closely interwoven with Sri Rama's life and achievements that it is well-nigh impossible to think of any one without the other. In fact, the most popular picture of Sri Rama, i.e., of Sri Rama Pattabhisheka includes Sita, Hanuman and all his brothers. And in the bringing out of the greatness of all these partners of his life-drama, Rama's instinctive recognition of their merit and virtues played no mean part. He would always be the first to openly appreciate the unique and noble traits in others' character. Even for Kaikeyi, who was responsible for his banishment to forest, Rama had only words of kindness. And as for Ravana, the abductor of his wife, Rama's unstained praise of his erudition and prowess at once lifts the story of Ramayana to heights unsurpassed in the annals of human history.

Spiritual and Religious Significance: The Ramaayana, the Rama story, teaches two lessons: the value of detachment and the need to become aware of the Divine in every being. Faith in God and detachment from objective pursuits are the keys for human liberation. Give up sense objects, and you gain Rama. Sita gave up the luxuries of Ayodhya so she could be with Rama during His exile. When she cast longing eyes on the golden deer and craved it, she lost Rama's presence. Renunciation leads to joy; attachment brings about grief. Be in the world, but not of it.

Rama's brothers, comrades, companions, and collaborators are all examples of people saturated with dharma. Dasaratha is the representative of the merely physical, with the ten senses. The three qualities (gunas) —serenity, passion, sloth (sathva, rajas, thamas)— are the three Queens. The four goals of life (purusharthas) are the four sons. Dharma (Rama), Artha (Lakshmana), Kama (Bharatha) and Moksha (Shatrughna). These four aims of man have to be systematically realised, always with the last one, Moksha, clearly before the eye. Sugriva is discrimination (viveka). Vali is despair. Hanuman is the embodiment of courage. The bridge is built over the ocean of delusion. The three demon (rakshasa) chiefs Ravana, Kumbhakarna, and Vibhishana are personifications of the passionate, slothful, and serene (raajasic, tamasic, and satvik) qualities. Sita is the awareness of the Universal Absolute (Brahmajnaana), which the individual must acquire and regain while undergoing travails in the crucible of life. With these to help him, Rama seeks the Truth and succeeds. That is the lesson of the Epic to every man.

The entire Ramaayana is like a game of chess. The scene, in the Ramaayana, is a kind of battlefield, where the forces of right and wrong are waging war. Rama represents righteousness and Ravana represents unrighteousness. The battle between the two is the war fought on the battlefield.

Ravana taught a great lesson to the world. He exclaimed: "Oh men! Do not live as I have lived and ruin your lives." What is the root cause of Ravana's ruin? Unable to conquer his desires, unwilling to get rid of his impulses, he ruined his entire clan. His sons were killed, his brother and other kinsmen were killed, and ultimately his country itself was reduced to ashes. Ravana confessed, "In the end I ruined myself." This was Ravana's message to his countrymen in his last moments.

Only by suppressing desires does a man manifest his humanness. A man who is unable to put an end to his desires puts an end to himself. By his good conduct, a good man achieves greatness. Ravana sought to achieve greatness but did not strive to lead a good life.

From time immemorial, every individual in Bharat (India) has regarded Sri Rama's life as an ideal and has sought to sanctify every moment of his life by living up to it. Sri Rama incarnated as a human being to promote peace and happiness in the world. "Rama is the very embodiment of righteousness (*Ramo Vigrahavaan Dharmah*)." It was as if righteousness itself had incarnated on earth. Dharma and Rama are inseparable.

The word Rama has the triple power of destroying sins, conferring peace, and dispelling ignorance. When you utter the word "Ram", you first open the mouth with the sound "Ra". All your sins go out when your mouth is open. When you utter "M" by closing the mouth, the entry is barred against the sins that have gone out. Everyone should recognize the sweetness, sacredness, and divinity enshrined in the name Rama. It is good to utter the name Rama with full understanding of all that it signifies.

Fasting: Some observe a strict fast on this day. The diet of such a person would include potatoes made in any form without *haldi* (turmeric), garlic, ginger or onion. He can also eat fruit and root vegetables of any kind. Curd, tea, coffee, milk, and water are also permitted. On the face of it Sri-Ramnavmi appears to be just a festival commemorating the reign of a king who was later deified.

But even behind present-day traditions there are clues which unmistakably point to the origin of Ramnavmi as lying beyond the Ramayana story.

A huge fair is held in Ayodhya (*Ram Janam Bhumi*) on Ram Navami day, where thousands of devotees gather to celebrate this festival.

In Andhra Pradesh: Ram Navami is a major festival celebrated with great religious fervour and devotion. It is celebrated for 10 days from the *Chaitra saptami* to the *Bahula Padyami* that fall in the month of March and April. *Rambhaktas* (devotees of Rama) visit temples where Rama's birthday is celebrated by the re-enactment of his marriage to Sita. For this reason Ram Navami is also called the *Kalyanotsavam*.

In Other Parts of South India: Besides the usual fasting and prayers, a most delightful tradition that is practised as a part of the Ram Navami celebrations in south India is the narration of stories. Talented storytellers are known to narrate episodes of the Ramayana adding local flavour and humour to it. This is essentially a folk tradition and still continues in villages and small towns.

The Sun is considered to be the progenitor of Rama's dynasty, which is called the Solar Dynasty (*Raghukula* or *Raghuvamsa* – *Raghu* means Sun and *Kula* or *Vamsa* mean familial descendant). Rama is also known as *Raghunatha, Raghupati, Raghavendra* etc. That all these names begin with the prefix Raghu is also suggestive of some link with Sun-worship. The hour chosen for the observance of the Lord's birth is that when the Sun is overhead and is at its maximum brilliance. In some Hindu sects, prayers on Ramnavami day start not with an invocation to Rama but to Surya (Sun). Again the syllable *Ra* is used in the word to describe the Sun and brilliance in many languages. In Sanskrit, Ravi and Ravindra both mean "Sun".

None but the righteous can be truly happy. None but he who has the correct sense of duty and the will for its implementation can be said to live worthily. One must be imbued with a definite conviction about the supremacy of moral principles, ethical values and spiritual ideals. These ought to guide one's day-to-day actions and serve as powerful means for the culture of the human personality. That is the purpose of life. That is the way to Self-realisation. That is the message and the mission of Lord Rama's fife on earth.

Devotion to God is not a simple emotion. It is the result of intense dispassion and purity of heart and attitude. You should strive your utmost to possess the good qualities that are extolled in the Ramayana and exemplified in the life of Lord Rama. Otherwise, emotion may rise up in you temporarily to a kind of ecstasy, but you will not experience divine consciousness thereby. Devotion is a fruit which ripens gradually through the processes of self-restraint and virtue. Without intense dispassion there can be no real Sadhana for Self-realisation. Only after detachment from the world of things, is it possible to attain the Supreme Godhead.

Devotion has absolutely nothing to do with age, caste, creed, position or sex. Generally, the worldly-minded people say: "We will practise meditation and devotion when we retire from service." This is a serious mistake. How can you do serious Sadhana after squeezing out all your energy in working? How will you be able to practise the strict Yogic discipline in your old age? Is there any certainty in life? No, the spiritual seeds of discipline and devotion must be sown in you while you are young, while your heart is tender and untainted. Then only will it strike a deep root, blossom forth and bear fruit when you become old and retire. Only then can you bravely face the god of death and meet him with a smile!

I shall tell you the means of attaining the final release from the great cycle of births and deaths. Devotion to Lord Rama is a great purifier of the heart. From devotion arises knowledge. From knowledge comes the realisation of the pure Self. Knowing this perfectly, one goes to the Supreme Abode and merges in the Supreme Self.

Without first developing devotion to Rama who is the Self, who lives in the hearts of all beings, who is all bliss and who is peerless, how can man cross the ocean of worldly life which has sorrow, pain and misery for its waves?

Do thou therefore worship Lord Rama who is Vishnu and the consort of Sita who is Lakshmi. Abandon all foolishness and enmity. Take to the service of Lord Rama. The Lord is extremely fond of those who have surrendered themselves to Him. He has given this promise in the Ramayana: "To anyone who once takes shelter under Me and solicits 'I am Thine', I bestow fearlessness from all beings. This is My vow".

Even a great sinner who is full of evil qualities and who is fond of other people's wealth, is freed from all kinds of faults that pertain to worldly life if only he remembers the Lord always. He attains purity and goes to the supreme abode of the Lord.

The Name of Lord Rama is the greatest purifier of the heart. It wipes away all one's sins. Not only this, but it wipes away the sinful tendencies as well. The Name is sweeter than the sweetest of objects. It is the haven of peace. It is the very life of pure souls. It is the purifier of all purifying agencies. It quenches the consuming fire of worldly desires. It awakens the knowledge of God. It bathes the aspirant in the, ocean of divine bliss. Glory to Sri Rama and His Name!

O Devotee! recite His Name, sing His glory and serve His Lotus Feet. Enthrone in your heart Lord Rama of dark hue, whose image is reflected in the heart of Lord Shiva. Blessed is the pious soul who uninterruptedly drinks the nectar of Sri Rama's Name which has been churned out of the ocean of the Vedas, which removes the impurities of the Kali Yuga or the iron age, which lives constantly on the lips of Lord Shiva, which is a sovereign remedy or unfailing specific to cure the disease of worldly existence and which is the life of Mother Sita.

Ram-Nam burns ignorance, passion and sin. With or without knowledge, correctly or incorrectly, when the word "Rama" is pronounced it showers a rain of good upon the devotee. Sri Rama is Brahman who takes one across the ocean of worldly existence. Rama is one in across whom the Yogis sport, that is, the Self within.

Lord Shiva tells His consort Parvati: "This Ram-Nam is equal to the Lord's thousand Names, or repetition of the Mantra a thousand times".

I call this the anti-gossip tonic. When you find that you are wasting your time in gossip, repeat His Name several times. You can make up for the time lost, and the mind will be slowly weaned away from the habit of gossiping.

Sri Rama is also a wish-fulfilling tree. He will bestow upon you whatever you want! Just read what Lord Shiva further says:

"The seat of all good things, the destroyer of all impurities of this age of darkness, purer than purity itself, the food for the journey of aspirants on the path to salvation, their only resting place, the very life-breath of virtuous men, is the Divine Name of Sri Rama. So say the sages". On the auspicious Ramnavmi day take a firm resolve that you will repeat Ram-Nam with every breath and that you will endeavour to lead a righteous life.

Ramnavmi is one of the most important festivals of the Vaishnava sect of the Hindus. However, even those who adore Lord Shiva celebrate the occasion. Some observe a strict fast on the day. Temples are decorated and the image of Lord Rama is richly adorned. The holy Ramayana is read in the temples. At Ayodhya, the birthplace of Sri Rama, a big fair is held on this day.

In South India the Sri Ramnavmi Utsavam is celebrated for nine days with great fervour and devotion. Those talented in the art of story-telling narrate the thrilling episodes of the Ramayana. The Kirtanists chant the holy Name of Rama and celebrate the wedding of Rama with Sita on this great day. It is an extremely colourful ceremony, highly inspiring and instructive, too.

At the Sivananda Ashram, Rishikesh, Ramnavmi is celebrated for nine days as follows:

1. Spiritual seekers do as much Japa as possible. The sacred Mantras Om Sri Ramaya Namah or Om Sri Ram Jai Ram Jai Jai Ram are chanted.
2. Devotees read the whole of the Ramayana, either the Sanskrit version of Sage Valmiki or the Hindi version of Saint Tulsidas, during these nine days.
3. Those who cannot recite the entire epic may read this single verse which contains in a nutshell the story of the Ramayana: "Formerly, Sri Rama went to the forests, where Rishis did penance, and killed the illusive deer. Sita was carried away and Jatayu was killed. Rama met Sugriva, killed Vali and crossed the ocean. The city of Lanka was

burnt by Hanuman. The demons, Ravana and Kumbhakarna, were then killed. Thus is recited the holy Ramayana".

4. Devotees greet one another with "Sri Ram" or "Jai Ram-ji-ki".
5. Those who have adopted Lord Rama as their favourite Deity observe a fast, taking only milk and fruit for all the nine days. Some fast only on the Ramnavmi day itself
6. On the final or Ramnavmi day, there is a grand worship of Lord Rama in the gorgeously decorated temple. All the Vedic rituals including Laksharchana are performed.
7. A havan is also performed.
8. From four in the morning to late at night, there is Ram and Ram alone everywhere!
9. Leaflets, booklets and books relating to Lord Rama are distributed.
10. Special meetings are held in the evening at which discourses on the life and teachings of the Lord are delivered.
11. Earnest seekers take resolves to accelerate their spiritual progress.

O beloved seekers! Time is fleeting. Know the value of time. Time is most precious. Utilise every second profitably. Do not procrastinate. Abandon all idle gossiping. Forget the past. Live every moment of your life for the realisation of the divine ideal and goal. Unfold your latent faculties. Grow, evolve and become a superhuman or a dynamic Yogi. Struggle hard and reach the goal of life.

May you all attain the final beatitude of life through intense devotion towards Lord Rama! May you live immersed in the ecstasy of divine love! May Sri Rama who is as effulgent as a million suns and who is adored by the gods and devotees, protect you all! May the blessings of Lord Rama be upon you all!

Pooram

In Kerala life is a celebration. The festivals are cultural events which bring together people from all walks of life, all castes and creeds. These are perhaps the only occasions when one gets to watch the wealth of classical and folkarts of the land which are otherwise fast being relegated to memory.

Since the word pooram literally means a group or a meeting, it was believed that every year the dynastic Gods and Goddesses of neighboring provinces met together for a day of celebrations. Trichur Pooram, the Pooram of all Poorams, the most spectacular festival of this cultural capital celebrated at Vadakkumnathan Temple every year during April-May. Though non-Hindus are not allowed inside the temple, Kerala'.

Trichur Pooram, the mother of all temple festivals in the state, is essentially one of spectacles. The two devaswams- Thiruvampadi and Paramekkavu- explore and exploit every source at their command to make this annual festival a memorable one.It is celebrated with a colourful procession of caparisoned elephants, parasol exchanges, drum concerts, display of pyro-techniques and refreshing scenes of public participation .During the festival season, Trichur, popularly known as the temple town turns into a town of colour, music and mirth. The Pooram programmes extending about 36 hours begins with the ezhunellippu of the Kanimangalam Shasta in the morning followed by the ezhunnellippu of the other six minor temples on the Pooram Day. The ezhunnellippu programme which is considered to be a ritual symbolising the visit of the Devi from the Paramekkavu and Thiruvambadi temples to the Vadakkunnathan temple. A major event of the Pooram festival is the Panchavadyam in which about 200 artistes from the disciplines of Thimila, Maddalam, Trumpet, Cymbal and Edakka participate. Another major event of the pooram begins with the setting off of the 'Pandemelam' at noon in which about 200 artistes in the disciplines of drum, trumpets, pipe and cymbal participate. The grand finale of this festival of colour, music and fire works would be marked with a function of bidding farewell to the deities of the Thiruvambadi and Paramekkavu Devaswams in front of the Western Gate of the Vadakkunnathan Temple.

A noteworthy feature of the pooram festival is the participation of a cross section of people and elephants. The pachyderms emerge out in all their regalia with newly fabricated caparisons. They make their way through the milling crowds drawn from all religions, castes and creed to the accompaniment of ecstatic percussion ensembles. The exhibition of the paraphernalia of elephant decorative, commonly known as 'Aana Chamayal pradarsanam', the spectacular show of 'Kudamattom' in which parasols of myriad numbers, designs and colours are exchanged by the people atop the elephants. The Pooram festival is concluded with a spectacular fire works display, which is held in the three hours of the day after the Pooram. The Thiruvambadi and Paramekkavu Devaswams present many innovative patterns and varieties of fire works which make spectators going into raptures. This famous and mighty display of the magnificent display of fireworks add to the popularity of the Pooram festival.

The most striking feature of the Trichur Pooram is its very secular nature. The Muslim and Christian Communities actively take part in it and they play a very prominent role in the very conduct of the festival. Most of the pandals are the craft work of the experts from the Muslim community. For the two days of the festival, the CMS High School owned by the North Kerala Diocese of CST Church and located on the western part of the Swaraj Round, becomes virtually the Headquarters of the Thiruvampadi Devaswam. The temple elephants are tied in the school compound. The 'Aana Chamaya pradarsanam' is also held here. The parasols for the 'Kudamattom' are offered by the churches and their members. At a time when the secular fabric of the Indian Society is slowly disintegrating, one can not be myopic to the relevance of Trichur Pooram, the conduct of which should become worthy of emulation to other festivals in the country.

Thrissur Pooram – 'Pooram of all Poorams' : Thrissur Pooran, the pooram of all Poorams, falls in April every year. It is intrinsically a people's festival in all respects. It is different from other national festivals like the Kumbha Mela of Uttar Pradesh, the Vijayadashami pageantry of Mysore or the Rath Yatra of Orissa. Pooram is participated and conducted by people cutting across all barriers of religion and caste.The unique catholic nature of Pooram could be traced to its genesis two centuries ago when Sakthan Thampuran (1751-1805), the very architect of Thrissur, became the ruler of the erstwhile state Kochi. He took up the renovation of the

Vaddakkannathan temple temple complex which was enclosed by high walls. The four massive gopurams of the temple have been ascribed to him. At a time when nobody would have dared to look straight at the almighty Namboodiris, Sakthan Thampuran stripped of their powers and took over the administration of the temple that claimed an antiquity of more than three centuries.

Thrissur Pooram is considered to be the mother of all poorams, is a cultural highlight par excellence, celebrated in the Malayalam month Medam (April/May).

The two century old festival of spectacular procession of caparisoned elephants and enthralling percussion performances in a never ending succession is an 36 hours marathon event of incredible beauty, a feast for the eye and the ear, unfolding between 6 am to 12 noon the other day.

Different from the usual temple festival, Thrissur Pooram is participated and conducted by people across all barriers of religion and caste.

Historical Background: Before the advent of Thrissur Pooram, the largest temple festival during summer in central Kerala was the one-day festival held at Aarattupuzha, 12 km south of the town. Temples in and around Thrissur were regular participants of this religious exercise until they were once denied entry by the responsible chief of the Peruvanam area of Cherpu, known for its Namboodiri supremacy. As an act of reprisal and also in a bid to assuage their wounded feelings, Prince Rama Varma (1751-1805), also known as Sakthan Thampuran and enthroned as the ruler of the erstwhile Cochin state invited all these temples to bring their deities to Thrissur where they could pay obeisance to Lord (Sri) Vakunnathan, the deity of the Vadakunnathan temple. Further he directed the main temples of Thrissur, Thruvambadi and Pamamekkavu, to extend all help and support to these temples. It is this historical background that determines the course of the Pooram program and it is specifically the ruler's antipathy to the brahmin aristocracy to open Thrissur pooram for the common man.

Religious Background: Adhering to the medieval Peruvanam tradition, the festival is confined to the temples of Devi (goddess) and Sastha (divine combination of Shiva and Vishnu). Ten deities from the neighboring temples pay obeisance to the presiding deiety of Thrissur and only spectator of the Pooram events, Lord Siva at the Sree Vadakkunnathan temple, situated in the heart of the town. Principle participants are Paramekkavu and Tiruvambadi, close to the Vadakunnathan temple. Also participating and known as 'Cherupooram' are the suburban temples at Kanimangalam, Karamukku, Choorakkattukara, Laloor, Ayyanthole, Neithilakkavu and Chembukkavu,Panamukkampilly, altogether 8 deities. The sprawling Thekkinkadi maidan, en circling the Vadakumnathan temple, is the main venue of the festival.

Namboodiri: Brahmin: Pooram: Malayalam: Name of the Brahmin caste in Kerala the caste of the priests; the highest caste in the Hindu society the meeting point of all the arts language of Kerala.

Pooram is the most colourful of all the temple festivals of Kerala. It is celebrated in Thrissur at Vadakkumnathan temple in the month of Medam (April) where the regaining deity is Lord Shiva. Situated on a hillock right in the centre of the city, the spaciously laid out 'kshetram' or temple attracts thousands of devotees from all over the land during the Pooram festival. It is a magnificent spectacle with fireworks, umbrella showing competition and a splendid elephant procession.

The best elephants of the state from the various temples in Kerala are sent to Thrissur to participate in the Pooram festival. At 3' O Clock in the night spectacular display of fireworks begins. It lasts till 6' O clock in the morning. By afternoon the festival ends.

Pooram: When the Gods Meet: Thrissur is best known for its mammoth Pooram Festival, which is the most colourful and spectacular temple festival of Kerala. The legends and myths behind each festival of Kerala are many, varied and equally interesting. Since the word pooram literally means a group or a meeting, it was believed that every year the dynastic gods and goddesses of neighbouring province met together for a day of celebration. This usually happened on the pooram asterism of one of the spring months.

Pooram is the festival of festivals. It is conducted at the great Vadakkunnatha temple of Trissur. The Vadakkunnatha temple, which resembles a Japanese Shrine, is built in the ancient Kerala style with sanded courts, stone sculptures, a traditional auditorium and multi level roofs. In the evening of Pooram day, two lines of 13 elephants face each other, on the ground south to the temple. Each Pachyderm bears an umbrella holder, a peacock fan carrier and a yak-tail fly whisk wielder. Between the two lines of elephants stand percussion and wind orchestras. As each orchestra reaches a crescendo, a new display of brilliant ceremonial umbrellas blossoms over the elephants and the supporting crowd applauds. This continues till sunset when the elephants depart and late at night, the darkness explodes with a magnificent fireworks display.

The gods and their entourage arrived for the meeting on colourfully decorated tuskers. Even today, the converging of these divine processions at the festival venue is an awe inspiring sight. The Pooram draws to a close with mind-blowing fireworks displays in the evening and in the wee hours of the next morning. Some of the main Pooram celebrations are at Aratupuzha, Thrissur, Uthralikavu, Cheeramkulangara, Pariyanampetta, Mannarkad, Perumanam, Aryankavu, Mangottu, Medamkulangara, Kodikal, Thirumandhamkunnu etc.

Thrissur Pooram is held in the Malayalam month of Medam (April- May). Devotees and spectators from all parts of the state and even outside, throng the 'Pooram'.

Introduced during the reign of Sakthan Thampuran (1775-1790), the Raja of Kochi, Pooram is an assemblage of suburban deities before the presiding deity at the Siva temple in down town Thrissur. The Pooram celebration is held at the Thekkinkadu grounds.

Traditionally, two groups representing the main geographic divisions of Thrissur, Paramekkavu and Thiruvambadi, rival to add to the Pooram's grandeur. Both teams field face to face arrays of richly caparisoned elephants. And then 'Kudamattam', a competition in the swift and rhythmic changing of brightly coloured and sequinned parasols is conducted. The whole event takes place in rhythm with the traditional orchestra 'Pandimelam'.

Thrissur Pooram is the most colourful temple festival of Kerala, south India. Thrissur Pooram attracts large masses of devotees and spectators from all parts of the State and even outside.

Celebrated in Medom (April-May) it consists of processions of richly caparisoned elephants from various neighbouring temples to the Vadakumnathan temple, Thrissur. The most impressive processions are those from the Krishna Temple at Thiruvambadi and the Devi Temple at Paramekkavu which is quite a significant event for its devotees.

This festival was introduced by Sakthan Thampuran, the Maharaja of the erstwhile Cochin State. Perhaps, there is no other festival in Kerala that draws such an unbelievable number of people to a single event. However Vadakkunnathan is a mere spectator at this festival, lending its premises and grounds for the great event. The pooram festival is also well known for the magnificent display of fireworks. Fire works start in the early hours and the dazzling display last three to four hours.

The Pooram Festival is celebrated by two rival groups representing the two divisions of Thrissur Paramekkavu and Thiruvambadi vying with each other in making the display of fireworks grander and more colourful. Each group is allowed to display a maximum of fifteen elephants and all efforts are made by each party to secure the best elephants in South India and the most artistic parasols, several kinds of which are raised on the elephants during the display. Commencing in the early hours of the morning, the celebrations last till the break of dawn, the next day.

The procession of the Thiruvambadi Pooram to the grounds of Vadakkumnatha Temple and back is not only important, but also quite enlivening. The marvellous as well as magical effect of the Panchavadyam, a combination of five percussion and wind instruments is to be felt and enjoyed. Among the varieties of festivals celebrated in Kerala, *Thrissur Pooram* is the most thunderous, spectacular and dazzling. There are three temples participating in the event. It is an expression of popular fascination for sound and colour, and because of the pageantry, it appeals to all people. The images of the deities from all temples of the village are taken on elephants to the main temple. The climax of the festival is the exhibition of thirty elephants and the famous fireworks at 2.30 am local time.

Adhering to the medieval Peruvanam tradition, the festival is confined to the temples of Devi (goddess) and Sastha (divine combination of Shiva and Vishnu). Ten deities from the neighboring temples pay obeisance to the presiding deiety of Thrissur and only spectator of the Pooram events, Lord Siva at the Sree Vadakkunnathan temple, situated in the heart of the town.

Principle participants are Paramekkavu and Tiruvambadi, close to the Vadakunnathan temple. Also participating and known as 'Cherupooram' are the suburban temples at Kanimangalam, Karamukku, Choorakkattukara, Laloor, Ayyanthole, Neithilakkavu, Chembukkavu and Panamukkampilly altogether 8 deities. The sprawling Thekkinkadu maidan, en circling the Vadakumnathan temple, is the main venue of the festival its usually know as Thrissur Round.

Since the word pooram literally means a group or a meeting, it was believed that every year the dynastic Gods and Goddesses of neighboring provinces met together for a day of celebrations. Trichur Pooram, the Pooram of all Poorams, the most spectacular festival of this cultural capital celebrated at Vadakkumnathan Temple every year during April-May. Though non-Hindus are not allowed inside the temple, Kerala's grandest temple pageantry, which includes colourful processions of caparisoned elephants and a midnight fireworks display, parasol exchanges, drum concerts can be witnessed from the crowded streets of Trichur.

Commencing one morning the celebration goes on to late in the morning of the next day. It starts at 11' O clock as a procession of fifteen elephants from Thiruvambadi temple to Vadakunath temple and stands in a row on one side. The main elephant of the group will carry a statue of Krishna. At the same time another group of 15 elephants, will start from Paramekavu Bhagavathy temple stand in a row facing the other group. The leader of this group will carry the statue of the goddess. Thirty decorated elephant groups face each other in two rows while drums and nadaswarams (a flute like instrument) create a crescendo of music. It includes around 80 drummers and many other artists who are experts in playing various instruments. Then at around 2' O clock another crescendo of music starts under a tree called the 'Elanchithara Melam' which lasts for three hours. The artists play in a competitive spirit. The atmosphere is filled with music and even the elephants seem to enjoy the music by shaking their ears along with the rhythm of the drums. Around evening people carrying colourfully decorated umbrellas and venchamaramas (peacock-fan) gets ready on top of the elephants. Then the umbrella showing competition called the 'kudamattom' begins. They will inter change the umbrella aesthetically in rhythm of the music. This event evokes considerable enthusiasm from thousands of spectators. After this event, the elephants are taken back and the statues of Krishna and the goddess are returned to the temple. By night, the ground is lighted up by lamps. At 3' O Clock in the night spectacular display of fireworks begins. It lasts till 6' O clock in the morning. The display of fire works is between two parties representing the two divisions of Trichur, Paramelkavu and Tiruvuvampadi each puts forth its best, to make its display grander than that of the other. By afternoon the festival ends.

The gods and their entourage arrived for the meeting on colourfully decorated tuskers. Even today, the converging of these divine processions at the festival venue is an awe inspiring sight. The pooram draws to a close with mind-blowing fireworks displays in the evening and in the wee hours of the next morning. Some of the main Pooram celebrations are at Aratupuzha, Thrissur, Uthralikavu, Cheeramkulangara, Pariyanampetta, Mannarkad, Perumanam, Aryankavu, Mangottu, Medamkulangara, Kodikal, Thirumandhamkunnu etc.

Religious Programme: Following the ancient tradition, Thrissur Pooram is confined to the temples of Devi (goddess) and Sastha (divine combination of Shiva and Vishnu). Ten deities from the neighboring temples pay obeisance to the presiding deity of Thrissur. Chief participants are Paramekkavu and Tiruvambadi. Other participants called *'Cherupooram'* include Kanimangalam, Karamukku, Choorakkattukara, Laloor, Ayyanthole, Neithilakkavu, Chembukkavu and Panamukkampilly.

The festival extends for 36 hours beginning with ezhunellippu of the Kanimangalam Shasta in the morning, followed by the ezhunnellippu of the other six minor temples on the Pooram Day. Where *'ezhunnellippu'* is a ritual symbolising the visit of the Devi from the Paramekkavu and Thiruvambadi temples to the Vadakkunnathan temple. It may be noted that although this grand festival is known as Thrissur Pooram, it is in fact the conclusion of the eight-day Utsavams of nine temples.

Rituals and Celebrations: Major participants of the Pooram, Paramekkavu and Thiruvambadi provide a spectacular show of best of Kerala art and culture to the onlookers as they display their artistic prowess. The groups of artists vie with each to prove their mastery over their respective art and provide a rare show of talent to the spectators.

Massive and colourful processions are organised by temples, starting from Krishna Temple and Devi Temple. The groups enter the Vadakumnatha Temple through the western gate and take exit from the southern gate of the temple. This way they come face to face and the competition becomes open. A major attraction of the festival is *'Panchavadyam'*. Over 200 artists from various disciplines like Thimila, Maddalam, Trumpet, Cymbal and Edakka unleash their talent and leave the audience spell bound. Time of noon is reserved for another event called, *'Pandemelam'*, in which artists holding mastery of drum, trumpets, pipe and cymbal participate.

A procession of caparisoned elephants is the most enchanting facet of Thrissur Pooram. On the Pooram evening, two lines of 13 decorated elephants face each other, on the ground south to the temple. The best of elephants are selected for the procession and given a massive make over. They are painted, bejeweled and given a beautiful satin robe. Colourful silk parasols are the important parts of their get up. Each of the majestic pachyderm gets the honor of bearing an umbrella holder, a peacock fan carrier and a yak-tail fly whisk wielder. This exhibition of the paraphernalia of elephant decorative is called *'Aana Chamayal Pradarsanam'*. Commissioning of elephants and the parasols is vital and is done with utmost secrecy as winning the competition is a matter of pride for the organisors.

Space between the two lines of elephants is taken up by the orchestra consisting of percussion and wind instruments. Just when the orchestra reaches its crescendo, the parasols are changed with an even more colourful and exquisite one. The ceremony is called, *'Kudamattom'*. This is very exciting for the crowds who applaud whole heartedly every time the parasols change. The revelry continues till late in the evening. The deities of different temples arrive on the regally decorated elephants. The sight of the meeting of the different 'Gods' is brilliant and memorable one.

The festival concludes with the dazzling display of fire works. The bursting of crackers continues till the wee hours of the next morning. Shows by Thiruvambadi and Paramekkavu Devaswams are the most reputed and popular of all. Thus the festival which begins in the early hours of the Pooram morning concludes at the break of the dawn, the next day on a cheerful note.

Teej Festival

Held during the monsoons, July-August Teej is also dedicated to Lord Shiva and Parvati and this time it is married women who pray for a happy and long married life. Though celebrations are held all over the state, it is particularly colorful in Jaipur where a procession winds its way for two days through the Old City. It is the festival of swings which are decorated with flowers and hung from trees. Young girls and women dressed in green clothes sing songs in celebration of the advent of the monsoon. The Teej idol is covered with a canopy whereas the Gangaur idol is open.

Teej is celebrated mainly by the women folk of Rajasthan. Married women who idolize Parvati for her devotion to her husband Shiva celebrate Teej. The festivity revolves around singing and dancing in praise of Parvati. The rituals allow the women to pamper and enjoy themselves, to feast, to dress in the best of cloths, finery and jewellery, in fact to look the stunning best.

All over Rajasthan, even in remote villages, Jhoolas (swings) are hung from trees and decorated with leaves and flowers. Ladies and girls can be seen enjoying on these swings, playing games, singing folk songs and applying Mehandi (henna) on their palms. In Jaipur an idol of Goddess Parvati (Teej Mata) is taken out in a royal procession from the city palace so that the general public can have a chance to pay homage to the Goddess. Antique gilt palanquins, bullock carts pulling cannons, chariots, gaily decorated elephants with silver haodas, horses, camels, brass bands, and group of dances all form a part of this grand spectacle. The Pamaquin of Goddess Paravati is carried by 8 men dressed in red color. This kilometer long procession winds its way through the lanes of the old city. Local people come in huge numbers, dress in their best traditional clothes. Space is at a premium as people perch on top of building, windows even trees to catch a glimpse of Goddess. A huge band of urchins follows the Pamaquin to grab these offerings. A lot of merriment prevails during the Teej procession. Groups of men and women can be seen singing dancing and playing musical instruments. Men and women dressed as gods and Goddess also join in the procession.

History: According to Hindu mythology, on the 3rd day (teej) after the new moon in the month of Shravan Goddess Parvati went to the house of lord Shiva, her husband and was united with him. This day is celebrated as Teej all over India and especially so in Rajasthan. Apart from its mythological origins this festival also heralds the arrival of the rainy season. In the month of Shravan the long awaited monsoon finally arrives in Rajasthan bringing relief to the parched land. Like a magic wand it transforms the hot, dusty and barren summer landscape of Rajasthan into the fertile green beehive of activity. The Teej festivities also celebrate this rejuvenation.

Raksha Bandhan

Raksha Bandhan (*the bond of protection* in Hindi) or *Rakhi* is a Hindu festival which celebrates the relationship between brothers and sisters. It is celebrated on the full moon of the month of Shravana and in 2006 it falls on August 9.

The festival is marked by the tying of a rakhi, or holy thread by the sister on the wrist of her brother. The brother in return offers a gift to his sister and vows to look after her. The brother and sister traditionally feed each other sweets.

It is not necessary that the rakhi can be given only to a brother by birth; any male can be "adopted" as a brother by tying a rakhi on the person, whether they are cousins or a good friend. Indian history is replete with women asking for protection, through rakhi, from men who were neither their brothers, nor Hindus themselves. Rani Karnavati of Chittor sent a rakhi to the Mughal Emperor Humayun when she was threatened by Bahadur Shah of Mewar. Humayun abandoned an ongoing military campaign to ride to her rescue.

The rakhi may also be tied on other special occasions to show solidarity and kinship (not necessarily only among brothers and sisters), as was done during the Indian independence movement.

Origins: The origin of the festival is mostly attributed to one of following mythological incidents:

1. Indra's fight with Vritra - Indra, the king of *devtas* (gods), had lost his kingdom to the *asura* (demon) Vritra. At the behest of his Guru Brihaspati, Indra's wife Sachi tied a thread around her husband's wrist to ensure his victory in the upcoming duel.
2. Draupadi and Krishna during the *Rajsuya yagya* - After Shishupal's death, Krishna was left with a bleeding finger. Draupadi, the wife of the Pandavas, had torn a strip of silk off her sari and tied it around Krishna's wrist to staunch the flow of blood. Touched by her concern, Krishna had declared himself bound to her by her love. He further promised to repay the debt manifold, and spent the next 25 years of his life doing just that. For all that Draupadi was the daughter of a powerful monarch, sister to a legendary warrior, and wife to five warrior princes, Krishna remained the only man she could ever truly depend on.

Rani Karnawati and Emperor Humayun: The ealiest origins of Raksha Bandhan in documented history can be traced to the medieval era. During this period the Rajputs were fighting Muslim invasions. Rakhi at that time was a spiritual symbol associated with protection of the sister. History has it that when Queen Karnawati the widow of the then King of Chittor realised that she could in no way defend the invasion of the Sultan of Gujarat, Bahadur Shah, she sent a rakhi to Emperor Humayun. The Emperor touched by the gesture, accepted the rakhi thereby accepting Queen Karnawati as a "sister" and immediately started off with his vast troops to protect Queen Karnavati.

Alexander The Great and King Puru: One of the oldest legendary references to the festival of Rakhi goes back to 300 B.C. At this time Alexander the Great, was invading India. Alexander was shaken by the fury of the Indian king Puru in his first attempt. Upset by this, Alexander's wife, who had heard of the Rakhi festival, approached King Puru. King Puru accepted her as his sister and when the opportunity came during the war, he refrained from fighting Alexander.

Vrita-Indra: The origin of this festival is usually traced back to the mythological incidents of Indra's fight with Vritra-Indra that resulted in Indra's loss. Then, his wife had tied a thread around his wrist and empowered it with divine powers to make sure Indra emerged victorious in the duel that followed.

Krishna and Draupadi: Another incident is the one that concerns Krishna and Draupadi, the wife of the Pandavas. She had torn a strip of silk off her sari and tied it around Krishna's wrist to stop the flow of blood Krishna was so touched by her action that he found himself bound to her by love. He promised to repay the debt and then spent the next 25 years doing just that. Draupadi inspite of being married to 5 great warriors and being a daughter of a powerful monarch only trusted and depended wholly on Krishna.

King Bali and Goddess Laxmi: According to another legend the Demon King Bali was a great devotee of Lord Vishnu. Lord Vishnu had taken up the task to guard his kingdom leaving his own abode in Vaikunth. Goddess Laxmi wished to be with her lord back in her abode. She went to Bali disguised as a Brahmin woman to seek refuge till her husband came back.

During the Shravan Purnima celebrations, Laxmiji tied the sacred thread to the King. Upon being asked she revealed who she was and why she was there. The king was touched by her goodwill for his family and her purpose and requested the Lord to accompany her. He sacrificed all he had for the Lord and his devoted wife.

Thus the festival is also called Baleva that is Bali Raja's devotion to the Lord. It is said that since then it has been a tradition to invite sisters in Shravan Purnima for the thread tying ceremony or the Raksha Bandhan

Yama and the Yamuna: According to another legend, Raksha Bandhan was a ritual followed by Lord Yama (the Lord of Death) and his sister Yamuna. Yamuna tied rakhi to Yama and bestowed immortality. Yama was so moved by the serenity of the occasion that he declared thar whoever gets a rakhi tied from his sister and promised her protection will become immortal.

Raksha Bandhan Celebrations in India: While Rakhsa Bandhan is celebrated all over the country, different parts of the country celebrate the festival in different ways with a different significance.

Tying of Rakhi: Perhaps the single most important way of celebrating Raksha Bandhan is by tying the rakhi. A sister ties a rakhi to the wrist of her brother. The tying of a rakhi signifies her asking of her brother for his protection and love for the sister. The brother is turn, accepts the rakhi, confirms his love and affection for his sister and shows this with gifts and money. It is a family event where all members of family, dressed in finery, gather and celebrate. The tying of rakhi is followed by a family feast.

Rakhi Purnima: Rakhi is celebrated as Rakhi Purnima in North India as well as in parts of Northwest India. The word "Purnima" means a full moon night.

Nariyal Purnima: In western India and parts of Maharashtra, Gujarat, Goa and Karnataka, this day is celebrated as Nariyal Purnima. On this day an offering of a coconut (nariyal) is made to the sea, as a mark of respect to Lord Varuna, the God of the Sea. Nariyal Purnima marks the beginning of the fishing season and the fisherman, who depend on the sea for a living, make an offering to Lord Varun so that they can reap bountiful fish from the sea.

Avani Avittam or Upakarman: In southern parts of India including Kerala, Andhra Pradesh, Tamil Nadu and Orissa this day is celebrated by the Brahmin community as Avani Avittam. On this day they change their sacred threads or Janeyu.

Kajari Purnima: In central parts of India such as Madhya Pradesh, Chattisgarh, Jharkand and Bihar this day is celebrated as Kajari Purnima. It is an important day for the farmers and women blessed with a son. On the ninth day after Shravana Amavasya, the preparations of the Kajari festival start. This ninth day is called Kajari Navami and varied rituals are performed by women who have sons until Kajri Purnima or the full moon day.

Pavitropana: In parts of Gujarat, this day is celebrated as Pavitropana. On this day people perform the grand pooja or the worship of Lord Shiva. It is the culmination of the prayers done through out the year.is a unique Indian festival dedicated to the angelic love between a brother and a sister. Rakhi or Raksha Bandhan is the day of love, care and bonding signified by a thread that is tied around the wrist of the brother by his loving sister. Raksha Bandhan means the bond of protection – a vow that is made by the brother in return of eternal love from his sister.

The festival of Rakhi is observed on the full moon day of the Hindu month of Shravan. Rakhis are generally made of silk with gold and silver threads and are beautifully embroidered with glitter and decorated with semi precious stones. It is also the time when gifts are exchanged, wishes given and blessings showered for a safe, secure and loving time ahead. Rakhi or Raksha Bandhan is known by many names like Vish Tarak - the destroyer of venom, Punya Pradayak - the bestower of boons, and Pap Nashak - the destroyer of sins. In the parts of Northern India, Rakhi Purnima is also called Kajri Purnima or even Kajri Navami. This is the time when wheat or barley is sown and the goddess Bhagwati is worshipped. In the other parts of India like the western states the festival is called Nariyal Purnima or the Coconut Full Moon.

History of Rakhi there are many legends regarding the origin of the festival of Rakhi. According to one, it was a raksha thread that made Lord Indra victorious against the demon king 'Daitya Raj'. Again, it is said that it was Krishna who asked Yudhishthir to wear a Rakhi for protection during the epic battle of Mahabharata. Alexander's wife is believed to have tied a rakhi to the king Puru or Porus. In return he is believed to have promised to protect her and her husband. In the battle when Puru had the opportunity to strike Alexander, his promise is believed to have restrained him from delivering a fatal blow. During Mughal times the custom of tying Rakhis helped bind the Hindu Rajputs and the Mughal rulers of Delhi together. During India's freedom struggle, Rabindra Nath Tagore called all Indians – Hindu, Muslim, Sikh and Christians – to tie Rakhis, demonstrating their unity at the face of turbulent times. Although today rakhi celebrations center on the brother-sister relationship, it was not always so. In the olden days the rakhi thread was tied for protection or raksha. Anybody, a wife, a daughter or a mother could tie this rakhi thread.

The Rishis tied rakhi on the wrist of the people who came seeking for their blessings. The sages also use to tie this sacred thread to themselves to safe guard them from evil. Rakhi – thus – has always signified a bond of love, protection, security and unity. It is much more than just a celebration of brotherly love – Rakhi actually encompasses the broader arena of universal brotherhood and peace. Rakhi Celebrations. Rakhi is celebrated all over the world. Sister wait for their brothers with a warm heart, an auspicious Rakhi thali, rakhi thread, sweets and lovely rakhi gifts for their brothers. In case of long distance relationships, Rakhis are brought online and sent to brothers anywhere in the world. Brothers too send return gifts to their beloved sisters. With wishes and blessings, gifts and greetings, love and unity – Rakhi – the festival of love – is unique in its own way.

The chaste bond of love between a brother and a sister is one of the deepest and noblest of human emotions. 'Raksha Bandhan' or 'Rakhi' is a special occasion to celebrate this emotional bonding by tying a holy thread around the wrist. This thread, which pulsates with sisterly love and sublime sentiments, is rightly called the 'Rakhi'. It means 'a bond of protection', and Raksha Bandhan signifies that the strong must protect the weak from all that's evil.

The ritual is observed on the full moon day of the Hindu month of *Shravan*, on which sisters tie the sacred Rakhi string on their brothers' right wrists, and pray for their long life. Rakhis are ideally made of silk with gold and silver threads, beautifully crafted embroidered sequins, and studded with semi precious stones.

The Social Binding: This ritual not only strengthens the bond of love between brothers and sisters, but also transcends the confines of the family. When a Rakhi is tied on the wrists of close friends and neighbors, it underscores the need for a harmonious social life, where every individual co-exist peacefully as brothers and sisters. All members of the community commit to protect each other and the society in such congregational Rakhi Utsavs, popularized by the Nobel laureate Bengali poet Rabindranath Tagore.

The Friendly Knot: It won't be wrong to say the fashionable friendship band in vogue today is an extension of the Rakhi custom. When a girl feels a friend of the opposite sex has developed a kind of love too strong for her to reciprocate, she sends the guy a Rakhi and turns the relationship into a sisterly one. This is one way of saying, "let's just be friends", without hurting the other person's soft feelings for her.

The Auspicious Full Moon: In Northern India, Rakhi Purnima is also called Kajri Purnima or Kajri Navami, when wheat or barley is sown, and goddess Bhagwati is worshipped. In Western states, the festival is called Nariyal Purnima or the Coconut Full Moon. In Southern India, Shravan Purnima is an important religious occasion, especially for the Brahmins.

Rakhi in History: The strong bond represented by Rakhi has resulted in innumerable political ties among kingdoms and princely states. The pages of Indian history testify that the Rajput and Maratha queens have sent Rakhis even to Mughal kings who, despite their differences, have assuaged their Rakhi-sisters by offering help and protection at critical moments and honoured the fraternal bond. Even matrimonial alliances have been established between kingdoms through the exchange of Rakhis.

History has it that the great Hindu King Porus refrained from striking Alexander, the Great because the latter's wife had approached this mighty adversary and tied a Rakhi on his hand, prior to the battle, urging him not to hurt her husband.

Rakhi: Rituals like Rakhi, there is no doubt, help ease out various societal strains, induce fellow-feeling, open up channels of expression, give us an opportunity to rework on our role as human beings and, most importantly, bring joy in our mundane lives. Shravan purnima's second festival is Raksha Bandhan. This is an ancient tradition. Bhavishya Purana refers to a battle between gods and demons, and Indra (the king of the gods) was feeling depressed. At that time Indra's wife Sachi took a thread, charged it with sacred verses or Mantras for protection and tied it on Indra's hand. Through the strength of this thread Indra conquered his enemies. Since then till today this festival is celebrated.

Through the passage of time festivals are undergoing modifications. Raksha Bandhan is also known as Rakhi. Rakhi has become a sacred festival for sisters and brothers. Sisters tie them to brothers. Priests tie them to people of his congregation. During the middle ages, if a woman tied a Rakhi on the hand of any man, then it became imperative for him, as his religious duty of the highest order, to protect that woman. That man would put his life at stake to protect the honour of that woman.

In those days, many Rajputs sacrificed their lives to protect their spiritual sisters. Humayun received a Rakhi from the queen Karmavati of Chittor and for that, Humayun carried out his sacred brotherly duty and protected her by opposing his own soldiers.

According to ancient traditions, it is customary to have protection threads that are charged with sacred verses (Mantras) and sanctified with rice, durva grass etc.; to have these tied by people who know the Vedas or by near and dear ones. This protection thread saves from sins on the one hand and removes diseases on the other hand. By tying this thread, protection is afforded for a full one year and all kinds of fears are removed.

Nowadays Rakhis are decorated with soft silky threads of various colours, and also with ornaments, pictures, gold and silver threads etc. These Rakhis enhance the artistry of the people. Within these Rakhis reside sacred feelings and well wishes. It is also a great sacred verse of unity. Acting as a symbol of life's advancement and a leading messenger of togetherness.

Each person should celebrate with enthusiasm this sacred festival of Rakhi or Raksha Bandhan. (Raksha = protection. Bandhan = tie).

Two important festivals are celebrated during the bright fortnight in the month of Shravan. One is known as Upakarma and the other as Raksha Bandhan.

The annual "festival" of Raksha Bandhan, which is meant to commemorate the abiding ties between siblings of opposite sex, usually takes place in late August, and is marked by a very simple ceremony in which a woman ties a rakhi — which may be a colorful thread, a simple bracelet, or a decorative string — around the wrist of her brother(s). The word "raksha" signifies protection, and "bandhan" is an association signifying an enduring sort of bond; and so, when a woman ties a rakhi around the wrist of her brother, she signifies her loving attachment to him. He, likewise, recognizes the special bonds between them, and by extending his wrist forward, he in fact extends the hand of his protection over her. The thread-tying ceremony is sometimes preceded by the woman conducting *aarti* before her brother, so that the blessings of God may be showered upon him, and this is to the accompaniment of her enunciation or chanting of a mantra, which may be in Sanskrit or one of the other Indian languages. In Punjabi, for instance, the mantra says: "Suraj shakhan chhodian / Mooli chhodia beej / Behen ne rakhi bandhi / Bhai tu chir jug jee", which can be roughly translated as follows: "The sun radiates its sunlight / the radish seeds / I (the sister) tied the rakhi / brother, may you live long." After the conclusion of the ceremony, she places a sweet in her mouth, and he might return the gesture. The brother bestows a small gift upon his sister, generally in the form of a small sum of money, such as Rupees 51, 101, 251, or 501.

It is doubtless possible, from a feminist perspective, to view raksha bandhan as another expression of patriarchal culture, however well-intentioned. It is, after all, the brother who extends his protection to his sister, and the woman who, in a manner of speaking, agrees to place herself under the protection of her brother. Against such a reading, one could well argue that the festival seeks to celebrate simply the affectionate ties between siblings of opposite sex, and that the brother-sister nexus is, comparatively speaking, innocent. This is scarcely to say that the relationship is devoid of power, or that there are not habitual practices and customs which define the relationship. But the real significance of raksha bandhan may lie elsewhere. Though it has been common in most societies for the woman to leave her natal home at marriage for her husband's home, in India this is firmly entrenched as a social practice, and has often had undesirable consequences. Women who are subjected to harassment or life-threatening behavior on account of dowry by the husband's family have often been reluctant to return to their natal home, and similarly parents are reluctant to take back their married daughters on account of the immense stigma attached to the return of a married daughter.

There is ample evidence to suggest that the problem of dowry has unquestionably been aggravated by the social sanction placed upon married daughters residing in their natal home. Consequently, raksha bandhan can be viewed as an occasion for reasserting a woman's ties to her natal home. The brother conveys a message to his sister that she has not been abandoned by her biological kin; similarly, the woman conveys a message to her husband's family that she can well count upon her natal family to come to her assistance.

Though in principle raksha bandhan is an observance between biological siblings of the opposite sex, the practice often extends more generally to people of the opposite sex who are not biologically related, or who are not related as siblings. On raksha bandhan day, a number of women may tie the rakhi around the Prime Minister's wrist (unless the Prime Minister be a woman), and similarly soldiers can expect to have women tie rakhis around their wrists. Thus, from ads placed on the occasion of raksha bandhan in the *Times of India* (Mumbai, 25 August 1999), col. 3: "Let's break the traditions of Sisters sending Rakhis to their Brothers this time and approach the widows of Kargil Heroes with Rakhis to tie", and "Let us all send a Thread to our Brave Soldiers in Kargil so that they shred their Pakistan opponents. Satnam Kaur." Everywhere, especially in north and western India, females might tie a rakhi around the wrist of boys and men without sisters. A man might acquire a *muh boli behen*, that is a sister who in every respect is such except in biological fact; or a woman may tie a rakhi around the wrist of her male first cousin who is without sisters. Imagining a person of the opposite sex as a sibling is certainly one way of obscuring the problem of sexual desire, and Indian texts are rife with the observation that men should look upon women as their sisters and mothers.

Raksha bandhan is not entirely a pious affair, though sentimentality doubtless prevails. It has, thankfully, also become an occasion for some jest, humor, and mild ribaldry. Rakhi advertisements from the *Times of India*, Mumbai (25 August, 1999), suggest that some men construe "raksha bandhan" truly as an occasion for taking their responsibilities as a protective brother seriously, as in this advertisement which deploys the familiar metaphor of the sheltering banyan tree: "Your Brother Banyan Tree will protect 5 branches Saroja, Vijaya, Laxmi, Thangam, Lalitha on auspicious Raksha Bandhan Day. A.R. Parshuram" (col. 3). A similar sentiment, with the sacred as its central trope, is expressed by this woman: "Dear Brother. Accept my blessing and affection through this sacred thread which tightens our relationship better" (col. 6).

The supposition that a sister stands in place of a mother comes across in some ads: "Dear Sister Ruta, they say mothers couldn't be everywhere everytime, so God made sisters. Ani" (col. 5), and "My Loving Sister, for me you're like both mother & father. You're next to God & your love is next to Divinity. Rays of your love & blessings enlivened me like Rays of the Ultimate. Symbol of love & sacrifice, I adore your feet today. Deeyech" (col. 7). But alongside the expression of these more conventional sentiments, one might consider the humor of the ad from one "Feh": "Dear Bro. Nirlek. You are the perfect Brother to have — good height, strong built, lots of money, and no brain" (col. 5), or the lampooning of India's family planning programs: "Adarniya [Respected] Bachelor Padhanmantriji [Prime Minister] no solution for population control? Try popularising Raksha-Bandhan day all throughout India. Love. Joekar" (col. 7).

The delicate cord tied by the sister to the brother on this day pulsates with this sublime sentiment. History and legends of Bharat abound in touching episodes of ladies seeking protection from far-off, unacquainted heroes, though the Raakhi. A story is told of Alexander's wife approaching his mighty Hindu adversary Pururavas and tying Raakhi on his hand, seeking assurance from him for saving the life of her husband on the battlefield. And the great Hindu king, in the true traditional Kshatriya style, responded; and as the legend goes, just as he raised his hand to deliver a mortal blow to Alexander, he saw the Raakhi on his own hand and restrained from striking.

A more poignant instance is of the princess of a small Rajput principality. It speaks of the spell the Raakhi had cast even on those of alien faiths. The princess sent a Raakhi to the Moghal Emperor Humayun to save her honor from the onslaught of the Gujarat Sultan. The emperor who was engaged in an expedition against Bengal, turned back and hastened to the rescue of his Raakhi sister. But, alas, to his utmost sorrow, he found that the kingdom had already been overrun and the princess had committed Jauhaar, i.e., leaped into the flames to save her honor.

The sister-brother relationship highlighted by the Raakhi goes far beyond the mere personal protection of a female from a male. It also implies the basic element of an amicable and harmonious social life where all members of the society look upon themselves as brothers and sisters and as children of one common motherland.

The congregational Raakhi function carries this social content. Particularly, the tying of Raakhi to the sacred Bhagavaa Dhwaj at the start of the function signifies this social and cultural aspect. Not only do the participants in the function develop a sense of love and affection amongst themselves but they also affirm their loyalty and devotion to the society of which they are the children. Their commitment to protect each other and also the society as a whole is emphasized through this simple ceremony.

In the Hindu tradition the Rakshaa has indeed assumed all aspects of protection of the forces of righteousness from the forces of evil. Once, Yudhishthira asked Sri Krishna how best he could guard himself against impending evils and catastrophes in the coming year. Krishna advised him to observe the Rakshaa Ceremony. He also narrated an old incident to show how potent the Rakshaa is.

Once, Indra was confronted by the demon king - the Daitya-raaja - in a long-drawn battle. At one stage, the Daitya-raaja got better of Indra and drove him into wilderness. Indra, humbled and crest-fallen, sought the advice of Brihaspati, the Guru of

Gods. The Guru told him to bide his time, prepare himself and then march against his adversary. He also indicated that the auspicious moment for sallying forth was the Shraavana Poornima. On that day, Shachee Devi, the wife of Indra, and Brihaspati tied Raakhis around Indra's right-wrist. Indra then advanced against the Daitya-raaja, vanquished him and reestablished his sovereignty

It is not merely that the spirit of Rakshaa manifests itself on occasions of mortal peril to the life and honor of the beloved ones or to the society. It is not like the Home Guards or the militia which are expected to come to the rescue of the people in times of war or natural calamities. No, it is far more deep and all-encompassing. It is like the flow of bloodstream through every limb and organ of the body, carrying strength and nourishment to every cell thereof. As a result, even a small wound anywhere in the body is promptly attended to by the entire body. Every other limb spontaneously scarifies a part of its blood and energy to heal that wound and keep that organ healthy and strong.

'Daridradevo bhava, moorkhadevo bhava.'

The boon asked of God by the King Rantideva who, when his kingdom was ravaged by famine, gave away his last morsel of food to a hungry man and the last sip of water to a thirsty dog, remains the eternal heart-beat of every devout Hindu:

Na twaham kaamaye raajyam na swargam naapunar bhavam |

Kaamaye duhkhataptaanaam praaninaam aarti naashanam ||

"Oh Lord, I desire not kingdom nor the heavens nor even moksha. All I desire is to remove the suffering from the afflicted beings." It is only when this type of attitude towards one's less fortunate brothers and sisters permeates society that exploitations of the weak by the strong will end. Powers of intellect and body, and of material wealth and influence will then be utilized for the uplift and service of others. A Sanskrit Subhaashita says,

Vidyaa vivaadaaya dhanam madaaya shaktih pareshaam paripeedanaaya |

Khalasya sadhorvipareetam etat jnaanaaya daanaaya cha rakshanaaya ||

For the wicked, learning is for dry arguments, wealth is for satisfying vanity, strength for harassing others, but in the case of holy men these are for imparting knowledge, offering charity and protecting others.

In short, Raksha Bandhan affords a most auspicious occasion to recharge ourselves every year with the true spirit of service and sacrifice for the welfare of the society, and find therein the highest spiritual fulfillment of human life.

Scriptural Origin

- The Bhavishya Purana cites a story that the devas once battled with the danavas (demons) for twelve years. However, the devas lost, including the mighty Indra. So they prepared to fight again. On this occasion, Indrani tied a raksha on her consort Indra, after extolling Raksha Bandhan's glory. Indra then attained victory.
- During the Mahabharat war, Queen Kunti tied a raksha on her grandson Abhimanyu to protect him in battle.
- When the demon King Bali's devotion won over Lord Narayan, he was compelled to leave his abode, Vaikunth, to stay in Bali's kingdom in Sutal. When Lord Narayan failed to return, his distressed consort Lakshmi arrived in Sutal on Shravan Purnima. She accepted Bali as her brother by tying a raksha on him. In return, Bali asked her to wish for a boon. She requested Narayan's return. She grieved that despite having a consort she was experiencing premature widowhood in Narayan's absence. However, the Lord had pledged to eternally protect Bali, by guarding his door. To resolve his dilemma, Brahma and Shiva agreed to guard Bali for four months each, while Vishnu (Narayan) would guard him for the auspicious four months Chaturmaas - beginning from Ashadh Sud Ekadashi and terminating on Kartik Sud Ekadashi, usually from Mid-July to Mid-November. The festival of Raksha Bandhan commenced when Lakshmiji tied the 'rakhadi' ('rakhee' in Hindi) on Bali Raja. Since Bali Raja offered devotion by sacrificing everything to the Lord, the day is also known

as 'Bali-eva' or 'Baleva' for short. Therefore when Brahmin priests perform puja rituals, they chant a famous mantra while tying the 'nada chhadi' (raksha) on a devotee:

Yena baddho Balee raajaa daanavendro mahaabalah |

Tena twaam anubadhnaami rakshe maa chala maa chala | |

It means, "I am tying a Raksha to you, similar to the one tied to Bali, the powerful king of the demons. Oh Raksha, be firm, do not waver." The mantra recalls how the demon king Bali had become powerful with the Rakhi on. The power of the mantra is supposed to protect the wearer from evil influences. This shows how dependent and secure a sister feels when she has a brother. Tying this Rakhi or Raksha signifies the restrengthening of the bond between the siblings of opposite sexes.

How this simple, annually recurring act of tying the Rakhi on one's wrist can evoke such strong and intense emotions in a person is indeed surprising. It seems almost like an unspoken pledge, exchanged between a brother and a sister cementing their fraternal relationship and reinforcing their protective bond against all ills and odds.

Raksha Bandhan day starts with a festive mood in every Indian home. Rakhis are made or bought a day before the festival. Traditional goodies and dishes are prepared early in the morning. After an early bath, the offering Puja (worshipping of god) takes place. The sister then offers "aarti" (a traditional way of worshipping) to her brother and ties the thread on his right wrist. Traditional "tilak"or vermilion powder on the forehead of the brother is put and the brother blesses the sister. The tradition of giving gifts and presents is also an important part of this festival. The brother gifts his sister a gift after she ties the Rakhi on his wrist. This gift acts as a token of love and affection of the brother towards the sister. Sometimes sisters also demand for a gift of their own choice to keep it as a loving memory of that very day. However, the blessing bestowed by the brother itself is regarded as the biggest gift for the sister. Treating her brother along with her entire family, the goodies and eatables that have been prepared follows next. The normal rituals are followed with great devotion and dedication.

India shows its unity among diversity in its various ways of celebrating Raksha Bandhan too. Rakhi is mostly celebrated in the northern part of India. The celebration of Raksha Bandhan is more or less the same in this region. But the other parts of India celebrate this festival in various other ways. The rituals and customs followed differ with region to region.

The festival of Raksha Bandhan is also known as Narial Poornima or Coconut Full Moon in Mumbai's famous beaches. Coconuts are thrown into the sea to propitiate the Sea God, Varuna, who is the chief object of worship on this occasion. The 'three eyes' of the coconut are believed to represent the three-eyed Shiva and hence the religious significance. In fact, Hindus consider it auspicious to break a coconut in front of a deity before embarking upon any important venture.A similar practice is followed in some other places in order to offer Puja to the God of rain and water, Lord Varuna.

Raksha Bandhan is called Avani Avittam in South India. This is the time of "upakarmam," and is celebrated in various ways. It falls on the full-moon day of the month of Shravan (August–September). It is an important Hindu festival. On this day, Hindu Brahmans wear a new holy thread and offer libations of water to the ancient Rishis. The day is also set apart for Brahmins to change their sacred thread they wear. Thus, though the rituals and customs followed are different from region to region, the festivities of the Indian festivals have always been present in all the festivals. The characteristics like jauntiness, zeal, customs and rituals, traditional cuisines are also very much present in all the festivals here.

The festival of Raksha Bandhan is very significant in a Hindu society. Hindu society values relationships to a great extent. Raksha Bandhan not only helps in strengthening the relationship between brothers and sisters, it also strengthens the relationship of the society in general. This simple ceremony affirms the people's loyalty and faith not only amongst themselves, but also for the society. Celebration of festivals creates a feeling of unity and belongings in the minds of the people involved to it.

The passing of time and the concept of globalization have influenced the festivals and the ways of celebrating it. Today tying of Rakhi is not confined to the siblings alone. The concept has been widened and Rakhi is tied to anybody whom a girl wants to be a sister of Nowadays, Raksha Bandhan day is also a day for some of the girls to visit the orphanages or prisons to tie Rakhi to the inmates of the orphanage and jails. This is a total humanitarian approach. This kind act gives the fated Rakhi brothers a feeling of hope that there are people who love and care for them too.

To conclude, Raksha Bandhan stirs up one of the deepest and noblest emotions in the human breast—the abiding and chaste bond of love between the brother and the sister. The delicate cord tied by the sister to the brother on this day pulsates with this sublime sentiment. The sister–brother relationship highlighted by the Rakhi goes far beyond the mere personal protection of a female from a male. It also implies the basic element of an amicable and harmonious social life where all members of the society look upon themselves as brothers and sisters and as children of one common motherland.

"Raksha" means protection, "bandhan" means bound or binding. Raksha bandhan, the festival to celebrate the immaculate love between brothers and sisters is falling on August 19, 2005. India has always been known for its colorful festivals and its celebratory fervor. Fresh flowers, exchange of gifts, tying rakhis, new clothes, meeting new and old friends and offering of sweets. All these sum up a typical Indian celebration. Although the significance of these festivals varies with each occasion, they are observed, without exception, with great pomp and joy. The basic characteristics of Indian festivals are the gaiety, enthusiasm, feasts, customs, rituals, and prayers to God. Some of these festivals are related to family and relationship bonding. Raksha Bandhan is one of the festival that strengthen the bond of relationships through obeying of various rituals and customs related to them. They keep the emotional bonding of the family members. Say, between husband and wife, in-laws, or brother and sisters alive and intact. Around mid-August, on Shravan Purnima, Hindus all over celebrate *Raksha Bandhan.* "Raksha" means protection, "bandhan" means bound or binding. In North India, the occasion is popularly called Raksha Bandhan or Rakhi, the tying of an amulet. On this day, sisters tie an amulet, the Rakhi, around the right wrist of their brothers

praying for their long life and happiness. In some places in medieval India, where women felt unsafe, they tied Rakhi round the wrists of men they could count upon, regarding them as brothers. In South India, RAKSHA BANDHAN is called *Avani Avittam*. The Raksha Bandhan full moon day is a household festival for the men, where the sacred thread is ceremoniously changed. The festival of Raksha Bandhan is similar to *Karthikay* in Kartika (October-November) in South India. On this day, sisters offer food to brothers to wish them a long life. The festival is an occasion to strengthen the bond between a brother and a sister.

Narali Purnima: On the full moon day of Shravan, after one or two months of heavy rains and strong winds, the sea becomes calm. On this day boats are allowed to launch into the sea again. But before doing so the sea is worshipped by throwing a coconut ("naral") into the water. In this way Varun, the god of the water, is worshipped.

The Coconut as "Prasad": The coconut is a fruit full of symbolism. It is known as "Shriphal", or "divine fruit". Within its hard shell it contains food and drink, the two essential elements God has placed in creation for man's nourishment. The hard shell expresses God's desire that man should enjoy the fruits of the earth through personal effort. The coconut is the most common fruit used as an offering to God. The effort needed to break the shell represents the element of sacrifice. The kernel and the water are first offered to God and then shared with all those present, and also taken home to be shared with relatives and neighbours as "prasad", or food blessed by God.

NAGPANCHAMI

Hinduism as a religion is many-sided yet bound by a common search for Truth and to Hindus it means a way of life and a fellowship of faiths. With the advent of the Aryans, it originated as a simple form of worship of the forces of Nature, drawing in its system action in social organisations, local cults, deities diverse beliefs and modes of worship.

Nag-Panchami is an important all-India festival and is celebrated on the fifth day of the moonlit-fortnight in the month of Shravan (July /August). This is the time when serpents invariably come out of their holes that get inundated with rain-water to seek shelter in gardens and many times in houses. As such they pose a great danger to man. May be therefore, snakes are worshiped on this day. Right from the times when mankind started acquiring some sort of culture, Sun and Snake have been invoked with prayers and ritual worship in most of the countries. In India even before the Vedic times, the tradition of snake-worship was in vogue.

In ancient India, there lived a clan by the name of "NAGAS" whose culture was highly developed. The Indus Valley civilisation of 3000 B.C. gives ample proof of the popularity of snake-worship amongst the Nagas, whose culture was fairly wide-spread in India even before the Aryans came. After the Naga culture got incorporated into Hinduism, the Indo-Aryans themselves accepted many of the snake deities of the Nagas in their pantheon and some of them even enjoyed a pride of place in the Puranic Hinduism. The prominent Cobra snakes mentioned in the Puranas are Anant, Vasuki, Shesh, Padma, Kanwal, Karkotak, Kalia, Aswatar, Takshak, Sankhpal, Dhritarashtra and Pingal. Some historians state that these were not snakes but Naga Kings of various regions with immerse power.

The thousand-headed Shesh Nag who symbolises Eternity is the couch of Lord Vishnu. It is on this couch that the Lord reclines between the time of the dissolution of one Universe and creation of another. Hindus believe in the immortality of the snake because of its habit of sloughing its skin. As such Eternity in Hinduism is often represented by a serpent eating its own tail.

In Jainism and Buddhism snake is regarded as sacred having divine qualities. It is believed that a Cobra snake saved the life of Buddha and another protected the Jain Muni Parshwanath. To-day as an evidence of this belief, we find a huge serpent carved above the head of the statue of Muni Parshwanath. In medieval India figures of snakes were carved or painted on the walls of many Hindu temples. In the carves at Ajanta images of the rituals of snake worship are found. Kautilya, in his "Arthashastra" has given detailed description of the cobra snakes.

Fascinating, frightening, sleek and virtually death-less, the cobra snake has always held a peculiar charm of its own since the time when man and snake confronted each other. As the cobra unfolded its qualities, extra-ordinary legends grew around it enveloping it in the garble of divinity. Most of these legends are in relation with Lord Vishnu, Shiv and Subramanyam.

The most popular legend is about Lord Krishna when he was just a young boy. When playing the game of throwing the ball with his cowherd friends, the legend goes to tell how the ball fell into Yamuna river and how Krishna vanquished Kalia Serpent and saved the people from drinking the poisonous water by forcing Kalia to go away.

It is an age-old religious belief that serpents are loved and blessed by Lord Shiv. May be therefore, he always wears them as ornamentation around his neck. Most of the festivals that fall in the month of Shravan are celebrated in honour of Lord Shiv, whose blessings are sought by devotees, and along with the Lord, snakes are also worshiped. Particularly on the Nag-Panchami day live cobras or their pictures are revered and religious rights are performed to seek their good will. To seek immunity from snake bites, they are bathed with milk, haldi-kumkum is sprinkled on their heads and milk and rice are offered as "naivedya". The Brahmin who is called to do the religious ritual is given "dakshina" in silver or gold coins some times, even a cow is given away as gift.

In Bengal and parts of Assam and Orissa the blessings of Mansa, the queen of serpents are sought by offering her all the religious adoration. Protection from the harmful influence of snakes is sought through the worship of Mansa who rules supreme over the entire clan of serpents. On this occasion snake-charmers are also requisitioned to invoke the Snake Queen by playing lilting and melodious tunes on their flutes. In Punjab Nag-Panchami is known by the name of "Guga-Navami". A huge snake is shaped from dough, which is kneaded from the contribution of flour and butter from every household. The dough-snake is then placed on a winnowing basket and taken round the village in a colourful procession in which women and children sing and dance and onlookers shower flowers. When the procession reaches the main square of the village all the religious rites are performed to invoke the blessings of the snake god and then the dough snake is ceremoniously buried.

In Maharashtra, Hindu women take an early bath wear their "nav-vari" - nine yards-sarees, put on ornaments and get ready for the "puja" of Nag-Devata. Snake charmers are seen sitting by the roadsides or moving about from one place to another with their baskets that hold dangerous snakes that are their pets. While playing the lingering melodious notes on their flutes, they beckon devotees with their calls - "Nagoba-la dudh de Mayi" (give milk to the Cobra Oh Mother!) On hearing that call, women come out of their houses and then the snake-charmers take out of the snakes from their baskets. Women sprinkle haldi-kumkum and flowers on the heads of the snakes and offer sweetened milk to the snakes and pray. Cash and old clothes are also given to the snake-charmers. Bowls of milk are also placed at the places which are likely haunts of the snakes.

Elderly women draw pictures of five-headed cobras on wooden planks, recite mantras and pray. The daughters wash the eyes of their fathers with rose flowers dipped in milk and then receive gifts from their fathers. In Hindu homes frying any thing on this day is forbidden by tradition.

The most fantastic celebrations of Nag-Panchami are seen in the village of Baltis Shirale which is 70 kilometres from Sangli and 400 kilometres from Mumbai. There people pray to live cobras that they catch on the eve of this pre-harvest festival. About a week before this festival, dig out live snakes from holes and keep them in covered earthen pots and these snakes are fed with rats and milk. Their poison-containing fangs are not removed because the people of this village believe that to hurt the snakes is sacrilegious. Yet it is amazing that these venomous cobras do not bite instead protect their prospective worshipers.

On the day of the actual festival the people accompanied by youngsters, dancing to the tune of musical band carry the pots on their heads in a long procession to the sacred-temple of goddess Amba and after the ritual worship the snakes are taken out from the pots and set free in the temple courtyard. Then every cobra is made to raise its head by swinging a white-painted bowl, filled with pebbles in front. The Pandit sprinkles haldi-kumkum and flowers on their raised heads. After the puja they are offered plenty of milk and honey.

After all the obeisance is rendered to the goddess and the ritual puja is over, the snakes are put back in the pots and carried in bullock-carts in procession through the 32 hamlets of Shirala village where women eagerly await outside their houses for "darshan" of the sacred cobras. One or two cobras are let loose in front of each house where men and women offer prayers, sprinkle puffed rice, flowers and coins over them, burn camphor and agarbattis and perform "aarti". Girls of marriageable age regard the cobras as blessings of good luck in marriage. Some courageous girls even put their faces near the cobra's dangerous fangs. Behold the wonder the cobras do not bite them!

Director of the Madras Snake Park thoroughly examined these cobras and confirmed that neither the fangs nor the poison had been extracted. This truly is something so wonderful that it cannot be possibly explained by man's rational thinking.

In the evening the open space adjoining the temple of Amba holds a popular fair. Pots containing the cobras are placed on an erected platform and the lids are removed. The cobras raise their heads and spectators look on spell-bound. Vast crowds arrive from Kolhapur, Sanghli, Poona and even from foreign lands to see this wonderful spectacle and enjoy in the fair. The following day the snakes are released in the jungle.

There is one popular legend telling how this festival started. Once Guru Gorakhnath while passing through his village saw a woman praying before a clay-cobra idol. He turned it into a living snake and told her not to be afraid of snakes. Since then this Baltis Shirale and its neighbouring regions worship snakes. Guru Gorakhnath's temple is on a nearby hillock. Tribals in the interior parts of Maharashtra perform acrobatics and magic shows on the streets. Crowds collect around them to see and touch the snakes which the tribals bring in their baskets to show them off. There are snake-temples in our country with idols of snake-gods. In these temples cobras are also reared and live snakes are worshipped on Nag-Panchami day. Serpents are worshipped on Shravan Shukla Panchami. On this day, on both the sides of door 2 idols of serpents are made of cowdung. In this vow, on the Chaturthi day one should take food only once a day. One should fast on the Panchami day and should take food only in the evening..

One should make an idols of a 5 hooded serpents of silver, gold, mud or wood pens and using Turmeric and Sandal wood pastes as ink. On the Panchami day porridge, Panchamrit (milk, curd, ghee, honey and sugar), lotus flowers, incense etc are offered and the god is accordingly worshipped. In serpents, Ananta, Vasuki, Shesh, Padma, Kambal, Karkotok, Ashvatar, Dhifrashta, Shankpal, Kaaliya, Takshak and Pingal these 12 serpent are the most important ones. Every month one serpent is prayed and worshipped and the (Brahman) person who performs the worship, should be offered food. On the day of Nag Panchami the Brahmin should be offered cows and gold. Some also offer a silver serpents on betel leaves. The person who performs worship of the serpents on Panchami day should not dig the ground. By observing this vow, one is freed from the fear of snakes and serpents and earns plenty of money.

Nag Panchami is celebrated across India in various ways. In Mumbai, cobras are venerated and fed sweetened milk, usually by women. Tourists can hope to see more snake charmers than usual on the streets and could indulge in a little cobra feeding.

While Christian myth sees snakes in a wholly negative light, Hindu culture reveals a mixed response to the reptiles, a combination of fear and worship. In its positive aspects, the cobra is associated with gods like Shiva (who drapes one around his neck) and Vishnu (who reclines on one). This festival reflects Hinduism's dual attitude in its combination of adoration and appeasement

Nag Panchami is celebrated throughout India; however, more festivities are seen in the south than in the north. The village of Baltis Shirale, which is situated approximately 400 kilometers (approximately 250 miles) from Mumbai, conducts the most outstanding of all the celebrations. Reportedly, the largest collection of snakes in the world can be found in Baltis Shirale. Visitors from all over the world gather in the village to worship live snakes. Interestingly, despite no venom being removed from the snakes, no one has ever been bitten. Other popular areas of worship during the Nag Panchami include:

- Adiesha Temple in Andhra Pradesh
- Nagaraja Temple in Kerala
- Nagathamman Temple in Chennai
- Hardevja Temple in Jaipur.

Important *Aspects of Nag Panchami This* so called "snake day" has several important components. In addition to offerings made to the snakes throughout the country during worship and celebration, men and women celebrate the day in these ways: • Cobras are bathed in milk and offered rice as this is thought to offer immunity from their bites.

- Women often partake in early baths of milk and wear colourful saris.
- Pots of milk and flowers are placed next to holes that are believed to contain snakes as an offering of devotion. If a snake actually drinks the milk it is thought to be the ultimate sign of good luck.
- Mansa, the Queen of Snakes, is worshiped in most parts of Bengal during Nag Panchami.
- In the Punjabi region, a large dough snake is created and then paraded around the village. The parade is colourful with plenty of singing and dancing; at the end of the parade the snake is buried. Nag Panchami is referred to as "Guga-Navami" in Punjab.
- Snake charmers sit alongside the roads of Maharashtra and encourage women to offer milk, flowers and haldi-kumkum (a powdered offering of tumeric and vermillion) to the dangerous snakes the snake charmers carry.

Naga Panchami is a Hindu festival celebrated by Hindus in most parts of India. It is celebrated on Panchami in Shravan month. On this day, they worship Nâga Devata (Cobras). Cobras are considered devine in Hindu mythology. People go to temples and snake pits and they worship the snakes. They offer milk, and silver jewelry to the Cobras to protect them from all evils. It is on the fifth day of the bright half of the Shravan that Naga Panchami, or the festival of snakes, is celebrated. The setting sun is witness to mile-long processions of gaily-decorated bullock carts, cheerfully trundling to the nearby Shiva temple. The excitement and merry-go-round of a fair takes over, lasting well into the night. The snakes that the men had captured from the deep forests the week before can now return to where they came from.

Snake worship no doubt owes its origin to man's natural fear of these reptiles. Hindu books are filled with stories and fables about snakes, and pictures and images of them meet you at every turn. Worshippers search for holes where snakes are likely to be found. When they have found a hole, they make periodic visits, placing before it milk, bananas, and other food that the snake is likely to fancy.

Because of its cyclical moulting, the serpent is believed to be immortal by the Hindus, and eternity is thus illustrated in the form of a serpent eating its tail. Temples have also been erected in honour of snakes. There is a particularly famous one in Mysore, at a place called Subramania, which is also the name of the great snake (it is on this snake that Lord Vishnu reclines while sleeping in the sea), so often mentioned in Hindu fables.

The Naga culture was fairly widespread in India before the Aryan invasion, and continues to be an important segment of worship in certain areas. After the invasion, the Indo-Aryans incorporated the worship of snakes into Hinduism, as is apparent in prevailing worship and mythology. The thousand-headed Ananta is Vishnu's couch and also holds up the earth, while snakes play an ornamental role in the case of Shiva.

Snake worship is more common in peninsular India than in the north. On this day, ploughing a field is forbidden. Legend has it that on this day, while tilling his land, a farmer accidentally killed some young serpents. The mother of these serpents took revenge by biting and killing the farmer and his family, except one daughter, who happened to be praying to the Nagas. This act of devotion resulted in the revival of the farmer and the rest of his family.

On this day, the women draw figures of snakes on the walls of their houses using a mixture of black powder, cow dung and milk. Then offerings of milk, ghee, water and rice are made. It is believed that in reward for this worship, snakes will never bite any member of the family.

In Maharashtra, snake charmers go from house to house carrying dormant cobras in cane baskets, asking for alms and clothing. This festival heralds the arrival of Ganesha, almost exactly one month later.

In Kerala, snake temples are crowded on this day and worship is offered to stone or metal icons of the cosmic serpent Ananta or Sesha. Altars in many Kerala homes have a silver or copper cobra that is worshipped and offered milk and sweets as families pray for the welfare of their children and for prosperity.

In Punjab, the festival is celebrated in September-October and is called Guga Naumi. A snake made of dough is taken round the village in a basket, and an offering of flour and butter is made from each house. The 'snake' is then buried.

In West Bengal and parts of Assam and Orissa, the snake deity worshipped on Naga Panchami is the goddess Manasa.

Lord Krishna and the Kaliya Snake: Nag Panchami is also connected with the following legend of Krishna. Young Krishna was playing with the other cowboys, when suddenly the ball got entangled in the high branch of a tree. Krishna volunteered to climb the tree and fetch the ball. But below the tree there was a deep part of the river Yamuna, in which the terrible snake Kaliya was living. Everybody was afraid of that part of the river.

Suddenly Krishna fell from the tree into the water. Then that terrible snake came up. But Krishna was ready and jumping on the snake's head he caught it by the neck. Kaliya understood that Krishna was not an ordinary boy, and that it would not be easy to overcome him. So Kaliya pleaded with Krishna: "Please, do not kill me." Krishna full of compassion asked the snake to promise that henceforth he would not harass anybody. Then he let the snake go free into the river again.

On Nag Panchami day the victory of Krishna over the Kaliya snake is commemorated. For this reason Krishna is known as "Kaliya Mardan". Snakes are believed to like milk. As this is the day of the serpents, devotees pour milk into all the holes in the ground around the house or near the temple to propitiate them. Sometimes, a small pot of milk with some flowers is placed near the holes so that the snakes may drink it. If a snake actually drinks the milk, it is considered to be extremely lucky for the devotee. The festival is celebrated with much enthusiasm by all, especially women.

As most rivers in India are in spate during the month of Shriven, poisonous snakes come out of their subterranean abodes and creep about in plenty all over the place. Many also float on flooded rivers running through the countryside. Mortality from snakebites must have been considerable to prompt people to worship the nagas to seek protection from them. Because of the fear, nagas were elevated to a divine status by the Hindus. The serpents are believed to have the capability to change their shape at will. When in human form, they are depicted as beautiful women and handsome men.

Naga Panchami is observed indifferent ways in different parts of India. It is one of the most ancient fasts, and finds mention in the Puranas. It is believed to be one of the most auspicious days of the entire year. According to the Bhavishya Purana, when men bathe the snakes called Vasuki, Takshaka, Kaliya, Manibhadra, Airavata, Dhritarashtra, Karkotaka and Dhananjaya with milk on the fifth day of the bright fortnight of Shriven, they ensure freedom from danger for their families.

In some parts of southern India, figures of snakes are drawn with red sandalwood paste on wooden boards, or clay images of snakes coloured yellow or black are purchased. These are then worshipped and offered milk. Snake charmers wander about with all sorts of snakes, to which people offer milk. The snake charmers are paid some money for allowing this Serpent worship developed gradually from the fear of serpents that must have taken a heavy toll on life, particularly at the beginning of the rainy season. In the Ashvalayana Grihyasutra, the Paraskara Grihyasutra and other Grihyasutras, a rite called Sarpabali or 'offerings to serpents' was performed on the full moon night of Shriven. However the reason that it was moved from the full moon night to that of the fifth night of the bright fortnight is not apparent. It may be due to the slight change in the time of the onset of the rains.

The Celebration of Nag Panchami: Nag Panchami is celebrated on the fifth day of the Hindu month of Shravan, which coincides with July and August in the Gregorian calendar.

During this time, snakes often seek refuge in houses as their holes in the ground become flooded with rainwater. Due to the danger they pose to humans, snakes are worshiped during this period to protect villagers from harm.

Nag Panchami is celebrated throughout India; however, more festivities are seen in the south than in the north.

The village of Baltis Shirale, which is situated approximately 400 kilometers (approximately 250 miles) from Mumbai, conducts the most outstanding of all the celebrations.

Reportedly, the largest collection of snakes in the world can be found in Baltis Shirale. Visitors from all over the world gather in the village to worship live snakes. Interestingly, despite no venom being removed from the snakes, no one has ever been bitten.

Other popular areas of worship during the Nag Panchami include:

- Adiesha Temple in Andrha Pradesh
- Nagaraja Temple in Kerala
- Nagathamman Temple in Chennai
- Hardevja Temple in Jaipur.

Important Aspects of Nag Panchami: This so called "snake day" has several important components. In addition to offerings made to the snakes throughout the country during worship and celebration, men and women celebrate the day in these ways:

- Cobras are bathed in milk and offered rice as this is thought to offer immunity from their bites.
- Women often partake in early baths of milk and wear colorful saris.

- Pots of milk and flowers are placed next to holes that are believed to contain snakes as an offering of devotion. If a snake actually drinks the milk it is thought to be the ultimate sign of good luck.
- Mansa, the Queen of Snakes, is worshiped in most parts of Bengal during Nag Panchami.
- In the Punjabi region, a large dough snake is created and then paraded around the village. The parade is colorful with plenty of singing and dancing; at the end of the parade the snake is buried. Nag Panchami is referred to as "Guga-Navami" in Punjab.
- Snake charmers sit alongside the roads of Maharashtra and encourage women to offer milk, flowers and *haldi-kumkum* (a powdered offering of tumeric and vermillion) to the dangerous snakes the snake charmers carry.
- In many villages, snake charmers carry pots containing cobras to a central temple where they are released and then worshiped with offerings of milk and rice.
- Mainly in the south of India, people worship figures of snakes made of clay or sandalwood as alternatives to the real-life versions.
- No Hindu home may fry anything on the day of Nag Panchami.
- Girls who are hoping to marry believe that the cobra offers good luck in their quest for eternal happiness.

Snake worship is popular in Himachal Pradesh. There are references to it in the *Mahabharata.* Man worships snakes either out of awe or out of reverence. He reveres snakes as they are considered the reincarnation of Lord Shiva. Himachalis worship snakes till *Janam Ashtami* when the snakes go into hibernation. Snakes come out of hibernation after *Shivratri,* but their worship begins after *Nag Panchami.* It is only after *Nag Panchami* that they become ferocious. In the rainy season, their holes get filled with water. Unable to stay there they come out and can even bite people. Hence people worship them out of awe. During these months of worship, festivals are held at various snake temples. Decorated shops sell paper-snakes. There are processions in market places. Live cobras are caught by experts and put into multi-coloured pictures. In some parts of Himachal small snake temples are made of cow dung. After whitewashing these, people make offerings to the *nag devta*. The offering is considered fit for Lord Shiva only when a live cobra passes by it.

There are snake temples in every nook and corner of Himachal but all are not famous. The ones at Nagani (Kangra), Bhagsu Nag (Dharamsala), Kamrah (Chachiot) in Mandi district, Chaiyad near Theog, Sapni (Kinnaur), and Naggar (Kullu) where a statue of Rana Guga Mal is worshipped, all deserve a mention. These temples attract a large number of devotees, including foreigners. The most-worshipped *nag devta* of Himachal is that of Kamru Nag whose mention can be found in the *Mahabharata*. Recorded in the history of Mandi state, it is also a god of rains. When Lord Krishna was advising Arjuna on how to fight and win the battle of Kurukshetra, a Yaksha appeared before the Lord. Realising that the Yaksha was not an ordinary one, the Lord gave him a tough test to find out the potency of his arrows: "I will be convinced if you can pierce every leaf of that enormous peepal tree with thy arrow!" When the Yaksha was preparing his arrow, the Lord plucked some leaves and hid them in his closed fists. To his surprise the arrow pierced even the leaves in his fists.

The Lord realised the Yaksha was none other than Rudra. Disguised as a Brahmin, the Lord again appeared before the Yaksha. When asked for *dakshana*, the Lord said: "Thy head alone can appease my hunger!" The Yaksha was taken in. He said: "Thou appease thy hunger, but please place my head on the tree on the lofty Kamru hill from where I can witness the battle of Mahabharata!" Situated at the top of the Kamru hill, this Nag temple stands in the midst of a thick forest. Surrounded by a few small shops and a government cafe, Bhagsu Nag temple is very famous. About 600 years ago, Raja Dharam Chand, the then king of the region, got this temple built. He also built the town of Dharamsala. The remains of his ancient fort can still be seen on a tall mountain facing the temple of Bhagsu Nag. Legend has it that a demon king, Bhagsu, was the ruler of Alvar in Rajasthan. Once a severe drought hit the region. Bhagsu promised his people that he would help them deal with the calamity. Travelling far and wide, he reached the Dull Lake near McLeodganj (Upper Dharamsala). Black mountains surround it.

There was plenty of water there, and snakes infested the area even during winters .Seeing this crystal clear water, Bhagsu Nath was thrilled. He collected the water in a big container and started towards Alvar. He could magically increase the small quantity of water if he reached his destination safe and sound. But the snakes soon realised that some water was missing from the lake. A grim fight ensued between the snakes and the King Bhagsu. The container fell down and the water started flowing in the form of *jaldharas* (waterfalls) which can still be seen at the water tank at Bhagsu Nag temple. Before killing Bhagsu, the snakes agreed to grant his last wish. Bhagsu wanted a temple to be built in his memory at that place. He also disclosed that the water falling from the *jaldharas* had medicinal value unknown to man. Tourists from Kashmir to Kanyakumari visit this temple throughout the year. Guga Zahir Pir whose *mahasmadhi* is worshipped at Naggar in Kullu district is believed to cure snake bites. Russian painter Nikolai Konstantinovich Roerick had made an impressive painting of Rana Guga Mal. Guga came to be known as a saint who could cure snake bites after he visited the holy shrines of Mecca and Medina. Guga was born after his sterile mother got a boon from Guru Gorakh Nath, an incarnation of Lord Shiva. His blue horse was born at the same time as the mare had eaten the seeds of the fruit eaten by Guga's mother. Both Guga and his magic horse were immune to serpents' bites. Guga was brave enough to defeat Mohammed Gaznavi in the battlefield. After killing his vile cousins, Guga entered *mahasmadhi* near Guga Marhi in Bikaner (Rajasthan). To console his weeping wife, Guga started visiting her (in the form of a spirit) at night. Seeing her widowed daughter-in-law adorning herself like a newly married bride every night, Guga's mother naturally grew suspicious. One night the mother caught Guga who promised her that he would emerge from the earth along with his horse.

But he asked her to keep this a secret. She, however spread the news. As a result the bodies of Guga and his horse which had partly come out of the earth turned to stone. These images are still worshipped. Strangely enough, at many snake temples of Himachal, the images of Lord Krishna, playing a flute, and Radha are worshipped. Children make drawings of Murlidhar and offer them to the snake images at various snake temples. Beginning with *Nag Panchami* festivals at snake temples carry on for many months. It is believed that if a person visits a snake temple then his family will become immune to snake bites.

KRISHNA JANMASHTAMI

Shravan vad 8 celebrates the birth of Lord Shri Krishna, one of the most venerated incarnations in the Hindu Dharma. Five thousand years ago, he incarnated, at the end of the third cosmic phase, 'Dwapar Yuga' and the beginning of the present, 'Kali Yuga'.

Purpose of Incarnation: In the Gita (4/78) the Lord has ordained:

"Yadaa yadaa hi dharmasya glanir bhavati Bharat;

Dharma sansthaapanaarthaaya sambhaavami yuge yuge."

In the Bhavishyottara Puran Shri Krishna himself extols the celebration of Janmashtami to Yudhishtir, the eldest of the five Pandavas.

He incarnated in Mathura (Uttar Pradesh) to vanquish the evil King Kansa and other evil elements who were harassing pious people. His second reason was to fulfil the pledge he had given to Vasudev and Devki. When they married Kansa heard a divine proclamation that the couple's eighth son would be his nemesis. To obviate this, Kansa imprisoned the couple and killed the first seven sons born to Devki. When Shri Krishna was born Vasudev placed him in a cradle and took the baby child through the river Yamuna. Thus the Lord survived and eventually vanquished Kansa and other evil elements.

Festival Sentiments: The first importance of Janmashtami is to observe dharma. Since we humans are all imprisoned in samsara, the Lord incarnates in this prison with us, establishes dharma and redeems us from maya. We can only win over maya if we seek the Lord's aid, as did Arjuna during the battle of Mahabharat. As sage Ved Vyas ordains: "Yato Krishnastato dharmaha, Yato dharmastato Jayaha."

i.e. Where there is Krishna, there is dharma, where there is dharma, there is victory. Since Duryodhana, leader of the Kauravs did not observe dharma, he did not have Krishna. No Krishna, no victory.

Surrenderance - 'Sharnaagati': During the battle Shri Krishna uttered 700 shloks in the form of the 'Bhagvad Gita' to convince the reluctant Arjun to fight. The Lord finally uttered the essence of his sermons in the following verse (18/66):

"Sarva dharmaan parityajya maamekam sharanam vraja,

aham twaa sarvapaapebhyo mokshayishyaami maa shuchaha."

i.e. O Arjun! Forsake all your personal beliefs and surrender to me. Do not lament for I shall deliver you from all sins.

Therefore a true spirit of Janmashtami is for devotees to implicitly surrender at the Lord's lotus-feet, while staunchly observing dharma.

Ideal Devotee: In the Gita (18/54), the Lord stipulates:

"Brahma bhootaha prasannaatmaa na shochati na kaankshati,

Samaha sarveshu bhuteshu madbhaktim labhate param."

i.e. One who becomes 'Brahmarup' and offers devotion to Parabrahma (God), he forever remains blissful and attains the highest glory of God. 'Brahmarup' simply means to become the ideal devotee like Arjun who represents 'Nar' to then worship Krishna - Narayan. Hence the murtis of Nar-Narayan. Similarly, Shri Krishna played the 'Maha Raas' traditional (stick folk dance) with the Gopis of Vrindavan because of their unalloyed love for him. Radha was the foremost among them.

Therefore devotees should develop 'Gopi-bhav', to become Radha-rup (like Radha) to worship Shri Krishna. Hence devotees everywhere also consecrate murtis of 'Radha-Krishna' in mandirs, worshipping the Lord with his consort or choicest devotee. In addition to such surrenderance, how should the devotee strive to attain 'Gopi-bhav' to please the Lord?

Satsang: In the Srimad Bhagwat (11/12/1,2), Shri Krishna himself propounds 'Satsang', which is another important principle in celebrating Janmashtami.

"I am not as pleased by endeavors such as: Yoga, Sankhya, scriptural study, austerities, renunciation, altruistic social deeds, donation, fasting, yagna, study of Vedic scriptures, observance of the laws of Dharma and Yama (part of yoga), as I am by Satsang."

'Satsang' means associating with a God realised Sadhu. This was exemplified by King Parikshit when he was cursed to die in seven days, by surrendering to Shukdevji, who was a God-realised sadhu.

Finally, after Shri Krishna's departure from earth, how did the Lord continue his manifestation? This question was posed by Shaunak and other rishis to Suta Purani (in the Bhagwat). He replied, "Dharma resided in the Lord's true sadhu who is the true beholder of Dharma." In the Bhagwat, Shri Krishna supports this when he revealed to Uddhavji: "O Uddhav! You are not any the lesser than me." Thus the Lord revealed Bhagwat Dharma to Uddhavji and since then propagated it through him. The true spirit then, in celebrating Janmashtami is for devotees to do Satsang through the Satpurush who is the beholder of Bhagwat Dharma- in order to realize God within.

Festival and Rituals

- People fast on this day, usually a waterless fast.
- They spend the day immersed in Shri Krishna's glory by reading, reciting and singing his divine leela especially in the evening in mandirs.
- At midnight, the Lord's birth hour, arti is performed. He is also installed in the form of 'Lalji' (child form) in a swing and devotionally offered many sumptuous food dishes. 'Makhan' (butter) is especially included since Shri Krishna loved this in childhood. The traditional prasad is 'Panchajiri' - made of five ingredients: powdered ginger, 'suva', coriander, sugar and ghee. Other ingredients include poppy seeds (khaskhas) and dessicated coconut shavings.

Janmashtami is the birthday of Lord Krishna, the re-incarnation of Lord Vishnu who gave us the vital message of the Bhagwat Gita the guiding principles for every Hindu. Janmashtami is celebrated with full vigor all over the country. Janmashtami is celebrated in various parts of India to mark the birth of Lord Krishna. It is observed on the Ashtami day of the Shravan month according to the Hindu calendar. The temples of Vrindavan witness an extravagant and colourful celebration on this occasion. Raslila is performed to recreate incidents from the life of Krishna and to commemorate his love for Radha.

Lord Vishnu is invoked in his human incarnation as Krishna on his birth anniversary in the festival of Janmashtami. The idol of the infant Krishna is bathed at midnight and is placed in a cradle. Devotional songs and dances mark the celebration of this festive occasion all over Northern India.

On this day, in some parts of India, especially Maharashtra, youths celebrate it by breaking clay pots called 'Dahi-Handi', filled with curd and butter suspended high above the ground, young men and children form human pyramid to reach the pot and break it. This custom follows the habit of Lord Krishna who used to steal butter in this manner from villagers along with his friends. The reason for this is that Gokul; the place where lord Krishna spent his childhood used to generate a lot of milk and the people used to sell it in Mathura, thus depriving their children from milk and butter which is very essential for young boys and girls. In Maharashtra, Janmashtami witnesses the exuberant enactment of the god's childhood endeavors to steal butter and curd from earthen pots beyond his reach.

Krishna Janmashtami is observed on the eighth day of the dark half (*Krishna Paksha*) of the month of Bhadrapadha in the Hindu calendar, when the Rohini Nakshatram is ascendent. The Hindu calendar being lunar, these two events [the day being the eighth of the waning moon (*Krishna-paksha Ashtami*) and the *Rohini Nakshatram* being ascendent] may overlap for only a few hours. In such an event, the festival may be celebrated on different (but successive) days by different people, depending on their local or family traditions.

The pious begin the festival by fasting on the previous day (*Saptami*). This is followed by a night-long vigil commemorating the birth of Krishna at night, and his immediate removal by his father to a foster-home for safe-keeping. At midnight, the deity of the infant Krishna is bathed, placed in a cradle and worshipped. In the early morning, ladies draw patterns of little children's feet outside the house with rice-flour paste, walking towards the house. This symbolizes the entry of the infant Krishna into his foster-home. This custom is popular in some communities of South India. After ablutions, morning prayers and worship, the devout break their fast with Prasadam, food that has first been offered to God. During the fore-noon hours, the "Dahi-Handi" custom is celebrated in some parts of the deccan. This is followed by sumptuous mid-day feasts, where extended families customarily get together. Sweets made of milk and other dairy products, especially butter, are traditionally prepared on this occasion.

The festival is celebrated differently in North India. The temples at Vrindavan and Mathura witness a colourful, even boisterous celebration on this occasion, and festivities at these places may extend for several days. Devotional songs and dances mark the celebration. The Rasa Lila is performed to recreate incidents from the life of Krishna and commemorate his love for Radha.

Care is taken among certain circles not to imitate the Rasa Lila in a mundane way. It is said that one should not imitate the Rasa Lila even in dreams. The idea is that Krishna, or God's pastimes cannot be understood by the mundane mind-set and discussing them should therefore be avoided altogether. Krishna's pastimes with Srimati Radha can never be understood by materialistic people, they are transcendental and great care should be taken to present them in such manner.

While the Rasa Lila recreates the youthful Krishna's dalliance with the milkmaids of his native land, the "Dahi-Handi" tradition of Maharashtra re-enacts his childhood pranks, wherein Krishna and his young friends helped themselves to butter and other goodies in the houses of their neighbours. Clay pots called "Dahi-Handi", filled with curd and butter, are suspended high above the ground. To a constant chorus of "Govinda, Govinda" from all those present, teams of young men form human pyramids to reach the pot and break it, to the merriment of the youths and of the assembly. The festival is thus celebrated with great joy and communal togetherness by one and all.

Janmashtami celebrates the birth of one of the most famous Gods of Hindu religion, Bhagwan Krishna, on the eighth day (Ashtami) in the month of Sravana or Savana. Lord Sri Krishna was born on the 'Rohini' nakshatram (star). It is generally celebrated in the month of August-September according to the Christian Calendar. Legend has it that Sri Krishna was born on a dark, stormy and windy night to end the rule and atrocities of his maternal uncle, Kansa.

Position of Stars at The time of Birth: It was only on the eighth day of the second fortnight, in the month of Sravana when, the moon entered the house of Vrishabha in Rohini Nakshatra (star) that Lord appeared. According to Barhapatyamana, the month of Sravana corresponds to the month of Bhadrapada Krishnapaksha. Lord was born in the year of Visvavasu, appx. 5,227 years ago.

Celebrated for over Two Days: Janmashtami is celebrated for over two days as "Rohini" nakshatra and Ashtami may not fall on the same day. The first day known as Krishnashtami, as the birth of Bhagwan Krishna falls on the eighth day after Raksha Bandhan, which generally falls in the month of August. The second day is known as Kalashtami.

Welcome the Lord at Midnight: It is only at midnight between the first and the second day that birth of Sri Krishna took place. The actual festivities begin during midnight in this 48 hour period. The celebration reaches its peak at midnight, with the birth of Lord Krishna, with lot of hymns, arti taking place and blowing of the Conch (shankh), rocking the cradle of Lord. The idol of lord is bathed with Panchamrit (A mixture of milk, ghee, oil, honey and Gangajal). The Panchamrit is later distributed as Prasad to the devotees along with other sweets. While some Fast on the first day and break it at midnight for others the fasting continues for both days. The period coincides with rainy season.

Janmashtami is celebrated to welcome and enjoy Lord Krishna's birth. The birth of Lord Krishna took place when the various planets were in auspicious places. It is said that God chooses a particular time, as to when he will take birth as a human and the planetary systems are adjusted accordingly.

Born in Dwapur Yug (Iron Age): According to some scholars, Krishna was born on Wednesday,the eighth day of second fortnight in Sravana month in the year of Visvavasu around 3227 BC, also known as Dwapur Yug. July 19th 3228 BC to be more accurate. He lived for 125 years and disappeared on February 18th 3102 BC on the new moon night of Phalguna. His death was the onset of the current corrupt age known as Kaliyug.

Universal Happiness of all Forms of Life: From the time, Devki conceived Sri Krishna, she began to glow and exude divine light. The prison walls glowed with the aura of the new born infant. Atmosphere of peace and happiness prevailed all over, Forests were all green and full of trees with all kinds of beautiful flowers, rivers were all swollen due to joy, peacocks began to dance in sheer joy, people in all villages started being happy.

Objective of Krishna's Birth: The main objective of Lord Krishna's birth was to free Mother Earth from the wickedness of demons. Playing an important part in Mahabharata (legendary battle in Kurukshetra) and propagating the theory of bhakti and good karma were other important objectives.

Events Before The Birth of Sri Krishna: The people of Mathura were extremely unhappy with the wicked king Kansa who put his father, king Ugrasen in prison and declared himself the king of Mathura. It was to put an end to his evil ways and other demons that Lord Vishnu decided to take birth on Earth in human form. According to Akashvani (heavenly voice) at the wedding of his beloved sister Devki, Kansa got to know that the eighth child of his sister will take birth to kill him. So, in turn he rushed to kill his sister.

Kansa gave up the idea of killing after being assured by Vasudev that he will handover all his children to him. He put them in Prison. Kansa killed all the six infants as soon as they were born. The seventh child (Balram) was saved due to divine intervention, when he was transferred from Devki's womb to that of Rohini's (other wife of Vasudev).

Lord Krishna was born in a prison cell in the captivity of King Kansa. He took birth in divine form with lotus like eyes, his palms bearing the signs of a lotus and discus. He had a swastika sign on his sole. Wearing a yellow colored silk cloth, adorned with precious diamond earrings and a crown made of emeralds. Soon after the birth, a chain of events astonished Vasudev, when he saw the gates of the cell flow open and all the guards fast asleep. He immediately thought of Nand ,his close friend in Gokul and decided to handover his child to him in order to save him from the clutch of Kansa.

River Yamuna Bows To The Feet of Sri Krishna: The night of birth was witnessed by heavy rains which led to River Yamuna being in floods. As soon as the feet of Lord immersed in the river, the flow became normal and Yamuna made way for the Lord. Sheshnag, the serpent formed an umbrella to save the new born baby from rain.

Exchange of the Babies: Vasudev kept his child next to fast asleep Yashoda and took the baby girl lying with him back to Mathura. The baby girl is believed to be the sister of Lord Vishnu.

Disappearance of The Divine Child: On hearing the news of birth of the eighth child of Devki and Vasudev, Kansa rushed to the prison-cell and lifted the baby girl to kill her despite pleadings from Devki. However, instead of hitting the stone, the child flew up in the air and announced that the annihilator of Kansa was born and in safe hands.

Lord Krishna, the 10th incarnation of Lord Vishnu, took birth on earth with a purpose. The main objective of taking human form by the divine being was to rid mother Earth from the cruelties and increasing power of the demons. Life Span of Lord Krishna it is believed that Bhagwan Krishna lived on Earth with brother Balram for 125 years. The first ten years of his life were spent in the towns of Gokul and Vrindavan, in Northern India. The following years beginning in the 11th year of Lord's life till the age of 28 were spent in Mathura. Sri Krishna later established Dwarka, a city in Gujarat and lived the rest of his life there with his wife Rukmini and sons. Legends of Lord Krishna's Disappearance. According to researchers, Lord Krishna disappeared on 18th February 3102 BC. The period after his disappearance marks the beginning of

Kaliyug. It is said Bhagwan Krishna had predicted that exactly seven days after the disappearance of the Lord, the Golden city of Dwarka in Gujarat will drown in the sea. Indeed Dwarka city is said to have been merged in sea owing to torrential rain. There are quite a few reasons assigned to Lord Krishna's leaving his spirit for the heaven. They are as follows:

Fulfillment of Sri Krishna's Birth Objective Lord Krishna alighted on mother Earth with the primary objective of reducing the growing power of the demons and relieving people from their cruelties. The secondary objective was fighting the historical battle in Kurukshetra in order to deliver justice to Pandavas. Having accomplished his missions and establishing peace , it was time for Lord to end his life journey on Earth. Curse of Mother Gandhari Mahabharata, the historical battle fought in Kurukshetra resulted in the death of all the hundred sons of King Dhritarashtra and Gandhari. Lord Krishna is said to have visited Mother Gandhari to offer his condolence. In a fit of rage and sorrow, Mata Gandhari cursed Bhagwan Krishna that just as the Kaurava dynasty had ended fighting with each other, similarly the Yaduvanslu dynasty would end fighting and killing each other. Mother Gandhari felt that Sri Krishna didn't play a fair role in putting an end to the war.

Lord Krishna happily accepted the curse. Curse of Sages Vishwamitra and Narada. According to a folklore, Sage Vishwamitra and Sage Narada once visited the city of Dwarka to meet Lord Krishna. A few children of Lord Krishna dressed up Samba (Son of Sri Krishna and Jambavati) as a pregnant woman and asked the visiting sages to foretell what kind of a child Samba will bear. Feeling insulted, the sages cursed that Samba will give birth to an Iron rod which in turn will be instrumental in the fall of the Yaduvanshi Dynasty. The very next day, Samba gave birth to an iron rod. Lord Krishna's sons crushed it into powder and threw the bottle in the sea. However, one day the bottle was washed up the shore and the powdered iron took form of an arrow. Lord Krishna could foresee everything and as a last resort to save his Dynasty, prohibited liquor in the city of Dwarka. Eventually, the Yadavas became drunk and killed each other with iron rods. None of them survived. Lord Krishna was shattered to see the Dynasty perish.

Death of Balram: On seeing the end of Yaduvanshi clan, Lord Balram the elder brother of Sri Krishna sat under a tree and ended his life by breathing out life from his mouth in the form of a white serpent. Disappearance of Sri Krishna Lord Krishna was disillusioned with the fraternal killing among the Yaduvanshis. He went to a forest near Somnath in Bhalka Tirth to meditate. Jara, a hunter mistook the lord's feet to be a deer and accidentally shot him with the arrow. Lord Krishna's spirit left for heaven. Bhagwan Krishna's disappearance marks the beginning of the current debauched age, also known as Kaliyug.The great sage Vyas then wrote the famous 'Bhagawad Puran' to save the heritage and miracles of Lord Krishna. The story of Lord Krishna has since been passed from generation to generation.

Janmashtami Pooja Process: The festival of Janmashtami is considered a very pious day by Hindus. Lot of bhajan singing, hymn chanting and poojas are performed this day. Devotees queue all the major Krishna temples to seek his blessings. People perform elaborate poojas during the festival. They keep day long fast. Functions and prayer meetings are organised to share the glory of their favourite God. The general pooja process begins early in the morning with devotees giving a bath or abhishek to Bal Gopal's idol with gangajal, ghee, water, honey and curd. The idol is then adorned with new clothes (preferably in yellow colour), stone or other precious jewellery. Next, the idol of lord is offered bhog, the contents of bhog may vary. Fruits, kheer, pedha, milk, and milk products are made. There are devotees who offer chappan bhog (56 dishes) to Bal Gopal. Thereafter, special Krishna pooja is performed. The cradle containing the divine infant's idol is rocked, conch is blown. Devotees sing Krishna arti, some people read out 108 names of lord. They get totally immersed in the name and praise of Gopal. After the entire pooja is over, devotees break their fast by having panchamrit. The time of breaking the fast may vary, this is so, because the time of performing pooja also differs from place to place. While some devotees choose to perform pooja at midnight and break fast, others perform pooja in the evening and have food.

Performing Rasleela: One of the most important aspects of the festival Janmashtami is Rasleela. Rasleela is a divine sport (Kreeda), which Sri krishna played with his gopis on the banks of river Yamuna in Vrindavan. Radha was the most important gopi and closest to the Lord. Her love for Lord Krishna was complete and in its purest form. Sri Krishna was ten years old when he performed Rasleela. Rasleelas are particularly performed in the city of Vrindavan. According to Bhagavata Puran, Lord Krishna was loved immensely by gopis.

The love gopis felt for Lord was not carnal, it was prerna (Divine love). The love for Sri Krishna was so strong that gopis forgot all about their worldly chores. The gopis were totally merged in the love of god through the practice of constant smaran (remembrance). Performance *of Rasleela Lord* Krishna promised gopis that he will dance with all of them. So Bhagwan Krishna stood in the centre suurounded by gopis who danced and sang in the glory of Lord. Sometimes Sri Krishna would put his arms around the neck of gopis and all of them would dance together. All the demigods, like Gandharva, Yakshas were witness of the divine dance, as they threw flowers from the sky, giving their blessings. The gopis would rejoice with sheer bliss in the company of the lord and consider themselves fortunate Disappearance *of God during Rasleela Dancing* almost every full moon night during autumn made the gopis conceited.

They started considering themselves superior to other women who were not fortunate enough to be with Lord Krishna. One night during Rasleela, lord Krishna did the disappearing act to teach them a lesson of humility. Not finding Krishna amongst them, the gopis started feeling the agony of desertion. Overwhelmed with grief, they started searching for God and prayed him to come back. During their search for Lord they sang songs popularly known as *Gopika Gitam*. Lord returned after many pleadings. Rasleela *in its present form.* In the current age, Rasleela is performed only by Brahmin boys between the age of 10-13 years. The main theme of rasleela revolves around the formative years of Lord Krishna. There are five main raslilas performed like janamleela- details regarding the birth of Lord Krishna, Shankarleela, Putanaleela- Killing of demoness Putana, And Nagleela- killing of the dreaded serpent Kaliya. They are performed by professional troupes with utmost devotion and love. The troupe captivates the audience with their performance. Rasleelas are usually performed in the local language, Brajbhasa, which is somewhat similar to Hindi language and therefore easy to understand. At the end of the performance, devotees throng to touch the feet of the young boy dressed as Lord Krishna. The young boy ceases to be human for the devotees and becomes a divine being during the festival. Rasleelas are performed by various renowned theater groups, plays are stages with celebrities playing the lead roles to mark the birth anniversary of Lord Krishna.

Janmashtami in Mathura: The celebration of Janmashtami is at its peak in the city of Mathura-birth place of Lord Krishna. The city is about 145 kms from Delhi. Lord is said to have been born around 5000 years back to put an end to the evils of demons. The city of Mathura adorns a complete festive look and the devotional mood reaches its pinnacle. The main celebration takes place at the actual place of birth, now converted into a big temple known as Krishna Janma Bhoomi Mandir. Lord's idol is kept in a room also known as the 'Garbha Griha'. Devotees keep a day-long fast and break it at midnight after the birth time of Bhagwan Krishna. All through the day devotees remain immersed in the chanting of Shlokas and name of the Lord. Songs and hymns are also sung in the glory of Sri Krishna. The Birth of Lord Krishna at midnight is followed by performance of pooja and other ceremonies.

The idol of Lord Krishna is bathed with milk and curd and then rocked in the cradle. A popular belief of the inhabitants is that any wish made while rocking the cradle is fulfilled on this day. The entire Mathura echoes with the sound of the conch (shankh) and ringing of bells. Devotees pray and welcome the lord with slogans of 'Jai Shri Krishna'. After the prayers have been performed, Panchamrit, a mixture of honey, gangajal, curd, ghee is distributed. Lord is fed with the customary prasad of 'Chhapan Bhog' (Fifty six dishes). Devotees break their fast with 'Prasad' of the Lord. Lot of eatables made of milk and milk products are relished by the devotees. Kheer, Laddoo, Butter, Shrikhand and Singhare ki Poori are few of the main dishes prepared on the day. Performance of Rasleelas Rasleelas, a kind of dance drama are performed at various places in Mathura city both by professionals as well as amateurs. Rasleela is performed by young boys between the age of 10-13 years. The artist acting as Krishna takes the divine form for devotees who touch his feet in reverence. Jhanki (Tableau) Jhankis, cribs or scenes depicting the various stages of Life of Lord Krishna are a common sight during Janmashtami all over Mathura city. Jhankis depict various important activities of Lord Krishna right from the childhood like - Janmlila, Shankarlila, Putanalila and Naglila. Jhulanotsav and Ghatas. Another important feature of celebrations in Mathura city are Jhulanotsav and Ghatas. These are specially held only in Mathura City. During Jhulanotsav, Swings are put in courtyard of temples and houses to welcome Lord Krishna's birth. It symbolizes cradling of Lord Krishna. Ropes of swings are decorated with flowers to give a festive look. The celebration of Sri Krishna's birth will be incomplete without Ghatas, another month-long unique feature, wherein all the temples of Mathura City are decorated with the same colour according to the theme selected. Even The idol of Lord Krishna is adorned with the Clothes of same colour. Devotees put their and heart and soul in decorating the temples and their house to welcome the birth of Lord Krishna. Number of Visitors During Janmashtami An estimated 8 lakh devotees visit the birth city Mathura during Janmashtami. The number, however, keeps growing every year. One finds it difficult to find an accommodation during festival days, so devotees get prior reservations made. All the temples witness long queues and it becomes quite a task for the security to maintain law and order.

Janmashtami in Vrindavan: Vrindavan is quite a famous place for pilgrimage in North India. Just about 15 kms from Mathura, the birthplace of Lord Krishna, it houses nearly 5000 temples both ancient as well as modern. The holy town of Vrindavan is where Lord Krishna spent his formative years. The town situated on the banks of river Yamuna is also known for the famous rasleelas that Lord Krishna performed with his beloved gopis. During Janmashtami, the entire city gets immersed in the spirit of devotion. Euphoric celebrations among the devotees is a common sight. The sound of bhajans and chanting echo in the city. Rasleelas and staging of various plays It is said that the city of Vrindavan starts celebrating Janmashtami 7-10 days before the actual date of the festival. This is done by staging various plays and rasleelas at different places in the city. Professional artists enact various episode of Lord krishna's life. These plays are a huge drawers of devotees. Celebrations *at main Temples in Vrindavan Although* there are around 5000 temples in Vrindavan but the main temples are Banke Bihari Temple, Rangnathji Temple, Shri krishna Balram Temple, Radharaman Temple, ISCKON Temple etc. These temples have an itenarary for the entire day, with timings fixed for various ceremonies and poojas all day long. Darshans are open for devotees even during Abhishek (holy bath) of lord Krishna.

Madhuban during Janamashtami: According to legend in Vrindavan, Madhuban is the exact place where Lord Krishna is said to have performed rasleelas with his beloved Gopis more than 5000 years ago. A famous folklore associated with the place is that Lord Krishna till date ascends to perform rasleela with the gopis. Anyone venturing into the place during night either dies or becomes insane. Thus no localite ventures into Madhuban during night. The place becomes alive during Janmashtami with rasleelas being performed in the premises during the daytime. Fasting *by devotees Fasting* is another ritual followed by all the devotees religiously every year. Devotees observe all day long last and break it at midnight after the arrival of Lord Krishna. It is believed by devotees that fasts act as an offering that humans can make to the Lord and bring them closer to him. Devotees cook various dishes of milk and milk products to mark the occasion. This is so because Lord Krishna was quite fond of milk and butter. Popular dishes include Kheer, Pedha, Shrikhand and Singhare ki poori.

Janmashtami in Dwarka: Dwarka, meaning 'Door to Moksha (Salvation)' is a popular city of Gujarat. It was established by Lord Krishna with his elder brother Balram. The city is also known as Golden City. It was built by divine architect Vishwakarma in two days. The city is said to have been made up of diamonds and crystal, with palaces made of gold, emeralds and other precious stones. It was the abode of Lord Krishna for nearly a 100 years. After Lord Krishna's death, the city is believed to have been submerged in the sea.

The celebration of Janmashtami in the main Dwarkadhish temple is very famous in India. Devotees from all over India throng the city of Dwarka during Janamashtami. The celebration on Janmashtami follows the daily routine or *'Nitya Kram'* of Lord Krishna. Rituals are performed by Aboti brahmins, who are special brahmins performing these rituals for the past many centuries now.

The festival day begins with mangla arti performed in the morning. Mangla arti is always performed at 7 in the morning. Beginning with *'Banta Bhog'* (of milk and milk products) offered to Lord Krishna, followed by cleansing of his face with water, brushing of the idol's teeth. Then the first darshan of the day is allowed to the devotees.

Abhishek or Bath of Lord Krishna: Lord Krishna is given the holy bath between 8 - 10 am and devotees are given a chance to see the abhishek which happens only twice a year. The bath is given right after the mangla arti with Panchamrit (mixture of gangajal, ghee, honey, curd and sugar).

Adorning Lord Krishna (Shringar): After the bath, Lord Krishna is adorned with clothes and ornaments. Lord is made to wear Pitamber, a yellow coloured cloth. Ornaments consists of Chandanmala, Vyjantimala (garland) and Suparimala (Made of Betel nut). Makeup on the face of Shri Dwarkadhish is done and he is also adorned with shankh (Conch), Discus (Chakra).

Darshan and Shringarbhog: After the adornment of Shri Krishna, the curtains are removed and devoted are allowed to do the darshans of the Lord. This is Followed by offering of Shringar Bhog (Swees) to the Lord. During this time, the curtains are drawn again and the devotees are not allowed to see the Lord. The Shringarbhog is prepared in the temple premises.

Shayan bhog and Shayan arti: After the evening arti, Lord is offered sweets again, devotees are not allowed the darshans of the Lord during this time. Then it is time for Dwarkadhish to sleep. This happens around 9:00 pm. It is around 10:30 pm that darshans are opened again for the devotees during the Janmashtami celebrations.

Janmashtami by ISKCON: ISKCON is an acronym of International Society for Krishna Consciousness. The organization was founded by Swami Prabhupada, an ardent devotee of Lord Krishna. At the age of 69, Swami Prabhupada left for United

States. In 1965, ISKCON was established with its headquarter in New York. ISKCON is a monotheist faith organisation that believes Lord Krishna is supreme to all the other deities in Hinduism. The organisation is famous all over the world. ISKCON took the western countries by storm with its mantra chanting of "Hare Krishna Hare Krishna, Krishna Krishna Hare Hare; Hare Rama, Hare Rama Rama Rama Hare Hare".

Almost every year, Janmashtami is celebrated over two days by various communities of Hindus. Lord Krishna is believed to have been born at midnight so while Shaivyas celebrate it on the second day after midnight when Vasudevji took him to Gokul, The Vaishnavs choose to celebrate the festival on the first day. ISKCON too celebrates Janmashtami on the second day ie. the day after the birth of Lord Krishna.

Worldwide celebrations by ISKCON: ISKCON, celebrates Janmashtami festival at its various centres all over the world. Main Celebrations are held in the prominent cities of United States including New York. Discourses and lectures are organised to mark the festival and spread the accomplishments of Lord Krishna.

Festive Activities at ISKCON: An offering of 108 dishes to Lord Krishna known as 'Bhog' takes place at midnight and thereafter it is distributed among devotees. Viewing or darshan of the idol of Lord Krishna takes place. The idol is beautifully decorated with flowers. The platform on which the idol is kept is also equally laden with flowers. Thereafter, Abhishek (bathing) of the Lord takes place with milk, milk products and fresh fruit juices. This is followed by Bhajans (devotional songs) sung with various musical instruments in the glory of the Lord, dances are performed by devotees to rejoice the birth of Lord. Finally plays or dramas are held enacting the various phases and leelas of lord Krishna's life. Reading of Scriptures From Bhagawad Gita especially the episode of Birth of Lord Krishna is a special feature during Janmashtami.

Group Chanting of the Hare Krishna slogan takes place continuously and for a longer period than usual days. This is done to appease the Lord.

Celebration of Janmashtami in Brajbhumi: ISKCON organises 'Braj Mandal Parikrama' every year in the months of October-November. This involves a walking tour of nearly 84 miles to about 12 forests in Vrindavan and neighboring towns of Mathura, Barsana, Nandgaon, Gokul, Govardhan Hill and Radha kund. This traditional walk takes nearly a month to cover all the areas. Fanatics of Lord Krishna cover this distance barefoot though shoes are also allowed. This Parikrama is undertaken by the organization to promote Krishna consciousness as well as spirituality. Devotees from all over take active participation to make this event a success.

Krishna Bal Leela: Lord Krishna is one of the most loved and adored Gods of Hindu religion. The foremost reason of the glorification and reverence of Bhagwan Krishna is his Bal Leela. Bal Leela depicts various episodes between the period of his birth till the age of ten. Lord Krishna right from the time of his birth displayed the signs of his divine being.

Episode of Killing of Demoness Putana: According to legend, King Kansa wanted to kill Krishna as it was predicted that he would grow up to kill the King. So Demoness Putana went about killing all the male infants in Mathura and other neighboring towns in the move to kill the new born Lord Krishna. She took the form of a beautiful woman and smeared her breast with poison. While roaming from one town to another, she reached Nand baba's house, and saw Bal Krishna lying in the cradle. She then fled with the child and fed Lord Krishna her milk in the vain hope of killing him. Lord Krishna kept smiling and drinking the milk and after a while Putana shrieked with pain. It is said that while sucking the milk, Lord Krishna sucked her life thus killing her.

Episode of Overturning the Cart by Lord Krishna: As per a folklore, during one of the birth ceremonies of Lord Krishna, Mata Yashoda kept fast asleep Krishna under a cart full of milk . Lord Krishna started crying for milk after getting up, but Mata Yashoda didn't hear his cries so Lord Krishna kicked the cart with his feet and overturned it. The pots were shattered and milk started flowing into his mouth. When the story of overturned cart was narrated to Mata Yashoda, she could not believe it.

Episode of Displaying the Cosmos to Mother Yashoda: Legend has it that one day Mata Yashoda was cuddling Lord Krishna and playing with him. The child lying on his mother's lap yawned and opened his mouth. Mata Yashoda saw the whole universe in his mouth, the sun, the moon and all the stars, the sky, mountains, rivers, islands, oceans, all the continents, all living as well as non living beings.

Episode of Killing of Demon Trinivarta: It is believed that King Kansa sent one of his loyal servant, Demon Trinivarta to kill Lord Krishna. The demon took the form of a whirlwind and carried the child away. As soon as the demon reached the sky, he found it difficult to proceed further on account of the heaviness of the child. Unable to bear his own weight as well as the weight of the child, demon Trinivarta fell on the ground and met his fate. His took his original form after the death and Mata Yashoda was astonished to see her child lying on the dead demon.

Episode with the Fruit Seller: According to another famous folklore, Lord Krishna went to a woman fruit seller and asked her to give him some fruits in exchange for a handful of grains. The woman took the handful of grains from Lord Krishna and put in her basket and left. On reaching home, the woman was astonished to see her basket full of precious stones and gems instead of grains.

Episode of Omnipresent Lord Krishna: Bal Gopal was very mischievous and found great pleasure in playing pranks on gopis. He would steal their milk, butter, break their earthen pots to get butter. One day Lord Krishna, broke all the earthen pots of a gopi in order to get butter. On being caught red handed, the gopi went to mother Yashoda to inform her of her son's mischievous deeds. She was shocked to see the Lord standing next to his mother; Feeling embarrassed she left the place.There are many more popular Bal Leelas of God like the killing of demons Aghasura, Bakasura, brothers of demoness Putana. Mata Yashoda tying Lord Krishna with a rope but each time the rope would fall short by a few inches is another famous episode of Krishna Bal Leela.

Krishna Janmashtami is the celebration of the birth of Lord Shri Krishna, the incarnation of Lord Vishnu, believed to have been born about five thousand years ago in Mathura in 'Dwapar

Yuga'. This celebration is said to be revealed originally by the Sri Krishna himself to Yudhishthira, the eldest of Pandavas, as mentioned in the Bhavishyottara Puran. He was born to Vasudev and Devki, who were imprisoned by Devki's evil brother Kansa and was brought up by Nand and Yashoda. The birth of Lod Krishna is believed to be symbolic of our imprisonment in worldly illusions, where He took birth with us and led us to salvation and peace, vanquishing all evils depicted by Kansa in the story.

Hindus all over India observe fast on this day and recite the life story and teachings of Sri Krishna noted in the form of 'shlokas' in Bhagwad Gita. Temples of Lord Krishna are decorated most beautifully and children are adorned as Lord Krishna and Radhika, his spiritual beloved. Krishna Leela or the plays depicting scenes from Krishna's life, especially childhood, are performed. At midnight, when Lord Krishna was believed to have taken birth, an 'aarti' is performed and people break their fasts by feasting on sweets and delicious dishes prepared especially for the occasion. In many parts, the child Krishna is installed in a swing and offered sumptuous food, especially 'Makkhan' (butter) and 'Mishri' (sugar cubes).

Janmashtami (also known as Krishnastami or Gokulastami) is a festival dedicated to Lord Sri Krishna and commemorates his birth.His birthday falls on the eight day (Ashtami of Krishna Paksh) of a lunar fortnight i.e. 8th day after Raksha Bandhan, hence it is named as (Krishna+ashtami) which comes sometime in August and is celebrated over two days. The first day is Krishnashtami or Gokulashtami. The second day is called Kalastami or more popularly Janmashtami. At midnight between the first and second days the birth of Lord Krishna is replicated with pomp and ceremony. Delicacies are prepared from milk and curds that Krishna loved. The more popular ceremony of Dahi-handi breaking a pot full of milk and its derivativen takes place on the second day.

The temples of Vrindavan witness an extravagant and colourful celebration on this occasion. The image of the infant Krishna is bathed at midnight and is placed in a cradle, amidst the blowing of conch shells and the ringing of bells. Devotional songs and dances mark the celebration of this festive occasion all over

Northern India. Sri Krishna, the ninth incarnation of Lord Vishnu is the most popular avatar and all other deities are regarded as his manifestation. His story and his exploits (leela) are numerous and very well known. To the Hindu, he is the supreme statesman, warrior, hero, philosopher, teacher and god himself.

In Indian religion and culture Lord Krishna has a unique status as a divine personality, combining in himself the qualities of a hero and a statesman, a warrior and a philosopher.

He grew to enormous proportion in the race memory of the Aryans and came to be worshipped as an Incarnation of Lord Vishnu. The teachings of this Supreme Personality as delivered in His Immortal "Bhagavad Gita"- The Song Divine - to Arjun on the battlefield of Kurukshetra, stand out untouched through the ages. He has also been portrayed as a naughty child, an inspired cowherd, a destroyer of demons, an enthralling flute-player, a divine lover, and a clever diplomat - all rolled in one. No wonder then that his day of birth is celebrated throughout the country very enthusiastically.

In the month of Shravan - July / August /September- falls the festival of Janmashtami. Lord Krishna was born as the eighth Incarnation of Lord Vishnu. This is an important festival especially of the Vaishnavas who are devotees of Lord Vishnu.

The main object of the incarnation of Vishnu as Krishna, who was born on the 8th day of Shravan at midnight, was to destroy the cruel King Kansa of Mathura. After the marriage of his sister, Devaki to Vasudev, when Kansa was driving the bridal chariot there burst forth - a voice from heaven -an AKASHVANI - predicting that the 8th child of Devaki would kill him. Kansa immediately put behind bars his sister Devaki and her husband. In prison she gave birth to 6 kids when Kansa brutally killed, but when Devaki conceived for the seventh time, gods transformed the embryo to the womb of Rohini, Vasudev's second wife who gave birth to a son whom was named Balram. Balram was the incarnation of the Shesh Nag - the ten-headed cobra on whose back Lord Vishnu always rested and slept in "Kshirasagar"- the sea of milk. When Devaki gave birth to her eighth child the newly born baby changed himself into the form of Vishnu and commanded Vasudev to carry him to Nandgaon and place him besides Yasodha and bring back the baby girl whom Yashoda had delivered. Vasudev immediately obeyed and brought back the baby girl. Enraged Kansa smashed her on the wall but she escaped and flew away to heaven announcing -"Beware, your killer is alive".

Krishna grew up in Nandgaon amongst cowherds. His flute-playing not only maddened the "gopis" who danced around him but even the cows would come to him hearing his flute. As such Krishna is regarded as the god of song and dance and hence the main celebrations on this festival is "RASLILA" in imitation of Krishna's moonlight dance with the gopis in the fields of Vrindavan. The Dandiya or Garba dances of today originated from that "Raslila in Vrajbhoomi" on banks of river Yamuna.

On this auspicious day of Janmashtami a small idol of child Krishna is placed in a cradle and everyone swings the cradle to the tune of songs. Exactly at midnight, Krishna's birth is announced with ringing of bells and blowing of conch shells. The whole atmosphere becomes full of joy and exultation as Vishnu's incarnation Krishna is born to give security to the suffering humanity. Then "Naivedya" is offered a of a mixture of puffed rice, milk , curds and sugar and distributed as "prasad".

GANESH CHATURTHI

Ganesh Chaturthi is one of the most popular of Hindu festivals. This is the birthday of Lord Ganesha. It is the day most sacred to Lord Ganesha. It falls on the 4th day of the bright fortnight of Bhadrapada (August-September). It is observed throughout India, as well as by devoted Hindus in all parts of the world.

Clay figures of the Deity are made and after being worshipped for two days, or in some cases ten days, they are imnersed into water.

Lord Ganesha is the elephant-headed God. He is worshipped first in any prayers. His Names are repeated first before any auspicious work is begun, before any kind of worship is begun.

He is the Lord of power and wisdom. He is the eldest son of Lord Shiva and the elder brother of Skanda or Kartikeya. He is the energy of Lord Shiva and so He is called the son of Shankar and Umadevi. By worshipping Lord Ganesha mothers hope to earn for their sons the sterling virtues of Ganesha.

The following story is narrated about His birth and how He came to have the head of an elephant:

Once upon a time, the Goddess Gauri (consort of Lord Shiva), while bathing, created Ganesha as a pure white being out of the mud of Her Body and placed Him at the entrance of the house. She told Him not to allow anyone to enter while she went inside for a bath. Lord Shiva Himself was returning home quite thirsty and was stopped by Ganesha at the gate. Shiva became angry and cut off Ganesha's head as He thought Ganesha was an outsider.

When Gauri came to know of this she was sorely grieved. To console her grief, Shiva ordered His servants to cut off and bring to Him the head of any creature that might be sleeping with its head facing north. The servants went on their mission and found only an elephant in that position. The sacrifice was thus made and the elephant's head was brought before Shiva. The Lord then joined the elephant's head onto the body of Ganesha.

Lord Shiva made His son worthy of worship at the beginning of all undertakings, marriages, expeditions, studies, etc. He ordained that the annual worship of Ganesha should take place on the 4th day of the bright half of Bhadrapada.

Without the Grace of Sri Ganesha and His help nothing whatsoever can be achieved. No action can be undertaken without His support, Grace or blessing.

In his first lesson in the alphabet a Maharashtrian child is initiated into the Mantra of Lord Ganesha, *Om Sri Ganeshaya Namah*. Only then is the alphabet taught.

The following are some of the common Names of Lord Ganesha: Dhoomraketu, Sumukha, Ekadantha, Gajakarnaka, Lambodara, Vignaraja, Ganadhyaksha, Phalachandra, Gajanana, Vinayaka, Vakratunda, Siddhivinayaka, Surpakarna, Heramba, Skandapurvaja, Kapila and Vigneshwara. He is also known by many as Maha-Ganapathi.

His Mantra is *Om Gung Ganapathaye Namah.* Spiritual aspirants who worship Ganesha as their tutelary Deity repeat this Mantra or *Om Sri Ganeshaya Namah.*

The devotees of Ganesha also do Japa of the Ganesha Gayatri Mantra. This is as follows.

Tat purushaaya vidmahe

Vakratundaaya dheemahi

Tanno dhanti prachodayaat.

Lord Ganesha is an embodiment of wisdom and bliss. He is the Lord of Brahmacharins. He is foremost amongst the celibates.

He has as his vehicle a small mouse. He is the presiding Deity of the Muladhara Chakra, the psychic centre in the body in which the Kundalini Shakti resides.

He is the Lord who removes all obstacles on the path of the spiritual aspirant, and bestows upon him worldly as well as spiritual success. Hence He is called Vigna Vinayaka. His Bija Akshara (root syllable) is *Gung,* pronounced to rhyme with the English word "sung". He is the Lord of harmony and peace.

Lord Ganesha represents Om or the Pranava, which is the chief Mantra among the Hindus. Nothing can be done without uttering it. This explains the practice of invoking Ganesha before beginning any rite or undertaking any project. His two feet represent the power of knowledge and the power of action. The elephant head is significant in that it is the only figure in nature that has the form of the symbol for Om.

The significance of riding on a mouse is the complete conquest over egoism. The holding of the *ankusha* represents His rulership of the world. It is the emblem of divine Royalty.

Ganesha is the first God. Riding on a mouse, one of nature's smallest creatures and having the head of an elephant, the biggest of all animals, denotes that Ganesha is the creator of all creatures. Elephants are very wise animals; this indicates that Lord Ganesha is an embodiment of wisdom. It also denotes the process of evolution—the mouse gradually evolves into an elephant and finally becomes a man. This is why Ganesha has a human body, an elephant's head and a mouse as His vehicle. This is the symbolic philosophy of His form.

He is the Lord of Ganas or groups, for instance groups of elements, groups of senses, etc. He is the head of the followers of Shiva or the celestial servants of Lord Shiva.

The Vaishnavas also worship Lord Ganesha. They have given Him the name of Tumbikkai Alwar which means the divinity with the proboscis (the elephant's trunk).

Lord Ganesha's two powers are the Kundalini and the Vallabha or power of love.

He is very fond of sweet pudding or balls of rice flour with a sweet core. On one of His birthdays He was going around house to house accepting the offerings of sweet puddings. Having eaten a good number of these, He set out moving on His mouse at night. Suddenly the mouse stumbled—it had seen a snake and became frightened—with the result that Ganesha fell down. His stomach burst open and all the sweet puddings came out. But Ganesha stuffed them back into His stomach and, catching hold of the snake, tied it around His belly.

Seeing all this, the moon in the sky had a hearty laugh. This unseemly behaviour of the moon annoyed Him immensely and so he pulled out one of His tusks and hurled it against the moon, and cursed that no one should look at the moon on the Ganesh Chaturthi day. If anyone does, he will surely earn a bad name, censure or ill-repute. However, if by mistake someone does happen to look at the moon on this day, then the only way he can be freed from the curse is by repeating or listening to the story of how Lord Krishna cleared His character regarding the Syamantaka jewel. This story is quoted in the *Srimad Bhagavatam.* Lord Ganesha was pleased to ordain thus. Glory to Lord Ganesha! How kind and merciful He is unto His devotees!

Ganesha and His brother Lord Subramanya once had a dispute as to who was the elder of the two. The matter was referred to Lord Shiva for final decision. Shiva decided that whoever would make a tour of the whole world and come back first to the starting point had the right to be the elder. Subramanya flew off at once on his vehicle, the peacock, to make a circuit of the world. But the wise Ganesha went, in loving worshipfulness, around His divine parents and asked for the prize of His victory.

Lord Shiva said, "Beloved and wise Ganesha! But how can I give you the prize; you did not go around the world?"

Ganesha replied, "No, but I have gone around my parents. My parents represent the entire manifested universe!"

Thus the dispute was settled in favour of Lord Ganesha, who was thereafter acknowledged as the elder of the two brothers. Mother Parvati also gave Him a fruit as a prize for this victory.

In the *Ganapathi Upanishad,* Ganesha is identified with the Supreme Self. The legends that are connected with Lord Ganesha are recorded in the Ganesha Khanda of the *Brahma Vivartha Purana.*

On the Ganesh Chaturthi day, meditate on the stories connected with Lord Ganesha early in the morning, during the Brahmamuhurta period. Then, after taking a bath, go to the temple and do the prayers of Lord Ganesha. Offer Him some coconut and sweet pudding. Pray with faith and devotion that He may remove all the obstacles that you experience on the spiritual path. Worship Him at home, too. You can get the assistance of a pundit. Have an image of Lord Ganesha in your house. Feel His Presence in it.

Don't forget not to look at the moon on that day; remember that it behaved unbecomingly towards the Lord. This really means avoid the company of all those who have no faith in God, and who deride God, your Guru and religion, from this very day.

Take fresh spiritual resolves and pray to Lord Ganesha for inner spiritual strength to attain success in all your undertakings.

May the blessings of Sri Ganesha be upon you all! May He remove all the obstacles that stand in your spiritual path! May He bestow on you all material prosperity as well as liberation!

Ganesha — the elephant-deity riding a mouse — has become one of the commonest mnemonics for anything associated with Hinduism. This not only suggests the importance of Ganesha, but also shows how popular and pervasive this deity is in the minds of the masses.

The Lord of Success: The son of Shiva and Parvati, Ganesha has an elephantine countenance with a curved trunk and big ears, and a huge pot-bellied body of a human being. He is the Lord of success and destroyer of evils and obstacles. He is also worshipped as the god of education, knowledge, wisdom and wealth. In fact, Ganesha is one of the five prime Hindu deities (Brahma, Vishnu, Shiva and Durga being the other four) whose idolatry is glorified as the *panchayatana puja*.

The devotees of Ganesha are known as 'Ganapatyas', and the festival to celebrate and glorify him is called Ganesh Chaturthi.

Significance of the Ganesha Form: Ganesha's head symbolizes the *Atman* or the soul, which is the ultimate supreme reality of human existence, and his human body signifies *Maya* or the earthly existence of human beings. The elephant head denotes wisdom and its trunk represents Om, the sound symbol of cosmic reality. In his upper right hand Ganesha holds a goad, which helps him propel mankind forward on the eternal path and remove obstacles from the way. The noose in Ganesha's left hand is a gentle implement to capture all difficulties.

The broken tusk that Ganesha holds like a pen in his lower right hand is a symbol of sacrifice, which he broke for writing the *Mahabharata*. The rosary in his other hand suggests that the pursuit of knowledge should be continuous. The *laddoo* (sweet) he holds in his trunk indicates that one must discover the sweetness of the *Atman*. His fan-like ears convey that he is all ears to our petition. The snake that runs round his waist represents energy in all forms. And he is humble enough to ride the lowest of creatures, a mouse.

How Ganesha Got His Head: The story of the birth of this zoomorphic deity, as depicted in the *Shiva Purana*, goes like this: Once goddess Parvati, while bathing, created a boy out of the dirt of her body and assigned him the task of guarding the entrance to her bathroom. When Shiva, her husband returned, he was surprised to find a stranger denying him access, and struck off the boy's head in rage. Parvati broke down in utter grief and to soothe her, Shiva sent out his squad (*gana*) to fetch the head of any sleeping being who was facing the north. The company found a sleeping elephant and brought back its severed head, which was then attached to the body of the boy. Shiva restored its life and made him the leader (*pati*) of his troops. Hence his name 'Ganapati'.

Shiva also bestowed a boon that people would worship him and invoke his name before undertaking any venture.

However, there's another less popular story of his origin, found in the *Brahma Vaivarta Purana*: Shiva asked Parvati to observe the *punyaka vrata* for a year to appease Vishnu in order to have a son. When a son was born to her, all the gods and goddesses assembled to rejoice on its birth. Lord Shani, the son of Surya (Sun-God), was also present but he refused to look at the infant. Perturbed at this behaviour, Parvati asked him the reason, and Shani replied that his looking at baby would harm the newborn. However, on Parvati's insistence when Shani eyed the baby, the child's head was severed instantly. All the gods started to bemoan, whereupon Vishnu hurried to the bank of river Pushpabhadra and brought back the head of a young elephant, and joined it to the baby's body, thus reviving it.

Ganesha, the Destroyer of Pride: Ganesha is also the destroyer of vanity, selfishness and pride. He is the personification of material universe in all its various magnificent manifestations. "All Hindus worship Ganesha regardless of their sectarian belief," says D N Singh in *A Study of Hinduism*. "He is both the beginning of the religion and the meeting ground for all Hindus."

During the festivals, a household worships an idol of Shri Ganesha. The worship happens for 1 day in South India, but in western states of Maharashtra and Goa, the worship may last from 2 to 10 days.

The main sweet-dish during the period are modaks, also known as modagam [kozhakottai] in South India and karanjis. A modak is a sort of dumpling made from rice flour with a stuffing of coconut, jaggery and some other condiments. It can be either steam-cooked or fried and the coconut can be fresh-grated or dried-grated. A karanji is similar but has the shape of the 4th day moon.

There are also public celebrations of the festival, with local communities (*mandals*) vying with each other to put up the biggest idol. The festival is the time for a lot of cultural activities like songs, dramas and orchestra. Legends say that Lord Ganapati (contraction of Ganesh pati - "Father Ganesh") was created by goddess Parvati, wife of Lord Shiva. Parvati created Ganesha out of the sandalwood paste that she used for her bath and breathed life into him. Letting him stand guard at the door she went to have her bath. However, while Parvati was taking her bath, Lord Shiva happened to come there and as Ganesha didn't know him, he didn't allow him to enter the house. As a result, Lord Shiva got angry and severed the head of the child and entered his house. But after realizing that he had beheaded his own son, Lord Shiva fixed the head of an elephant in place of Ganesha's head. In this way, Lord Ganesha acquired the image of the elephant-headed God.

According to the historian Shri Rajwade, records reveal that Ganesh Chaturthi was celebrated even during the reigns of Satavahana, Rashtrakuta and Chalukya. There are also references in historical records to similar celebrations during Peshwa times, Lord Ganapati being the family deity of the Peshwas. After the end of Peshwa rule, from 1818 to 1892 Ganesh Festival remained a family affair in Maharashtra.

It was around 1893, during the growth of nascent Indian nationalism, that the radical nationalist Bal Gangadhar Tilak began to organize the Ganesh Utsav as a social and religious function. Since then, Ganesh Chaturthi has been celebrated throughout Maharashtra with great community enthusiasm and participation.

Rooted in Tradition: From then onwards, this festive occasion has grown in acceptance and today, commands the respect of millions of citizens all over Maharashtra. Lokmanya Bal Gangadhar Tilak brought Ganesha as a deity out on the streets. It was a unique move by this freedom fighter, which he achieved with the Ganpati visarjana or immersion procession, wherein the mass output of several Ganesh mandals is taken out on a parade on the final day of the Ganesh festival and taken to be immersed.

This process was started in 1892 and is now prevalent virtually all over Maharashtra, with special emphasis on Bombay and Pune. Lokmanya Tilak attached this mass celebration to increase national awareness about the Freedom movement. Herein, neighbourhood Ganeshas are worshipped and brought to immersion sites, where huge crowds gather to bid him an emotional and frenzied farewell.

In Pune, as the sun sets over darkening rivers, the images are taken out in boats and as each one is immersed, a cry is raised asking him to return the next year. It is an emotional and public farewell to their beloved god as parthiva (of the earth), who like the Phoenix, will rise once again the following year.

A special puja is performed for Ganesha. The worship of the deity involves getting a corner ready to receive the god. Ganesha is invited with a special phrase and with material and verbal offerings, the puja begins. It involves the Panchamrit (five nectars), which includes milk, curd, ghee, honey and jaggery, with which the god's icon is bathed, cleansing in between with water.

Ganesha is then given a red garment and the sacred thread - saying it is silver. He is then smeared with red sandal paste and offered red or yellow flowers. A lamp is lit, bells chime and food is offered in six symbolic mouthfuls - not to the god's body, but to his five panchapranas or 'vital breaths' and the one beyond - the absolute.

During the festival, puja is performed twice every day - once in the morning and again in the evening. Ganesha is offered special leaves and flowers, 21 of each and white durva grass. The idol is formally installed on the first day and given life in the presence of Brahma, Vishnu and Shiva, and the Vedas. Touching the idol with blades of durva grass, he is brought to life step by step and made to go through 15 of the 16 rites of passage that each Hindu goes through in his lifetime. (The sixteenth one, which is for death, is omitted.)

The Ganesha mantra is chanted, followed by a Ganesha prayer. The last puja done, the family or congregation gathers around and rice grains are placed on the head of the idol, which is moved, symbolically unseating him.

As a matter of interest there are about 91 different figures of Ganesha according to research done by several scholars. The details of their make up may vary from figure to figure, but with no change in the main set-up. It is the enigma of certain striking variations in details that the sublime in the figures of Ganesha has to be sought for. Some figures are seen sitting with their trunks turned towards the left side, invariably reaching a bowl of modaks (a sweet edible and festive preparation), while in some figures, the trunks are seen turning towards the right and in yet others, the trunk is straight, hanging down, with or without a pot of nectar in the curve of their trunks.

In some images, Ganesha is seen standing, resting his right foot on a lion and his left foot on a mouse (his chosen mode of transport), while in some other images, his left foot is found resting on a mouse and his right foot lifted in an effort to touch the serpent girdle - his mount carrying a jewel in its mouth.

Environmentalists too have questioned the dumping of the idols made increasingly with chemicals which pollute the lakes and seas. On September 2004, the Chennai High Court imposed a temporary ban on such immersions. Every year there are at least a couple of casualties associated with accidents (while dumping the idols) or clashes associated with this.

On the day of the festival, it is placed on raised platforms in homes or in elaborately decorated outdoor tents for people to view and pay their homage. The priest, usually clad in red silk dhoti and shawl, then invokes life into the idol amidst the chanting of mantras. This ritual is the pranapratishhtha. After this the shhodashopachara (16 ways of paying tribute) follows. Coconut, jaggery, 21 modakas (rice flour preparation), 21 durva (trefoil) blades and red flowers are offered. The idol is anointed with red unguent (rakta chandan). Throughout the ceremony, Vedic hymns from the Rig Veda and Ganapati Atharva Shirsha Upanishad, and Ganesha stotra from the Narada Purana are chanted.

Swami Sivananda Recommends : On the Ganesh Chaturthi day, meditate on the stories connected with Lord Ganesha early in the morning, during the Brahmamuhurta period. Then, after taking a bath, go to the temple and do the prayers of Lord Ganesha. Offer Him some coconut and sweet pudding. Pray with faith and devotion that He may remove all the obstacles that you experience on the spiritual path. Worship Him at home, too. You can get the assistance of a pundit. Have an image of Lord Ganesha in your house. Feel His Presence in it.

Don't forget not to look at the moon on that day; remember that it behaved unbecomingly towards the Lord. This really means avoid the company of all those who have no faith in God, and who deride God, your Guru and religion, from this very day.

Take fresh spiritual resolves and pray to Lord Ganesha for inner spiritual strength to attain success in all your undertakings.

May the blessings of Sri Ganesha be upon you all! May He remove all the obstacles that stand in your spiritual path! May He bestow on you all material prosperity as well as liberation!

The Visarjan (immersion) Processions and Ceremony : The festival ends with the ceremony of immersion of the idols in the sea or rivers and wells. This ceremony which is called Ganesha-Visarjan which means immersion of Ganesha is as popular as the festival proper. During the immersion ceremony huge crowds move in a procession carrying idols of Ganesha towards the places of immersion. These processions which take place with great fanfare, begins in the afternoon and continue till the late hours of the night.

Ganesh Chaturthi is celebrated as the birthday of Lord Ganesh on the fourth day (Chaturthi) of the bright fortnight of Bhadrapada month of Hindu calendar. It is among the most celebrated of the festivals in India, and perhaps the only one involving general public (others only involve families and friends and are celebrated privately).

It is interesting to note that the festival was not celebrated until the times of Lokamanya Bal Gangadhar Tilak, who used it a great means to unite Hindus all over India and educate them the evils of colonization.

The festivities include fund-raising, building all kinds of innovative forms Ganesh idols, organizing public performances of music and dance, cooking grand feasts and making a lot of noise. The festivities end when the idol of the year is immersed in water (*visarjan*), accompanied by loud shouts of *Ganapati Bappa Moraya*!

Lokamanya Tilak (portrait - biography) visualized the cultural importance of this diety and brought in Ganesha Chaturthi as National Festival. It was an important festival during Peshwa rule in Maharashtra, but acquired more organized from all over India during the *Swaraj* movement (see Tryst with Destiny— The story of India's struggle for freedom remains as a guiding light for resolving the various conflicts around the globe). It made way for learned discourses, dance dramas, poetry recital, musical concerts bringing together all castes and communities who vied with enthusiasm in organizing this public festival. The all-pervading Gajanana (another name of Ganesh) has countless temples all over India and is worshipped with more affection than awe in every Hindu home.

Ganesha, the elephant-headed son of Shiva and Parvati is widely worshipped as the munificent god of wisdom. Ganesh Chaturthi is a festival in his honour and is celebrated in the states of Maharashtra, Tamil Nadu, Karnataka and Andhra Pradesh.

On the day of the Chaturthi, i.e. the last of the days dedicated to the elephant-headed god, thousands of processions converge on the beaches of Mumbai to immerse the holy idols in the sea. This immersion is accompanied by drum beats, devotional songs and dancing.

There is a curiously interesting tale about the birth of Ganesha. It is believed that once while Parvati was bathing, she created a human figure from some unguent and balm, gave him life and asked him to guard the door while she bathed. After a long period of meditation on Mountain Kailash (Shiva's abode), Shiva chose that very moment to drop by to see his better half, but was abruptly stopped by the man-god Parvati had posted at the door. Outraged by the cheek of this stranger, Shiva cut off his head only to discover that he had killed Parvati's son! For fear of enraging his wife, Shiva immediately dispatched his ganas (attendants) to get him the head of the first living creature they could find. Well, the first living creature happened to be an elephant. As instructed, the head was chopped off and brought back to Shiva, who placed it on Parvati's son's body, bringing him back to life. This elephant-headed god was welcomed into the first family of the Hindu heavens and named Ganesha or Ganapati, which literally means the chief of the ganas, or the attendants of Shiva. Ganesha is the foremost god of the Hindu pantheon. This brave guardian of the door to Parvati's bath is beheld today as the most auspicious God of new beginnings. He is worshipped during every festival and before people undertake a journey or embark upon a new venture.

You will also see him carefully guarding entrances to temples and homes, peeping out of calendars and happily gracing marriages and other such occasions.

Vinayaka (Ganesha) drives away all sorrows, difficulties, and miseries. He is the enemy of all obstacles. He will not allow any obstacles to come in the way. He is the destroyer of obstacles. He confers happiness and peace (on his devotees). He is the master of all these powers (intellect (buddhi) and fulfillment (siddhi, self-realization). What is this siddhi? When there is purity of mind, you achieve peace (which is siddhi). Vinayaka is thus the Lord of the intellect and self-realization. Hence, every human being should acquire control over the mind ... .

Vinayaka is the Lord of all learning (vidya). Does learning mean bookish scholarship? No. Everything pertaining to the cosmos is included in the term learning (vidya). Walking, talking, laughing, sitting, eating, strolling, thinking —every kind of activity is related to learning. Vinayaka is the master of every kind of learning. Today, learning is identified with acquisition of information. But apart from knowledge of the physical world, we have many other kinds of knowledge, relating to chemistry, the fine arts and other skills.

Vinayaka is the master of every kind of knowledge. Learning is related to the intellect (buddhi). It is not mere scholarship. Familiarity with books is not knowledge. One's entire life is a continuous process of learning. Any process of inquiry is related to learning. But basically our inquiry should be concerned with finding out what is transient and what is permanent. This is true knowledge.

Hence, today, students worship Vinayaka with zeal. Vinayaka is not the one who merely comes to the aid of those who read their books. He helps everyone at every step in life's journey.

In the verse (sloka) beginning with the words Suklaambaradharam Vishnum, only the form of the deity is described. But there is another inner meaning for the name Vinayaka. Suklaambaradharam means one who is clad in white. Vishnum means he is all-pervading. Sasivarnam means his complexion is grey, like that of ash. Chathurbhujam means he has four arms.

Prasannavadanam means he has always a pleasing mien. Sarvavighnopasaanthaye means for the removal of all obstacles. Dhyaayeth means meditate (on him). Vinayaka is the deity who removes all bad qualities, instills good qualities, and confers peace on the devotee who meditates on him. However, the Vinayaka-principle has only one meaning, which is relevant to everyone regardless of whether he is a believer or a non-believer. Vinayaka means that he is totally master of himself. He has no master above him.

He does not depend on anyone. He is also called Ganapathi. This term means he is the lord of the ganas —a class of divine entities. This term also means that he is the master of the intellect and discriminating power in man. He possesses great intelligence and knowledge. Such knowledge issues from a pure and sacred mind. This knowledge leads to wisdom (vijnaana). Because he is the master of intelligence (buddhi) and wisdom or realisation (siddhi), he is described as the Lord of Buddhi and Siddhi. Buddhi and Siddhi are referred to as the consorts of Vinayka.

The mouse is the vehicle of Vinayaka. What is the inner significance of the mouse? The mouse is considered as the embodiment of the sense of smell. The mouse is a symbol of the attachment to worldly tendencies (vaasanas). It is well known that if you want to catch a mouse, you place a strong-smelling edible inside the mouse-trap. The mouse also symbolises the darkness of night. The mouse can see well in the dark. As Vinayaka's vehicle, the mouse signifies an object that leads man from darkness to light. Thus, the Vinayaka-principle means that which removes all the bad qualities, bad practices, and bad thoughts in men and inculcates good qualities, good conduct and good thoughts.

Another name for Vinayaka is Vighneswara. Easwara is one who is endowed with every conceivable form of wealth —riches, knowledge, health, bliss, beauty, etc. Vighneswara is the promoter of all these forms of wealth and removes all obstacles to their enjoyment. He confers all these forms of wealth on those who worship him. Vinayaka is described as "the first deity who should be worshipped (prathama vandana)". ASinceeveryone in the world desires wealth and prosperity, everyone offers the first place for worship to Vighneswara.

Where are the ganas? What is their form? When you investigate this, you find that the five organs of perception and the five organs of action (jnaanendriyas and karmendriyas) are the ganas. The mind is the master over these ten organs. The intellect (buddhi) is the discriminating faculty above the mind. The ten senses, the mind, and the intellect together constitute the ganas.

In the word "gana" , "ga" stands for intellect (buddhi) and "na" means "Vaijnaana (the higher knowledge or wisdom)". Ganapathi is the Lord of the intellect and higher knowledge. The question may be asked, Are the intellect and higher knowledge present in the external world, or are they to be found within man? The answer is that he is present within each human being. There is no need to seek for him in the outside world. Ganapathi dwells in every human being in the form of intellect and wisdom.

When Ganapathi is described as "Parvathee thanaya", who is this Parvathee? Parvathee signifies Prithvi, Mother Earth. Everyone is a child of Mother Earth.

The meaning of "son of Parvathee (Parvatheethanaya)" is that Ganapathi, who is the Lord of the Ganas, is the son of Parvathee, who symbolizes the divine energy (sakthi).

The adoration of Parvathieeand Ganapathi is not of recent origin. Ganapathi is lauded at several places in the *Rig Veda*. This clearly shows that Ganapathi is as ancient as the *Vedas*.

In several places, Ganapathi is mentioned both in the *Vedas* and the *Upanishaths*. Many prayers are addressed to Ganapathi in the *Narayanopanishath*. There are also prayers to him in the *Thaithiriya Upanishath*. The Ganapathi Gayathri Mantra also figures in the *Upanishath*.

Ganapathi is called Vinayaka because there is no master above him. He is all powerful and independent. Without recognizing the esoteric significance of the Vinayaka Principle, people look only at the external form and offer worship in mundane terms.

What is the inner significance of worshipping the elephant-faced deity? The elephant is a symbol of might and magnitude. The elephant's foot is larger than that of any other animal. The elephant can make its way through the densest jungle. In this way, it signifies the quality of a leader who shows the way for others. The elephant is also known for its fidelity and gratitude. In any circumstance, it will not forget its master. Even in its last moments, if it hears the voice of its master, it will open its eyes and look for him. It will sacrifice its life for its master. These are the lessons man should learn from the elephant. Intelligence without gratitude is valueless. Every man should be grateful to those who have helped him.

Ganesh's Birth: Once Lord Shiva left his usual dwelling on Mt.Kailas in the Himalayas, to meditate in one of the caves in the same mountain. Two friends of Parvati, his consort, suggested that she should have a 'gana' - attendant of their own, since they were not too happy with Shivaji's 'ganas'. Parvati agreed. Soon after, using her divine powers, she created a son, naming him Vinayak. She instructed him to guard their home.

When Shivaji returned Vinayak prevented him from entering. After some bickering, Shivaji beheaded Vinayak with his 'trishul' (trident). When Parvati heard of this she lamented intensely. Shivaji realised his error. To set things right he sent his men to the forest to fetch the head of the first living thing they met. They encountered a baby elephant and returned with its head.

With his divine power, Shivaji placed the head over his son's body. Instantly Vinayak sprung to life. Henceforth Vinayak also earned the name of Gajaanan. 'Gaja' means elephant. Shivaji blessed him with a boon that people would first worship and offer him dedication in all their auspicious activities. Those who didn't would not attain success. Bhadarva Sud 4th is the day Parvati was offering the final pujan to the dead Ganeshji, when he resurrected.

Ganapati Vivaha (Marriage): When Shiva and Parvati decided to have their sons, Kartikeya and Ganesh married, they stipulated that he who circumambulated the earth first would be considered the best deity and would be married first. Kartikeya flew off on his vehicle - a peacock.

Poor Ganapati's vehicle was a mouse which was no match for a peacock. Being the choicest devotee of God, Parvatiji consoling him showed Ganeshji a simpler and quicker way. She advised him to cicumambulate the cow since she also symbolically represents another earth and he had reap the same benefit as going round the earth. Another reference cites him circumambulating his parents.

Consoling him, Parvati showed a short cut. She divulged that it was ordained in the scriptures that he who offered pujan to his parents and then circumambulated them received the same merit as he who went around the earth. Ganapati hence married first showing that one who obeys the wish of the choicest devotee of God or his parents attains his desired wishes. Hence Ganeshji is invoked first in all auspicious events, rites and rituals such as marriage, opening ceremonies, ground-breaking ceremonies, yagnas and so on.

The Shiva Puran cites another story. Prajapati had two daughters, Siddhi (wealth) and Buddhi (intellect). He approached Parvati and Shivaji for the girls' marriage to Kartikeya and Ganeshji. However both girls wished to marry only the latter. Thus they married him. Siddhi gave birth to a son named 'Shubh' (auspiciousness) and Buddhi to 'Labh' (merit).

Therefore when businessmen and merchants offer pujan to Ganeshji and Lakshmiji they write 'Shubh' and 'Labh' inside their account ledgers to invoke the two deities.

Sentiments: The first person to observe the 'vrat' (vow) of Ganesh Chaturthi was Chandra - the moon. After Ganeshji's fame as leader ('pati') of Shiva's 'ganas', hence Ganapati, he was travelling through the heavens. As he passed Chandra - who prided on his attractive features, he slighted Ganeshji's peculiar form. In return, Ganeshji cursed him, "You shall bear the fruit of your karma. Whenever somebody does your darshan he will be cursed too." Chandra begged for forgiveness. Ganeshji then advised him to observe the Ganesh Chaturthi vrat and was freed from the curse.

By being aware of the detrimental effects of false pride one should cultivate humility. The Skanda Purana mentions this sentiment of the festival.

The Vayu Puran advocates the observance of this festival by listening to the following relevant episode of Shri Krishna, to be relieved from false accusation:

When Shri Krishna was falsely accused of pilfering the Syamantak Mani (gem) he observed Ganesh Chaturthi and was freed from the false charge. This festival also inspires devotees to inculcate two virtues; obeying the commands of God and His choicest devotee, and consolidating faith in them, just as Ganeshji had faith and trust in Parvati regarding circumambulating his parents.

Names of Ganeshji : *Ekadant (one-toothed)*

- To scribe the Mahabharat Katha Ganeshji removed one of his tusks to carve a quill from it. He then scribed the epic on palm leaves as the sage Ved Vyas recited it. The scribing took three years!
- In south India there is a belief that when ploughing first began on earth, it was Lord Ganeshji who first ploughed using one of his tusks.
- In the Uttar Ramayan, Brahmand Puran and Padma Puran there is a reference of a battle between Ganeshji and Parshuram. During the duel, the latter's axe fractured one of Ganeshji's tusks According to the Brahmand Puran, it was his left tusk.

There are other names related to his body and virtues. A few commonly known are listed below:

- Lambodar - from the long - 'lambo', tummy - 'udar'.
- Gajkarna - from the large elephant 'Gaja' ears - 'karna.'
- Kapil - from his ruddy complexion.
- Vikat - heavy-bodied.
- Bhalchandra - having a Chandra (moon) on his forehead- 'bhal.'
- Dwaimatur - one who has 'dwi' - two, 'mata' - mother; Parvati - who gave birth to him and Malini - a demoness who nurtured him.
- Vakratund - one who breaks the ego of he who behaves anti-socially ('Vakra').
- Mudgal - In south India, a special 'Mudgal Puran' extols Ganapati's glory. It cites 32 names, while 'Shardatilak' lists 51 names.
- Vigneshwar - One who removes mayic obstacles - 'vignas'

Symbolism and Import

Since Ganeshji represents auspiciousness, his whole being has symbolic imports for devotees:

Large ears - signify listening to God's katha with great zeal.

Small eyes - to do the Lord's darshan minutely.

Large forehead - to develop great intellect to realise God.

Large stomach - depicts his great capacity to empathise with the woes of devotees.

Short legs - depicts patience.

Long trunk - symbolic of his deep scriptural wisdom.

Mouse as vehicle - a hyperactive creature, symbolic of our indriyas. Therefore Ganesh sitting on such a vehicle represents a deity of control over the indriyas.

Four arms - which hold: 'ankush' - symbol for control over the mind

'ladu' - for happiness

'pash' - axe to punish the indriyas and antahkaran

'ashirvad mudra' - blessings for the well being of humanity

Depending on the role of Ganapati, the number of arms varies, as do the type of objects.

Ganesha is the god of wisdom and prosperity and is invoked before the beginning of any auspicious work by the Hindus. It is believed that for the fulfillment of one's desires, his blessing is absolutely necessary. According to the mythology, he is the son of Shiva and Parvati, brother of Kartikeya - the general of the gods, Lakshmi - the goddess of wealth and Saraswati-the goddess of learning. There are numerous stories in Hindu mythology, associated with the birth of this elephant-headed god, whose vehicle is the Mooshak or rat and who loves Modaks (droplet shaped Indian sweet). Legend has it that Parvati created Ganesha out of the sandalwood dough that she used for her bath and breathed life into him. Letting him stand guard at the door she went to have her bath. When her husband, Shiva returned, the child who had never seen him stopped him.

Shiva severed the head of the child and entered his house. Parvati, learning that her son was dead, was distraught and asked Shiva to revive him. Shiva cut off the head of an elephant and fixed it on the body of Ganesha. Another tale tells of how one day the Gods decided to choose their leader and a race was to be held between the brothers- Kartikeya and Ganesh. Whoever took three rounds of the earth first would be made the Ganaadhipati or the leader. Kartikeya seated on a peacock as his vehicle, started off for the test. Ganesh was given a rat, which moved swiftly. Ganesh realised that the test was not easy, but he would not disobey his father. He reverently paid obeisance to his parents and went around them three times and thus completed the test before Kartikeya. He said, " my parents pervade the whole universe and going around them, is more than going round the earth." Everybody was pleasantly surprised to hear Ganesha's logic and intelligence and hence he came to be known as the Ganaadhipati or leader, now referred to as Ganpati.

There is also a story behind the symbolic snake, rat and the singular tusk. During one of his birthdays, His mother, Parvati, cooked for him twenty-one types of delicious food and a lot of sweet porridge. Ganesha ate so much that even his big belly could not contain it. Mounting his little mouse, he embarked on his nightly rounds. His mouse suddenly stumbled upon seeing a huge snake. To adjust His belly, Ganesha put the snake on as a belt around his stomach. All of a sudden, he heard laughter emanating form the sky.

He looked up and saw the moon mocking him. Ganesha infuriated, broke off one of his tusks and hurled it at the moon. Parvati, seeing this, immediately cursed the moon that whoever looks at it on Ganesh Chaturthi will be accused of a wrong doing. The symbology behind the mouse and snake and Ganesha's big belly and its relationship to the moon on his birthday is highly philosophic. The whole cosmos is known to be the belly of Ganesha. Parvati is the primordial energy. The seven realms above, seven realms below and seven oceans, are inside the cosmic belly of Ganesha, held together by the cosmic energy *(kundalini)* symbolized as a huge snake which Ganesha ties around Him. The mouse is nothing but our ego. Ganesha, using the mouse as a vehicle, exemplifies the need to control our ego. One who has controlled the ego has Ganesha consciousness or God-consciousness.

Ganapathi's position in the Hindu Pantheon: The Supreme Being manifested Himself as the holy Trinity of Brahma, Vishnu and Maheswara to undertake the functions of creation, sustenance and dissolution respectively of the entire universe. Their divine consorts respectively are Saraswathi, Mahalakshmi and Maheswari, Goddesses of learning, wealth and activity. All the above manifestations of Divinity have blessed Lord Ganesa, granting Him all their powers and attributes. They have also conceded to Him the first priority in any worship. In fact, the Gods themselves pray to Ganesa to bring success in their all endeavours.

Ganesa Tattwa or the Principle of the Manifestation: It is necessary that the devotee tries to grasp the significance of the system of his worship to improve his concentration and to avoid dissipation of his energy. The entire creation is made up of five elements, namely, ether, air, fire, water and earth and they have emerged in that order from the Absolute Reality. These elements operate in the human body from the five spiritual centres of Muladhara, swadhisthana, Manipura, Anahata and Visudhi in the reverse order of their emergence. These spiritual centers along with the sixth centre "Ajna" form the "shadchakra" (six energy points) in the sushumnanadi inside the backbone.

The lower centre, Muladhara, situated near the hip, is the seat of earth element (prithvi), the controlling deity being Ganapathy. The remaining higher centers are controlled by Brahma, Vishnu, Rudra, Jivatma and Paramatma, (Their seats being Swadhisthana, Manipura, Anahata, Vishudhi, and Ajna respectively. By constant sadhana and the grace of the respective deities starting from Ganesa, the individual soul is raised to higher levels in the realm of the Spirit, in the above order, enabling him to finally merge with the Ultimate Reality, dwelling in Brahmarandhra at the crown of his head in the form of Sadasiva.

Mantrajapa Sadhana: Ganesa Mantras are very powerful and they confer success to devotees, chanting them with deep faith and regularity.

On the 4th day of the bright half of Bhadrapad, the great festival of Ganesh or Ganpati is celebrated. This festival marked the birthday of Lord Ganesh. Ganpati is one of the most popular deities. He is worshipped by both Shaivites and Vaishnavites. Even Buddhists and Jains have respect for Ganpati. He is considered to be an avatar of both Shiva and Vishnu. To appreciate this occasion, one must go to Mumbai where preparations begin months in advance. Images of Ganesha are installed within homes as well as in places of assembly. Elaborate arrangements are made for lighting and decoration and Ganesha is fervently worshipped for about 7-10 days.

On the day of the Chaturthi, the last of the days dedicated to the elephant-headed god, thousands of processions converge on the beaches of Mumbai to immerse the holy idols in the sea. This immersion is accompanied by drum beats, devotional songs and dancing. Every year, the largest Ganesh idol is installed at Khairatabad in Hyderabad, which is more than 30 ft tall.The Ganapati Mahotsav or the Grand Festival of Ganesha is the principle festival in Bombay, the financial capital of India. In Bombay the largest of the 6000 or so Ganeshas are commissioned collectively by factories. Each of these idols can be upto 10 metres in height and are paraded on lorries decorated with multi-coloured lights. At the other end of the scale, little Ganeshas are placed in nukkads or street corners and in homes, and pujas are performed daily.

The festival was started by Shivaji , the great Maratha ruler, to promote culture and a feeling of nationalism amongst his subjects who were fighting against the Mughals.After his death the festival was celebrated but on a smaller scale. In 1894 when the British banned public assemblies the festivalwas revived by Lokmanya Bal Gangadhar Tilak who felt that this was way of spreading the freedom message through a legitimate religious festival. On full moon day every idol is taken down to the Chowpatty beach accompanied by hordes of people singing and dancing and is immersed in the Arabian Sea.

How the Brahma-Madhwa Vaishnava's observe Ganesh Chaturthi: The icon of Ganapati made of clay by artists of Udupi is brought to badage maalige during an auspicious period on that day. The entire area is decorated artistically with different kinds of decorations. A huge rangavalli of Ganesha is constructed in front of the icon. This is a feast to the eyes for the next four days.

After worshipping the special Ganapati icon for four days the icon is taken out in procession and then immersed in the Madhva-Sarovara.

At the entrance of the shrine also there is a small icon of Ganapati. Special worship is arranged there to the Lord Vishnu in the form of Sri Vishvambhara. The priests perform a sacrifice known as ganahoma. The Swamiji offers prasaada of Lord Vishvambhara to Ganapati and performs aarati.

A special icon of Ganapati made of five metals is present at Ananteshwara and is worshipped every day. Here also, the festival of Ganesha is celebrated with pomp.

I was going to mention it in the chapter containing the initial reference to Ananteshwara but because of incomplete memory of the story I didn't. It goes along the lines — the icon had been worshipped in a fort (can't remember where) and when the fort was attacked by marauding Muslims the icon was removed and eventually placed in the Ananteshwara temple for safe keeping. Even after the Muslims had been driven back, the icon remained in the Ananteshwara temple.

During Ganesha-chaturthi, special festivals are held here during the night and it is a magnificent sight. The whole of the temple is lit up with oil lamps and the people queue up to view the icon. Because of all the oil lamps this is the best time to view the icon.

DASHAHARA

This festival is observed twice a year, once in the month of Chaitra and then in Aswayuja. It lasts for nine days in honour of the nine manifestations of Durga. During Navaratri (the word literally means "nine nights") devotees of Durga observe a fast. Brahmins are fed and prayers are offered for the protection of health and property. The beginning of summer and the beginning of winter are two very important junctions of climatic and solar influence. These two periods are taken as sacred opportunities for the worship of the Divine Mother. They are indicated respectively by the Rama-Navaratri in Chaitra (April-May) and the Durga Navaratri in Aswayuja (September-October). The bodies and minds of people undergo a considerable change on account of the changes in Nature. Sri Rama is worshipped during Ramnavmi, and Mother Durga during Navaratri.

The Durga Puja is celebrated in various parts of India in different styles. But the one basic aim of this celebration is to propitiate Shakti, the Goddess in Her aspect as Power, to bestow upon man all wealth, auspiciousness, prosperity, knowledge (both sacred and secular), and all other potent powers. Whatever be the particular or special request that everyone may put before the Goddess, whatever boon may be asked of Her, the one thing behind all these is propitiation, worship and linking oneself with Her. There is no other aim. This is being effected consciously or unconsciously. Everyone is blessed with Her loving mercy and is protected by Her.

Durga Puja or Navaratri commences on the first and ends on the tenth day of the bright half of Aswayuja (September-October). It is held in commemoration of the victory of Durga over Mahishasura, the buffalo-headed demon. In Bengal Her image is worshipped for nine days and then cast into water. The tenth day is called Vijaya Dasami or Dussera (the "tenth day"). Processions with Her image are taken out along the streets of villages and cities.

The mother of Durga (that is, the wife of the King of the Himalayas) longed to see her daughter. Durga was permitted by Lord Shiva to visit her beloved mother only for nine days in the year. The festival of Durga Puja marks this brief visit and ends with the Vijaya Dasami day, when Goddess Durga leaves for Her return to Mount Kailas. This is the view of some devotees.

In Bengal, Durga Puja is a great festival. All who live away from home return during the Puja days. Mothers reunite with their sons and daughters, and wives with their husbands.

The potter shows his skill in making images, the painter in drawing pictures, the songster in playing on his instrument, and the priest in reciting the sacred books. The Bengalis save money throughout the year only to spend everything during the Puja days. Cloth is freely distributed to the Brahmins.

The woman of Bengal welcomes the Goddess with a mother's love and sends away the image on the last day, with every ceremony associated with a daughter's departure to her husband's home and with motherly tears in her eyes. This signifies the parting of Durga from Her beloved mother.

Durga Puja is the greatest Hindu festival in which God is adored as Mother. Hinduism is the only religion in the world which has emphasised to such an extent the motherhood of God. One's relationship with one's mother is the dearest and the sweetest of all human relations. Hence, it is proper to look upon God as mother.

Durga represents the Divine Mother. She is the energy aspect of the Lord. Without Durga, Shiva has no expression and without Shiva, Durga has no existence. Shiva is the soul of Durga; Durga is identical with Shiva. Lord Shiva is only the silent witness. He is motionless, absolutely changeless. He is not affected by the cosmic play. It is Durga who does everything.

Shakti is the omnipotent power of the Lord, or the Cosmic Energy. The Divine Mother is represented as having ten different weapons in Her hands. She sits on a lion. She keeps up the play of the Lord through the three attributes of Nature, namely, Sattwa, Rajas and Tamas. Knowledge, peace, lust, anger, greed, egoism and pride, are all Her forms.

You will find in the Devi Sukta of the *Rig Veda Samhita* that Vak, symbolising speech, the daughter of the sage Anbhirna, realised her identity with the Divine Mother, the Power of the Supreme Lord, which manifests throughout the universe among the gods, among men and beasts and among the creatures of the deep ocean.

In the *Kena Upanishad*, you will find that the Divine Mother shed wisdom on Indra and the gods and said that the gods were able to defeat the demons only with the help of the power of the Supreme Lord. The worship of Devi, the universal Mother, leads to the attainment of knowledge of the Self. The story in the *Kena*

Upanishad known as the "Yaksha Prasna", supports this view. It tells how Uma, the Divine Mother, taught the Truth to the gods. Goddess Shakti thus sheds wisdom on Her devotees.

Devi worship is, therefore, worship of God's glory, of God's greatness and supremacy. It is adoration of the Almighty. It is unfortunate that Devi is ignorantly understood by many as a mere blood-thirsty Hindu Goddess. No! Devi is not a vicious demoness nor is She the property of the Hindus alone. Devi does not belong to any religion. Devi is that conscious power of God. The words Devi, Shakti, etc., and the ideas of different forms connected with these names are concessions granted by the sages due to the limitations of the human intellect; they are by no means the ultimate definitions of Shakti.

The original or Adi Shakti is beyond human comprehension. Bhagavan Krishna says in the *Gita*: "This is only My lower nature. Beyond this is My higher nature, the life-principle which sustains the universe".

The *Upanishad* also says: "The supreme power of God is manifested in various ways. This power is of the nature of God, manifesting as knowledge, strength and activity".

Truly speaking, all beings in the universe are Shakti-worshippers, whether they are aware of it or not, for there is no one who does not love and long for power in some form or other. Physicists and scientists have now proved that everything is pure, imperishable energy. This energy is only a form of divine Shakti which exists in every form. A child is more familiar with the mother than with the father, because the mother is very kind, loving, tender and affectionate and looks after the needs of the child. In the spiritual field also, the aspirant or the devotee—the spiritual child—has an intimate relationship with the Mother Durga, more than with the Father Shiva. Therefore, it behoves the aspirant to approach the Mother first, who then introduces Her spiritual child to the Father for his illumination.

The Mother's Grace is boundless. Her mercy is illimitable; Her knowledge infinite; Her power immeasurable; Her glory ineffable; and Her splendour indescribable. She gives you material prosperity as well as spiritual freedom.

Approach Her with an open heart. Lay bare your heart to Her with frankness and humility. Be as simple as a child. Kill ruthlessly the enemies of egoism, cunningness, selfishness and crookedness. Make a total, unreserved, and ungrudging self-surrender to Her. Sing Her praise. Repeat Her Name. Worship Her with faith and unflinching devotion. Perform special worship on the Navaratri days. Navaratri is the most suitable occasion for doing intense spiritual practices. These nine days are very sacred to the Divine Mother. Plunge yourself in her worship. Practise intense repetition of the Divine Name, having a regular "quota" of repetitions per day, and the number of hours spent on it.

Devi fought with Bhandasura and his forces for nine days and nine nights. This Bhandasura had a wonderful birth and life. When Lord Shiva burnt Cupid with the fire of His "third eye", Sri Ganesha playfully moulded a figure out of the ashes, and the Lord breathed life into it! This was the terrible demon Bhandasura. He engaged himself in great penance and on account of it obtained a boon from Lord Shiva. With the help of that boon, he began harassing the worlds. The Divine Mother fought with him for nine nights (the demons have extraordinary strength during the night), and killed him on the evening of the tenth day, known as the Vijaya Dasami. The learning of any science is begun on this highly auspicious day. It was on this day that Arjuna worshipped Devi, before starting the battle against the Kauravas on the field of Kurukshetra.

Sri Rama worshipped Durga at the time of the fight with Ravana, to invoke Her aid in the war. This was on the days preceding the Vijaya Dasami day. He fought and won through Her Grace.

In days of yore, kings used to undertake ambitious expeditions on the day of the Vijaya Dasami. Those kings who did not go on such expeditions used to go out hunting in the deep forests. In Rajputana, India, even up to this date, people arrange mock attacks on some fort on Vijaya Dasami.

This day, however, has much to do with the life of Sri Rama. Nowhere in the history of the world can we find a parallel to the character of Sri Rama as a man, son, brother, husband, father or king. Maharishi Valmiki has exhausted the entire language in describing the glory of Sri Rama. And, we shall be rightly celebrating the Dussera if we make honest efforts to destroy the demon of our ego, and radiate peace and love wherever we go. Let us all resolve to become men of sterling character. Let us resolve and act. The story of Sri Rama is known in almost all parts of the globe, and if we but succeed in following even a hundredth part of His teachings, we shall make our lives more fragrant than the rose and more lustrous than gold!

Dussera can also be interpreted as "Dasa-Hara", which means the cutting of the ten heads of Ravana. So, let us resolve today to cut the ten heads—passion, pride, anger, greed, infatuation, lust, hatred, jealousy, selfishness and crookedness—of the demon, Ego, and thus justify the celebration of Dussera.

Religious observances, traditional worship and observances at times have more than one significance. Apart from being the adoration of the Divine, they commemorate stirring events in history, they are allegoric when interpreted from the occult standpoint and, lastly, they are deeply significant pointers and revealing guides to the individual on his path to God-realisation.

Outwardly, the nine-day worship of Devi is a celebration of triumph. This nine days' celebration is offered to the Mother for Her successful struggle with the formidable demons led by Mahishasura. But, to the sincere spiritual aspirant, the particular division of the Navaratri into sets of three days to adore different aspects of the Supreme Goddess has a very sublime, yet thoroughly practical truth to reveal. In its cosmic aspect, it epitomises the stages of the evolution of man into God, from Jivahood (the state of individualisation) to Shivahood (the state of Self-realisation). In its individual import, it shows the course that his spiritual practice should take.

Let us, therefore, examine in detail the spiritual significance of Navaratri.

The central purpose of existence is to recognise your eternal identity with the supreme Spirit. It is to grow into the image of the Divine. The supreme One embodies the highest perfection. It is spotless purity. To recognise your identity with That, to attain union with That, is verily to grow into the very likeness of the Divine. The aspirant, therefore, as his initial step, has to get rid of all the countless impurities, and the demoniacal elements that have come to cling to him in his embodied state. Then he has to acquire lofty virtues and auspicious, divine qualities. Thus purified, knowledge flashes upon him like the brilliant rays of the sun upon the crystal waters of a perfectly calm lake.

This process demands a resolute will, determined effort, and arduous struggle. In other words, strength and infinite power are the prime necessity. Thus it is the Divine Mother who has to operate through the aspirant.

Let us now consider how, on the first three days, the Mother is adored as supreme power and force, as Durga the Terrible. You pray to Mother Durga to destroy all your impurities, your vices, your defects. She is to fight with and annihilate the baser animal qualities in the spiritual aspirant, the lower, diabolical nature in him. Also, She is the power that protects your spiritual practice from its many dangers and pitfalls. Thus the first three days, which mark the first stage or the destruction of impurity and determined effort and struggle to root out the evil tendencies in your mind, are set apart for the worship of the destructive aspect of the Mother.

Once you have accomplished your task on the negative side, that of breaking down the impure propensities and old vicious habits, the next step is to build up a sublime spiritual personality, to acquire positive qualities in place of the eliminated demoniacal qualities. The divine qualities that Lord Krishna enumerates in the Gita, have to be acquired. The aspirant must cultivate and develop all the auspicious qualities. He has to earn immense spiritual wealth to enable him to pay the price for the rare gem of divine wisdom. If this development of the opposite qualities is not undertaken in right earnest, the old demoniacal nature will raise its head again and again. Hence, this stage is as important in an aspirant's career as the previous one. The essential difference is: the former is a ruthless, determined annihilation of the filthy egoistic lower self; the latter is an orderly, steady, calm and serene effort to develop purity. This pleasanter side of the aspirant's Sadhana is depicted by the worship of Mother Lakshmi. She bestows on Her devotees the inexhaustible divine wealth or Deivi Sampath. Lakshmi is the wealth-giving aspect of God. She is purity itself. Thus the worship of Goddess Lakshmi is performed during the second set of three days. Once the aspirant succeeds in routing out the evil propensities, and develops Sattwic or pure, divine qualities, he becomes competent to attain wisdom. He is now ready to receive the light of supreme wisdom. He is fit to receive divine knowledge. At this stage comes the devout worship of Mother Saraswathi, who is divine knowledge personified, the embodiment of knowledge of the Absolute. The sound of Her celestial *veena* awakens the notes of the sublime utterances of the *Upanishads* which reveal the Truth, and the sacred monosyllable, Om. She bestows the knowledge of the supreme, mystic sound and then gives full knowledge of the Self as represented by Her pure, dazzling snow-white apparel. Therefore, to propitiate Saraswathi, the giver of knowledge, is the third stage.

The tenth day, Vijaya Dasami, marks the triumphant ovation of the soul at having attained liberation while living in this world, through the descent of knowledge by the Grace of Goddess Saraswathi. The soul rests in his own Supreme Self or Satchidananda Brahman. This day celebrates the victory, the achievement of the goal. The banner of victory flies aloft. Lo! I am He! I am He!

This arrangement also has a special significance in the aspirant's spiritual evolution. It marks the indispensable stages of evolution through which everyone has to pass. One naturally leads to the other; to short-circuit this would inevitably result in a miserable failure. Nowadays many ignorant seekers aim straight at the cultivation of knowledge without the preliminaries of purification and acquisition of the divine qualities. They then complain that they are not progressing on the path. How can they? Knowledge will not descend until the impurities have been washed out, and purity is developed. How can the pure plant grow in impure soil?

Therefore adhere to this arrangement; your efforts will be crowned with sure success. This is your path. As you destroy one evil quality, develop the virtue opposite to it. By this process you will soon bring yourself up to that perfection which will culminate in identity with the Self which is your goal. Then all knowledge will be yours: you will be omniscient, omnipotent and you will feel your omnipresence. You will see your Self in all. You will have achieved eternal victory over the wheel of births and deaths, over the demon of worldliness. No more pain, no more misery, no more birth, no more death! Victory, victory be yours!

Glory to the Divine Mother! Let Her take you, step by step to the top of the spiritual ladder and unite you with the Lord!

At the Sivananda Ashram, Rishikesh, the following are the regular features during the Durga Puja celebrations:

1. A special ritualistic worship of the Mother is conducted daily, which includes the recitation of the *Durga Saptashati*.
2. Laksharchana for the Mother in the temple, with recitation of the *Sri Lalita Sahasranama*, is also conducted.
3. All are exhorted to do the maximum number of Japa of the Navarna Mantra, *Aim hreem kleem chaamundaayai vichche*, or the Mantra of their own tutelary Deity.
4. An elaborately decorated altar is set up for the evening Satsangs, with the picture of Mother Durga for the first three days, Mother Lakshmi for the next three days, and Mother Saraswati for the last three days. Many sacred verses from the scriptures are recited and many Kirtans are sung. The *Durga Saptashati* or the *Devi Mahatmya* is recited and explained in discourses. The function concludes with the formal floral worship and Arati. Sometimes scenes from the *Devi Mahatmya* are also enacted.
5. Earnest spiritual aspirants fast with milk and fruits only on all the nine days, or at least once in each of the three three-day periods.
6. Besides the books representing Saraswathi, all instruments and implements like typewriters, printing machinery, etc., are also worshipped on the ninth day.
7. On the Vijaya Dasami day, all aspirants *en masse* are given initiation into various Mantras according to their tutelary

Deities. Deserving aspirants are initiated into the holy order of Sannyas. Initiation in the study of the alphabets is given to young children, and to the old children also! New students commence their lessons in music, etc. During the morning Satsang the books which were worshipped on the ninth day are again worshipped and a chapter from each of the principal scriptures like the *Gita, Upanishads, Brahma Sutras, Ramayana,* and *Srimad Bhagavatam* is recited.

8. On the Vijaya Dasami day, there is Kanya Puja also. Nine girls below the age of ten are worshipped as the embodiment of the Divine Mother. They are fed sumptuously and, amongst other things, presented with new clothes.
9. On this last day a grand *havan* is conducted in the temple, with recitation of the *Durga Saptashati* and other verses in praise of the Divine Mother.

Durga, in Sanskrit means "She who is incomprehensible or difficult to reach." Goddess Durga is a form of Shakti worshiped for her gracious as well as terrifying aspect. Mother of the Universe, she represents the infinite power of the universe and is a symbol of a female dynamism.

Dushaharaa is the festival of Kshatriya. Right after Pitra Paksh of sixteen days, starts the second Nav Ratri of the year in Aashwin Maas. First Nav Raatri was in Chaitra Maas. This Nav Raatri is celebrated in the same way as it was celebrated in Chaitra Maas. Except that After the Chaitra Nav Raatri comes Ram Navamee, Lord Raam's birthday, and after this Nav Raatri comes Dushaharaa, the day Lord Raam killed Raavan the great demon.

During this Nav Raatri in every village, town, city, Ramleelaa drama is played in which the whole story of Ramaayan is retold. The tenth day, on the day of Dushaharaa (10th day) Lord Raam kills Raavan. Large fairs are arranged, and during the late evening (about after 5.00 pm) a life-like image of Raavan is built with wood, paper etc material and some fireworks are burned to depict the victory of Good on Evil.

In houses, Dushaharaa an image is drawn on the floor with cow dung, people worship it around noon, then take good food, take a nap, and then go to Dushaharaa fair. Kshatriya worship their weapons and Vaishya write the current prices of main items in a new book.

This day is important for farmers also. Farmers go out in their farms and try to see a bird called Neelkanth (a bird with blue throat). If they can find this bird in their farms, they feel lucky, because if this bird is there, they need not to worry about many kinds of natural worms and insects which may destroy their crop.

The Essentials of Durga Puja: The decorated puja platform with all the required essentials. Specific items are needed for each day of Durga Puja. There is a detailed method to worshiping Goddess Durga that are mentioned in the scriptures. Items which are needed for the ritual worship of the goddess should be collected beforehand so that the ritual is performed smoothly. The list of essentials of Durga Puja are:

Items needed for Kalparambho, the ritual performed before the commencement of the puja and Mahasna:

Food Offerings : Panchashasha (grains of five types - rice, mung or whole green gram, til or sesame, mashkalai or any variety of whole black leguminous seed, job or millet), panchagobbo (five items obtained from the cow - milk, ghee or clarified butter, curd, cow dung and gomutra), curd, honey, sugar, three big noibiddos, one small noibiddo, three bowls of madhupakka (a mixture of honey, curd, ghee and sugar for oblation), bhoger drobbadi (items for the feast), aaratir drobbadi mahasnan oil, dantokashtho, sugar cane juice, an earthen bowl of atop (a type of rice), til toilo (sesame oil).

Water Offerings: Ushnodok (lukewarm water), coconut water, sarbooushodhi , mahaoushodhi, water from oceans, rain water, spring water, water containing lotus pollen.

Puja Items: Sindur (vermillion), panchabarner guri (powders of five different colours - turmeric, rice, kusum flowers or red aabir, rice chaff or coconut fibre burnt for the dark colour, bel patra or powdered wood apple leaves), panchapallab (leaves of five trees - mango, pakur or a species of fig, banyan, betal and Joggodumur or fig), pancha ratna (five types of gems - gold, diamond, sapphire, ruby and pearl), panchakoshay (bark of five trees - jaam, shimul, berela, kool, bokul powdered in equal portions and mixed with water), green coconut with stalk, three aashonanguriuk (finger ring made of kusha).

Cloth Offerings: Gamcha or a piece of cloth to cover the pot, a dhoti for Vishnu, a sari each for bodhon and Chandi.

Decorative Items : Ghat or a pot, kundohari , a mirror, four arrows, tekatha or a triangular frame of wood, horitoki flowers (myrobalan), chandmala (garland with circular decorations), aashon (a mattress of jute or hay).

Other Items : Water camphor and perfumed sandal wood paste. soil - extracted from elephant tusks, from the teeth of the pig, from the horns of the ox, from the bank of rivers Ganga and Saraswati, from both the banks of a river, from a place where four roads intersect, from palaces, from the ant hill, from the mountains, Vishnu toilo.

Origin of Durga - The Mythology: Durga, a beautiful warrior seated upon a tiger.

Devi is the great goddess of the Hindus,the consort of Shiva and she is worshiped in various forms corresponding to her two aspects: benevolence and fierceness. She is Uma, "light"; Gauri, "yellow or brilliant"; Parvati, "the mountaineer"; and Jagatmata, "the-mother-of-the-world" in her milder guise. The terrible emanations are Durga "the inaccessible"; Kali, "the black"; Chandi, "the fierce"; and Bhairavi, "the terrible."

Descent of the Goddess: Durga, a beautiful warrior seated upon a tiger, was the first appearance of the great goddess. The circumstance of her miraculous arrival was the tyranny of the monster-demon Mahishasur, who through terrific austerities had acquired invincible strength. The gods were afraid of this water-buffalo bull because neither Vishnu nor Shiva could prevail against him. It seemed that the joint energy of Shakti was only capable of vanquishing Mahisha, and so it was the eighteen-armed Durga who went out to do battle.

Battlefield : She went to battle on her ferocious mount lion, armed with the weapons given to her by the other Gods. Durga is one of the angry and aggressive aspects of the goddess Shakti, whose role in Hindu mythology was to fight and conquer demons and also personify the Sakti or female aspect of any male deity. In the battle, she fought and killed the evil Mahishasura and restored heaven to the Gods. Since then the goddess is invoked for protection from the powers of evil. Durga Puja is observed in her honor, to celebrate her victory over evil.

Revered Mother: She has been worshiped from about 400 AD, but probably earlier, to the present. Her literary references are chiefly the Ramayana and Mahabharata, epic and Puranic texts, and she is mentioned by name in Vedic literature. In general, Durga is regarded in northern India as the gentle bride epitomizing family unity while in southern India she is revered more in her warrior aspect.

Navratri: Dandiya, the most awaited traditional dance festival of India.

Navratri, the festival of nights, lasts for 9 days with three days each devoted to worship of Ma Durga, the Goddess of Valor, Ma Lakshmi, the Goddess of Wealth and Ma Saraswati, the Goddess of Knowledge. During the nine days of Navratri, feasting and fasting take precedence over all normal daily activities amongst the Hindus. Evenings give rise to the religious dances in order to worhip Goddess Durga Maa.

1st - 3rd day of Navratri: On the first day of the Navaratras, a small bed of mud is prepared in the puja room of the house and barley seeds are sown on it. On the tenth day, the shoots are about 3 - 5 inches in length. After the puja, these seedlings are pulled out and given to devotees as a blessing from god. These initial days are dedicated to Durga Maa, the Goddess of power and energy. Her various manifestations, Kumari, Parvati and Kali are all worshipped during these days. They represent the three different classes of womanhood that include the child, the young girl and the mature woman.

4th - 6th day of Navratri: During these days, Lakshmi Maa, the Goddess of peace and prosperity is worshipped. On the fifth day which is known as Lalita Panchami, it is traditional, to gather and display all literature available in the house, light a lamp or 'diya' to invoke Saraswati Maa, the Goddess of knowledge and art.

7th - 8th day of Navratri: These final days belong to Saraswati Maa who is worshipped to acquire the spiritual knowledge. This in turn will free us from all earthly bondage. But on the 8th day of this colourful festival, yagna (holy fire) is performed. Ghee (clarified butter), kheer (rice pudding) and sesame seeds form the holy offering to Goddess Durga Maa.

Mahanavmi: The festival of Navratri culminates in Mahanavami. On this day Kanya Puja is performed. Nine young girls representing the nine forms of Goddess Durga are worshiped. Their feet are washed as a mark of respect for the Goddess and then they are offered new clothes as gifts by the worshiper. This ritual is performed in most parts of the country.

Mahalaya: People offering 'tarpan' in memory of their deceased forefathers. Mahalaya ushers in the aura of Durga Puja. The countdown for the Durga Puja begins much earlier, from the day of 'Janmastami'. It is only from the day of Mahalaya that the preparations for the Durga Puja reaches the final stage. The midnight chants of various hymns of 'Mahishasura Mardini' reminds one of the beginning of Durga Puja.

Mahalaya is an auspicious occasion observed seven days before the Durga Puja, and heralds the advent of Durga, the goddess of supreme power. It's a kind of invocation or invitation to the mother goddess to descend on earth - "Jago Tumi Jago". This is done through the chanting of mantras and singing devotional songs.

The day of Mahalaya is also the day of remembrance. On this day, people offer 'tarpan' in memory of their deceased forefathers. The banks of River Ganga becomes a sea of humanity. Priests are seen busy performing 'Tarpan' for devotees in groups. The rituals start from early down and end during the midday. Devotees and worshipers buy clothes and sweets to offer to their forefathers. 'Tarpan' is to be performed in empty stomach. After offering 'tarpan', people eat at the same place.

The festival of Dassehra, also known as Vijayadashmi, is one of the fascinating festivals of India and is celebrated with joy and enthusiasm. According to the great Hindu scripture, the Ramayana, Lord Rama performed chandi-puja (holy prayer). This was carried out in order to invoke the blessings of Durga Maa for the killing of Ravana, the ten-headed demon king of Sri Lanka who had abducted Seeta, wife of Lord Rama.

Durga Maa divulged the secret to Rama on how he could slay the great Ravana. Hence upon vanquishing the demon Ravana, Lord Rama with Sita and younger brother Laxmana, returned victorious to his kingdom of Ayodhya on the day which is called 'Diwali'. Revelers across northern India re-enact the legend at sundown in a performance called the Ramlila, featuring actors dressed as Rama shooting flaming arrows at effigies stuffed with firecrackers.

Dassera day is considered a most auspicious day. It is a time-honored belief that if any new venture is started on this day, it is bound to be successful. Hence, all the undertakings be it laying-in of foundation of a new building, opening of a new commercial establishment or even initiating a child into the world of learning-are started on this day. Also on this day implements of agriculture, manufacturer's machines, the intellectuals pens, the household articles, the children's school books are placed before the idol of Durga and worshiped.

The Beautiful Bengali Decoration Surrounding the Majestic Warrior : Sati, the consort of Shiva was the daughter of Daksha Prajaapati a descendant of Bhrama. Sati had married Shiva against the wishes of her father. Daksha was sponsoring a sacrifice and attendees came from various parts of the universe. He invited all of the gods and goddesses except his son in law Shiva. Against Shiva's wishes, Sati attended this sacrifice and was insulted by her father. Unable to bear this insult, Sati immolated herself. Enraged at the insult and the injury, Shiva destroyed Daksha's sacrifice, cut off Daksha's head and when pleaded by other gods, replaced it with that of a goat and restored him to life.

Still berserk with grief, he picked up the remains of Sati's body, and danced the dance of destruction throughout the Universe. The other gods intervened to stop this dance, and the disk of Vishnu cut through the corpse of Sati, whose various parts of the body fell at several spots all through the Indian subcontinent and formed the sites of what are known as Shakti Peethas today.

Shiva was finally pacified when the last piece fell off from his shoulder. Narayana revived sati as Uma for a new life. Ever since peace was restored, Uma, with her children, Ganesh and Kartick, and with her two 'sakhis' - Jaya and Bijaya, comes to visit her parent's home each year during the season of 'Sharat' or autumn when Durga Puja is celebrated.

The worship of Devi Durga in the month of Ashwin is called 'Akalbodhan'- an uncustomary time for commencement of the worship. It is so called since the period of this worship differs from the conventional period (during the spring - 'Basanta'). Ramayana says that when Rama was engaged in the fierce battle with Ravana, he wanted to secure the blessings of victory from Devi Durga. He held the puja to evoke the goddess during autumn to his dire plight, thereby worshiping Durga untimely (in Akal). Hence this puja is called Akalbodhon.

It was customary to worship Durga with 100 neel kamals (blue lotuses). Rama could gather only 99 of them; he offered one of his eyes as a substitute of the 100th lotus. Pleased with his devotion Durga blessed him. The battle started on Shaptami and Ravana was killed at the Shandhikshan (in between) Ashtami and Navami; he was cremated on Dashami. Therefore the four days of the puja that we celebrate ends in the triumph of the good over evil.

Region: West Bengal, Bihar, Uttar Pradesh, Delhi & Madhya Pradesh : During Durga puja or Durga Puja (commonly called in West Bengal), the idols of Goddess Durga are worshipped for nine days in beautifully decorated 'pandaals'. It is a public festival. On the tenth day, the 'Visarjan' or immersion of idols in sea waters is performed. During this time, in various parts of India, the 'Ram-Leela' is performed. Ram-Leela is a stage inaction of Ramayana, the story of Lord Rama. Durga puja has come to be associated with a grand exhibition of cultural functions.

In towns and villages, the evenings are replete with jatra, theatre, song, music, dance programmes, sports, physical and cultural competitions etc which everyone is free to attend. Community feasts are held. The immersion ceremony (vijaya), provides an impressive finale.

Region: Gujarat, Punjab and Maharashtra: Navratri is a festival of worship, dance and music celebrated over a period of nine nights. Devotees perform the 'devi-sthaapna' in their homes wherein they invite the Goddess and perform 'pooja-path' for nine days. Gujaratis perform their traditional dances 'Garba' & 'Dandiya-Raas' during Navratri. The women-folk dance in a circle, singing 'Garbas' or traditional songs.

'Dandiya-Raas' is played with wooden sticks or 'dandiyas'. Apart from Gujrat, Garbas are performed in other states & cities like Mumbai. Young men-women wear colourful traditional dresses and play Garba with great enthusiasm.The mood of Navratri is very colourful & unique.

Region: Kullu Valley, Himachal Pradesh : The annual mela or festival takes place in the Kullu Valley - also known as the Valley of the Living Gods, in North India. The festival celebrates the triumph of the God Ram over evil. The Rath Yatra of the idol of Lord Ragunath is led by the Kullu Raja and village deities, and is known as the running of the Gods. The procession starts a week of religious ceremonies, cultural activities, socializing and shopping at the huge bazaar, or market, that comprises most of the mela ground.

Dussehra at Kullu: commences on the tenth day of the rising moon, i.e. on 'Vijay Dashmi' day itself and continues in seven days. The birth of Dussehra in Kullu lay in royal fads and it nourished on religious, social and economic factors and ultimately came to be well established, because of the inborn love of the hill-men for fun, frolic, displayed in community singing and dancing. Numerous stalls offer a verity of local wares. This is also the time when the International Folk Festival is celebrated.

Region: Mysore, Karnataka: In Mysore, Dussehra is easily the most popular festival. It is celebrated on a grandiose scale here. Elephants are decked up with robes and jewelery and taken in processions through the streets of the city. In fact, many people visit Mysore from all over the country to watch this colorful event. There is also a floating festival in the temple tank at the foot of Chamundi Hill and a procession of chariots around the temple at the top.

The Dussehra of Mysore or Mysore Dassara as it is famously called is a 10-day long festival. On the day of Dussehra, a procession of caparisoned elephants carrying the idol of goddess Chamundi is taken through the city. The festival is celebrated in a grand style with scores of cultural performances in the great Durbar Hall of the Maharaja's Palace. On Vijaydashami, the 10th day of the festival, a colorful procession featuring caparisoned elephants winding through the gaily-decorated streets of the city, mark the occasion.

Region: Tamil Nadu, Karnataka and Andhra Pradesh: Bommai Kolu is traditionally a women's festival that Tamilians celebrate during Dasshera. Every year, a series of steps is set up and kolu bommai or dolls are displayed. These dolls typically depict gods or village scenes and weddings. A kolu can be as simple or as elaborate as one likes. The woman of the house invites other women to come inspect the kolu, eat a few snacks, exchange a little gossip and go home with a couple of small goodies.

During this time, the girls and women make rounds from house to house during those nine days of Navrathri. Sundal is a delicious confection made from bean sprouts and coconut that is traditionally served at kolu. Women set up decorated planks in a corner and place on it all the dolls in the house. This beautiful clay figurines of gods and goddesses are worshipped during Navaratri, viewing art as Divinity. Women traditionally exchange gifts of coconuts, clothes and sweets.

The ninth day is also the day of the Ayudha Puja. After the slaying of Mahisasura and other demons by Chamundeswari, there was no more use for her weapons. So the weapons were kept aside and worshipped. This Ayudha puja is being celebrated since ancient times. The importance of Ayudha Puja on this occasion may also be due to the fact that on the Vijayadasami day, Arjuna took back his weapons which he had hidden in a Vani tree in order to lead a life in disguise for the promised period of exile. It is believed that one who begins or renovates his learning to work on the Vijayadasami day will secure a grand success as Arjuna did in Kurukshetra war.

The Ayudha Puja is a worship of whatever implements one may use in one's livelihood. On the preceding evening, it is traditional to place these implements on an altar to the Divine. If one can make a conscious effort to see the divine in the tools and objects one uses each day, it will help one to see one's work as an offering to God. It will also help one to maintain constant remembrance of the divine. In India it is customary for one to prostrate before the tools one will use before starting one's work each day; this is an expression of gratitude to God for helping one to fulfil one's duties.

The tenth day or Vijayadasami is also the day of Vidyaramba or beginning of study when children usually begin to learn the alphabets. On the Vijayadasami day after a Puja in the morning, the Books and implements are removed from the room and this ceremony is called 'Puja Eduppu'. The time for the break up of the puja marks the beginning of learning and work. Learning and work commence at this auspicious moment.

Literates, in general write the alphabets on sand and read a few sentences from sacred books. Similarly the craftsmen and other skilled workers do some work using their implements. At this auspicious moment the children for the first time are given instructions to write the first few alphabets on rice or sand. They are thus initiated into the world of knowledge. This is called 'Ezhuthinu Iruthu' and according to custom only after this ceremony child becomes entitled to write or read.

The Goddess Saraswathi is worshipped as the Goddess of Learning, the deity of Gayathri, the fountain of fine arts and science, and the symbol of supreme vedantic knowledge. On the Durgashtami day, a ceremony called Poojavaipu is performed in the evening in Kerala. In a village, generally, it is done only in certain households, in temples and also sometimes in the village schools. The Brahmin houses and the houses which enjoy reputation for learning, mainly take the lead in celebrating the festival. The members of other houses in the village attend the ceremony performed in these houses or institutions.

In a well-decorated room, books and grandhas (holy books) are tastefully arranged with a picture or an image of Goddess Saraswathi in front. In certain poaches weapons and implements are kept by the side of books and garandhas. Then a Puja is performed to Saraswathi during which fruits, beaten rice, roasted paddy (malar), jaggery etc, are offered to Her. These offerings are distributed among those present when the Puja is over.

Just before the Pujavaipu, all studies and work which mainly require skill, are suspended. The following day is known as Mahanavami and it is totally devoted to the worship of Saraswathi. Pooja is performed both in the morning and in the evening. Many more items such as rice, payasam, thirali, etc are also offered to Devi.

The ten-day Saraswati festival, also known as Dussehra or Navaratri, is held September-October. It's celebrated throughout India but takes on special significance in Kerala. Young children are taken to the temples and, before an image of a goddess-celebrated in Kerala as Saraswati, the goddess of wisdom and learning - they are introduced to the letters of the alphabet.

Region: Maharashtra : In ancient times kings used the feast of Dasara to cross the frontier and fight against their neighboring kingdoms. This border crossing is known as "Simollanghan". Thus Dasara also marks the beginning of the war season.

This was also the day to worship the weapons. According to legend, Pandav went to dwell in the forest. On the way he hid his weapons in the hole of a "shami" tree. After one year he returned from the forest and on Dussehra day he took again his weapons and worshipped the shami tree and the weapons. Hence the custom of worshipping weapons on this feast.

People decorate the entrances of their homes with torans, flower studded strings, and worship the tools of trade, vehicles, machinery, weapons and even books. As the evening falls, the villagers cross the border, and worship the Shami tree. The leaves of the Apta tree are collected and exchanged among friends and relatives as gold.

Durga's mode of journey to the earth is detailed in scriptures. The modes, an elephant, a horse, palanquin, boat all signify luck or omen which influence the life on earth.Goddess Durga visits the earth for only four days but seven days prior to puja starts the Mahalaya. From this day starts 'Devipaksha' when people pray for their demised relatives and take holy dip in the Ganges. This ritual is known as 'Tarpan'. Puja Rule according to Bengali calender. Days are counted based on sunrise and sunset while 'Tithi' depends on the rising and setting of the moon. Sandhi Puja is performed counting 'Tithi'. Sasthi, Saptami, Nabami and Dashami pujas are performed after sunrise even if they fall in the previous evenings.This year the goddess arrives on a boat and departs on an elephant. Goddess Durga's arrival on a boat signifies good harvest, growth and prosperity while her departure on an elephant indicates greenery and prosperity through out the year. Dates : Festivities commence on the first night in the month of Ashwin (September / October). Nine nights are spent in worship and the tenth day is devoted to goddess Durga, who occupies a special position in the Hindu pantheon of gods and goddesses.

Durga is Shakti, the cosmic energy that animates all beings. According to a Puranic legend attached to this day, demon Mahishasur vanquished the gods and their king, Indra, who approached the Holy Trinity, Brahma, Vishnu and Shiva. They in turn sought the help of the divine mother Durga who, equipped with lethal weapons, riding a ferocious lion, in all her awesome majesty, killed Mahishasur. This day, thus, also celebrates the magnificence and omnipotence of Goddess Durga. Practice : Durga pooja is celebrated extensively in North India where beautiful idols of the Mother Goddess are worshipped in elaborate pandals for nine days, and on the tenth day, these are carried out in procession for visarjan (immersion) in a river or pond. The face of the goddess remains covered until the bodhon (unveiling) ritual is performed on Sasthi - the sixth day of the moon. It is Sarat, or autumn, and Nature adorns herself to welcome the advent of the Mother Goddess, Durga. Rabindra Sangeet, dances and various programmes form a part of the celebrations.

The Goddess is worshipped as a kumari or young girl, and reveals herself in her true form Mahasaptami (the seventh day of the moon). On Mahastami (eighth day) and Mahanavami (ninth day) the celebrations reach a fever pitch. On Dashami (tenth day) the idol of Durga is immersed in water. The ten-armed goddess dazzles the devotees with her splendour and appearance of fiery valour during her short stay every year. In the older days of zamindars (landed aristocracy) there used to be a Barwari pooja financed by the local zamindar who usually had a huge Nat

Mandir or Mandap (out-hall) for pooja purposes, where the entire village congregated. All found employment of some kind - from the Brahmins performing the rites to various artisans of lower castes. Even women had their share of work in the preparations. The time of immersion is a sad occasion and the Devi is repeatedly requested to return to shower bliss on devotees whenever invoked.

The festival sees a boom in pre-pooja sales. All trade and commerce gears up to meet the challenge of coping with the frenetic shopping spree. Whole communities of artisans spend their busiest time to ensure the netting of a sizeable income that will sustain them for several months to come. It is a time of activity and employment for all. Artisans build the mammoth pandal (a pandal constructed in 1994 as a replica of the Belur Math, was almost 90 ft high, required 3500 bamboo poles, 5000 planks of wood and over 2000 metres of cloth and cost Rs 5 lakh.). Weavers are kept busy, as are the craftsmen who model the exquisitely chiseled features and limbs of each figure in the pooja tableau from clay; electricians who ingeniously devise the decorative illuminations (everything of topical interest from the dinosaurs of Jurassic Park to World Cup football, to nuclear testing is portrayed); the dhaakis whose unsurpassed virtuosity finds expression in frenzied pounding on huge barrel-shaped drums, invoking an almost hypnotic rapture. Everybody is involved, and there is profit and fun for all.It is a time of prosperity also for publishing houses - the pooja Editions capitalize on the festive mood of the reading public. From big established dailies to little magazines, all thrive this season.

There is also a big demand for audiocassettes, which are Pooja Hits. Today pooja pandals seem to sprout like mushrooms - practically one every 100 yards. Apart from loudspeakers blaring forth pop and Hindi film music and other forms of entertainment (there are also cultural programmes), there is a fierce competition among organisers to compete with and outdo each other in the extravagant and lavish show they put up. Pooja committees are known to spend in lakhs on attractive pandal decor. Galaxies of twinkling lights make Technicolor pageants out of the dingiest lanes. The para poojas become grander still each year, as the poojas are an occasion people look forward to. Money is not a constraint, as people donate generously. Poojas are a convenient occasion for fun-loving denizens to forget their cares and let their hair down. Multitudes throng the streets - people from all communities are agog - shopping, gorging themselves or gazing on Durga who is a shimmering vision - power personified - tresses streaming, a flickering tongue of flame. Durga Pooja is celebrated with more fervour by Bengalis than any other community in India. With the Bengali, Bijoya evokes sentiment. It is a time of renewal of ties of kinship with friends and relatives. Thus Kolakuli echoes the Id embrace among Muslims. Durga Pooja is a festival Bengalis celebrate without religious inhibition. The nine days of pooja are synonymous with the Navratras and the tenth day is celebrated as Vijayadashmi in some parts of India.

Rituals: Durga pooja is celebrated extensively in North India where beautiful idols of the Mother Goddess are worshipped in elaborate pandals for nine days, and on the tenth day, these are carried out in procession for visarjan (immersion) in a river or pond. The face of the goddess remains covered until the bodhon (unveiling) ritual is performed on Sasthi - the sixth day of the moon.

The Goddess is worshipped as a kumari or young girl, and reveals herself in her true form Mahasaptami (the seventh day of the moon). On Mahastami (eighth day) and Mahanavami (ninth day) the celebrations reach a fever pitch. On Dashami (tenth day) the idol of Durga is immersed in water. The ten-armed goddess dazzles the devotees with her splendour and appearance of fiery valour during her short stay every year.

It is the time of the Durga Puja, celebrating the ten-armed goddess of fertility and the third embodiment of the Devi, Durga. It was Durga who vanquished the buffalo-demon Mahishasura. The festivities start with the first day called Mahalaya. It is also the day of the beginning of the countdown to the Durga Puja, which is celebrated in most households apart from the gaily-decorated puja mandaps that are erected in almost every locality. It is a common belief that Ma Lakshmi brings peace and prosperity to the households that celebrate the puja. Goddess Durga is called by various names on each day of the Navaratri festival:

Day 1: Shaila Putri

Day 2: Brahmacharini

Day 3: Chandraghanta

Day 4: Kooshmanda

Day 5: Scandamaata

Day 6: Kaatyayini

Day 7: Kaalaraatri

Day 8: Mahagowri

Day 9: Siddhidaatri

She is worshipped on all the days with special pooja. The fifth day, Lalithapanchami is considered a very auspicious day. On this day, Sharada pooja is done, where everyone worships his or her books and anything connected to learning. On Durgashtami, Durga Havana is performed, and on Mahanavami, Ayudha Pooja is performed. On this day, people worship their respective tools of work, and their vehicles too.

It is believed that if Goddess Durga is worshipped during Navaratri with devotion and dedication, the devotee will be bestowed with Her blessings, which will bring about prosperity in all that he/she does.

The various kinds of Poojas conducted during Navaratri are:

- Sharada Pooja
- Pustaka Pooja
- Lalitapanchami Vrata
- Durga Pooja
- Durgadeeta Namaskara
- Chandika Parayana
- Navadurga Poojane
- Durga Havana
- Chandika Havana
- Laxminarayana Hradaya Parayana
- Kumkumarchane

- Ayudha Pooja
- Yantra Vaahana Pooja

The story of the creation of this goddess is also very interesting. The gods in heaven decided to create an all-powerful being to kill the demon king Mahishasur who was ready to attack them. At that very moment a stream of lightning dazzled forth from the mouths of Brahma, Vishnu and Mahesh and it turned into a beautiful, magnificent woman with ten hands. Then all the gods furnished her with their special weapons. Those weapons and armour are very artistically carved in the ancient sculptures of this goddess in Java. The image of Durga, the Eternal Mother destroying the demon, Mahishasur on Chamundi Hills near Mysore is symbolic of the final confrontation of the spiritual urge of man with his baser passions. This goddess Durga as Lord Shiva's Consort represents two forms of female energy - one mild and protective and the other fierce and destructive. Dassera festival is also known as Durgotsav and during the ten days, the many splendoured goddess Durga is worshipped in one of her many forms differently in different regions. With religious rituals and chantings of mantras followed by "KATHA" or story-telling told by Pandits who by reading passages from religious texts awaken religious fervour in the minds of the listeners. In Bengal and the neighbouring states of Assam and Orissa Durga devi is worshipped by name of Kali as a symbol of Shakti before whom animal sacrifices were made. Her dance of conquest is famous in our ancient texts. As per the orthodox Hindu conceptions, the personality of one deity cannot be entirely separated from that of another. As such in some regions all the three principal goddesses - Durga, Lakshmi and Saraswati are worshipped during this festival, each for 3 days of the Navaratri.

As per our great epic Mahabharat, Pandavas after wandering in the forest for 12 years, hung their weapons on a Shami tree before entering the court of king Virat to spend the last one year in disguise. After the completion of that year on Vijayadashmi the day of Dassera they brought down the weapons from the Shami tree and declared their true identity. Since that day the exchange of Shami leaves on Dassera day became symbols of good, will and victory. The founder of the Hindu Swarajya Chatrapati Shivaji before any military expedition always invoked the blessings of Durga in the form of his goddess Bhawani. The Sikh guru Gobind Singh introduced the worship of Durga into his cult of the sword. This festival has immense mythological significance. As per Ramayan, Ram did "chandi-puja and invoked the blessings of Durga to kill Ravana, the ten-headed king of Lanka who had abducted Seeta and had charmed life. Durga divulged the secret to Ram how he could kill Ravana. Then after vanquishing him, Ram with Seeta and Laxman returned victorious to his kingdom of Ayodhya on Dassera day. Therefore, the festival of Durgotsava and Dassera is celebrated more in honour of Prabhu Ramchandra than Durgadevi in many regions of India and recitations from Ramayan and dances and dramas depicting the exploits of Ram assume great importance.

These Ramlila shows are very popular in Uttar Pradesh, Madhya Pradesh and to an extent in Maharashtra and effigies of king Ravana, his brother, Kumbhakarna and his son, Meghnath are burnt. During the pre-British period, the powerful Hindu rulers used to celebrate Dassera in right royal fashion and start military expeditions on this Dassera day against their enemies or recalcitrant vassals. With the arrival of the British, Hindu rulers could not indulge in military activities yet Dassera was celebrated with the old pomp and pageant of full military parades of all arms in the capitals of Hindu states when the Rajas and Maharajas personally took the salute, Trumpets blared militant notes, war drums sounded their loudest and soldiers looked martial. The procession of Dassera taken out in Mysore is always remembered for its grandeur. With independence and the disappearance of princely states these ancient pageants are dying out and Dassera is becoming more democratic than regal. Dassera day is considered a most auspicious day. It is a time-honoured belief that if any new venture is started on this day, it is bound to be successful. Hence, all the undertakings be it laying-in of foundation of a new building, opening of a new commercial establishment or even initiating a child into the world of learning- are started on this day. Also on this day implements of agriculture, manufacturer's machines, the intellectuals pens, the household articles, the children's school books are placed before the idol of Durga and worshipped.

The revolutionaries who followed the "CULT OF THE BOMB" to free their motherland from the slavery of the British imperialism looked up to Durgadevi for success in their mission. Even to-day in free India, Durga's blessings are invoked and Dassera is celebrated all over the country. These celebrations involve inter-Asia visits to temples like Meenakshi at Madras, Kamakshi at Conjivaram, Annapurna at Benares, Mumbadevi and Mahalaxmi at Mumbai and signify the triumph of good, of piety and devotion over all the forces of evil.

Following is the recipe for preparing MALPUAS Ingredients: 3 cups of fine wheat flour1 cup fine semolina (Suji) 2 cups grated jaggery (gur)2 Tablespoons ghee 1 Tablespoon peppercorns 2 cups milk1 Lime 1 Tablespoon curd Pinch each of salt and soda. Method: 1. Place the flour & the semolina in a dekchi along with the milk, curds, jaggery and the pinch of salt. 2. Beat at least for 5 to 7 minutes so that the mixture becomes light and fluggy. 3. Pound the peppercorns coarsely & add to the mixture. 4. Heat 2 tablespoons of ghee and pour over the mixture. 5. Mix well, cover the dekchi and let stand for 7/8 hours in a warm place. 6. The mixture would have risen by this time. Stir it well. If it is thick, add a little milk or water to bring it to the pouring consistency. 7. Add and blend in it the pinch of soda and juice lime. 8. Place a deep frying pan with lot of ghee in it, when it is heated lower the fire, gently put in 1 tablespoon of the ready balter into the heated ghee. 9. Fry to a golden brown colour on both sides. 10. While frying splash to make it porous and crisp. 11. Take out with a slotted spoon & place in a strainer so that the extra ghee drips down. 12. Thus fry all the Malpuas. They can be stored for a week or so.

The worship of Durga in the autumn (*Shôrot*) is the year's most major festival in Bengal, Orissa, Tripura and other parts of East India as well as in Bangladesh. *Puja* means "worship," and Durga's Puja is celebrated from the sixth to tenth day of the waxing moon in the month of *Ashshin*, which is the sixth month in the Bengali calendar. Occasionally however, due to shifts in the lunar cycle relative to the solar months, it may also be held in the following month, *Kartik*. In the Gregorian calendar, these dates correspond to the months of September/October.

In the Krittibas Ramayana, Rama invokes the goddess Durga in his battle against Ravana. Although she was traditionally worshipped in the spring, due to contingencies of battle, Rama had to invoke her in the autumn (akaal bodhan). Today it is this Rama's date for the puja that has gained ascendancy, although the spring puja, known as Basanti Puja, is also present in the Hindu almanac. Since the season of the puja is *Shôrot* (autumn), it is also known as *Sharodia*.

The pujas are held over a five-day period, which is traditionally viewed as the coming of the married daughter, Durga, to her father, Himalaya's home. It is the most important festival in Bengal, and Bengalis celebrate with new clothes and other gifts, which are worn on the evenings when the family goes out to see the *pandals* (temporary structures set up to venerate the goddess). Although it is a Hindu festival, many religious groups participate in the ritual. In Kolkata alone more than a thousand *pandals* are set up, all clamouring for the fickle attention of the populace. Across the world, Durga Puja serves as a community gathering and a connection to roots for the widespread Bengali diaspora. Tokyo has nearly ten Pujas, and North America has several hundred. Bangladesh, with its 10% Hindu population celebrate the puja in many temples, with more than 100 pujas taking place in the capital Dhaka alone.

History: A considerable literature exists around Durga in the Bengali language and its early forms, including *Durgotsavnirnaya* (11th century), *Durgabhaktitarangini* by Vidyapati (14th century), etc. Durga Puja was popular in Bengal in the medieval period, and records exist of it being held in the courts of Rajshahi (16th century) and Nadia (18th century). It was during the 18th century, however, that the worship of Durga became popular among the landed elite of Bengal. Prominent Pujas were conducted by the banyans enriched by British rule, including Nabakrishna Deb, translator for Robert Clive, who initiated an elaborate Puja at his Shobhabazar residence. Today, the culture of Durga Puja has shifted from the princely houses to *Sarvojonin* (literally, "involving all") forms.

Durga puja mood starts off with the Mahalaya. Bengalis traditionally wake up at 4:00 AM in the morning listening to the enchanting voice of Birendra Kishore Bhadra on All India Radio.

During the week of Durga Puja, in the entire state of West Bengal as well as in large enclaves of Bengalis everywhere, life comes to a complete standstill. In play grounds, traffic circles, ponds — wherever space may be available — elaborates structures called *pandals* are set up, many with nearly a year's worth of planning behind them. The word *pandal* means a temporary structure, made of bamboo and cloth, which used to be the venue of the worship of the goddess.

Durga Puja Pandal in Kolkata: Somewhere inside these complex edifices is a stage on which Durga reigns, standing on her lion mount, wielding ten weapons with her ten hands. This is the religious center of the festivities, and the crowds gather to offer flower worship on the mornings, of the sixth to ninth days of the waxing moon fortnight. Ritual drummers, carrying large leather-strung *dhaaks* show off their skills during ritual dance worships called *aarati*. On the tenth day, Durga the mother returns to her husband, Shiva, ritualized through her immersion into the waters.

Today's Puja, however, goes far beyond religion. In fact, visiting the *pandals* recent years, one can only say that Durgapuja the largest outdoor art festival on earth. In the 1990s, a preponderance of architectural models came up on the *pandal* exteriors, but today the art motif extends to elaborate interiors, executed by trained artists, with consistent stylistic elements, carefully executed and bearing the name of the artist.

The sculpture of the idol itself has evolved. The worship always depicts Durga with her four children, and occasionally two attendant deities and some banana-tree figures. In the olden days, all five idols would be depicted in a single frame, traditionally called *pata*. Since the 1980s however, the trend is to depict each idol separately.

At the end of six days, the idol is taken for immersion in a procession amid loud chants and drumbeats to the river or other water body, and it is cast in the waters symbolic of the departure of the deity to her home with her husband in the Himalayas. After this, in a tradition called *Vijaya Dashami*, families visit each other and sweetmeats are offered to visitors (*Dashami* is literally "tenth day" and *Vijay* is "victory").

Kerala: In Kerala, Durga Puja signifies the beginning of formal education for every child aged 3-5 years. While puja goes on in the temple for all ten days, it is only the concluding three days which are really important. Ashtami is the day of Ayudya Puja, when all the tools at home are worshiped. Custom dictates that no tools be used on this day. On navami, day, Goddess Saraswati is honored by worshiping the books and records at home.Thousands throng the Saraswati temple at Kottayam during this period to take a dip in the mysterious holy pond whose source is yet unknown. Large gatherings are also seen at the famous temples at Thekkegram (Palghat), in which there are no idols—only huge mirrors. A devotee finds himself bowing before his own reflection which indicates that God is within us.

Kashmir: Hindus are a minority in Jammu and Kashmir but they celebrate their festivals with pomp and show. These days, festivities are subdued, though. The favorite deities of Kashmir are Lord Shiva and Serawali Ma Durga, the one who rides the tiger. Pundits and Muslims alike vouch that Navratri is important. No big pandals here, each Hindi house-hold does the pooja at home. All the adult members of the household fast on water. In the evenings, fruit may be taken. As elsewhere, Kashmiris grow barley in earthen pots. They believe that if the growth in this pot is good, there is prosperity all year. The most important ritual for Kashmiri Pandits is to visit the temple of guardian goddess Kheer Bhawani on all nine days. On the last day of Navratri, an aarti is held at the temple after which people break their fast. On Dussehra day, Ravana's effigy is burnt.

Durga Pooja has some fond memories related to childhood. Initial ones are those of my native place. Later, we were not so frequent in visiting the village during Durga Pooja and it had not remained that interesting either. But at one point of time, it was almost a custom in our family that almost everyone would gather in our village during this time. Needless to say the place looked really cheerful then. Even the married daughters of the families would not stay at their in-laws place during Durga Pooja. They will come there with their children and stay here, most of the times accompanied by their husbands too all along. And it was not the case with just our family, but almost all the families in the locality. The Pooja of our village was quite famous in the villages nearby.

We were usually the ones to reach the last, since my father's job would not give him break before *saptami* or *ashtami*, unlike the jobs of many of our relatives. And usually, this was the only time in the year when I would visit the village. So, to me, the picture of always elucidates the picture of a place filled with people. I woud not glamourize it and be honest, being the shy and introvert person I was as child, the experience was not usually a very interesting one for me. But today, sitting here in the hostel, wondering what to do with this occasion called Durga Pooja, I can not help but feel nostalgic about those days, which probably will never come back. People have scattered all around, the aspirations of lives have changed (not that I bemoan it!) and things won't even be the same again.

There was this tradition (familiar to people almost all over India) of inviting young girls to eat. The feast is called "Kumari Bhoj" (Feast for virgin girls). Now, unfortunately for me, most of the families would have this feast for all the 10 days of Puja. Since, I would always reach late, I was not in the regular list of people :(. Sometimes, when people increased the number on *Ashtami* or *navami,* I may also end up getting an invitation. At other times, it would be out of sheer consideration and formality - "Oh! So Jaya has also come. Bring her along." Being the person I am, loss of the opportunity to eat was not really a loss (was more a relief, given the choosy nature I had with respect to what I did and did not eat), but when on *Dashami,* all my cousin sisters would return with the money and sometimes clothes they get after *Kumari Bhoj,* I did not used to feel a pang of envy. Not that I ever said anything.

Dahsami was a good day even for me. All the elders of the family (those who are earning) would give all the kids money for visiting the fair. And here, there even a late-comer like me was not at a disadvantage. In fact, this town-bred, shy, out-of-place girl was often at an advantage because she won't pressurize anyone. So, people used to get more generous at times, I would receive some amount secretly too. (Blame me for not being ethical) Especially from *kakka* (tau jee - dad's elder brother). The system was such that older children will get more money. There would usually be groups according to the age. And those on the border would try their best to get counted in the upper group so that they will be eligible for a higher amount!

Even before *Dashami,* we would go to the *Durga Sthan* (the temple of Goddess Durga) daily. Now, most of the things at the place and in the fair was hardly of any interest to me. My cousin sisters would go mad after the posters, song-books etc. I would usually end up spending very little, except on some the story books that were available. The normal ice cream that was available was not something I felt like eating (I had no qwality walls-upbringing then, but even for my small-town-taste, it was not up to the mark). However, there was a higher priced curd ice cream, which tasted quite well. I would usually have that.

The village used to be a very quiet and safe place then. There would be these drama shows (done by the people of the village themselves) all night and everyone including women (even the newly wed daughter-in-laws, who would usually be under strict *parda*) and kids would go there. No need of the group of women being escorted by men.

Then there was *Nisha Pooja*. This would involve an offering of all 56 *vyanjans* (dishes) at the *Durga Sthan* and would go on for all night. Almost all the adults and the kids who could manage it, would be there in the temple for the whole night.

Even at our home, there used to be celebrate rituals of the worship for the 10 days. The eldest man of the family would preside over the rituals. The second one of the four siblings of my grand-father's generations, was an avid devotee of Durga. We, kids, used to call him *Pooja-Baba* (Pooja= Worship, Baba = Grandfather). In those early days, he wasthe one who would preside over the things. Those ringing of *ghantas* (do not know exactly what is the English name for this instrument) along with the chorus recitation of *"Na mantram, na yantram"* by the whole family is something that would overwhelm even someone who knows nothing about the whole celebration.

Several things have changed since then. The village was not as safe a place afterwards. The clash of unemployed-youth-turned-into-trouble-makers of two nearby villages had made things really scary at one point of time. Every other month we would hear of someone or the other getting killed. This appears to have improved over time, however. However, in that period, some charm was lost and lost for ever. Now, more and more people are town and city bound. Several amongst those who would look at my discomforts in the village with skepticism, have themselves gone out to live in cities like Delhi and Mumbai and now find the lack of electricity in the village such a big trouble. Their kids are faring worse than I did! Again am not bemoaning the changes. Has led to at least some initiatives at personal level in the village to live in a better way. A proper toilet was never considered a necessity in the village in those days.

People can not manage to come every year now. Many have permanently settled outside and find it difficult to leave their homes for extended periods of times. The schools and homeworks and exams of the kids are big deterrents. It's good. The kids will aspire for a yet between life. However, as many people do not gather in my village now. Kids do not clout to be considered in the higher age-group, while getting money to go to the fair. Girls are no as crazy after the posters.

The cheap clothes given during the *Kumari Bhoj* are not as attractive. People demand better fashion and aesthetics. Now, the sisters do not buy the clothes of the same pattern on any occasion, which was so common earlier. It looks like a "band party". Those days people would go barefooted from the home to the temple. I found it very irritating as a child, but my mother would insist that I should not stand out. Last time when I went there, I followed the same practice and went out without a pair of slippers. Only to realize that everyone else was wearing it. A cousin sister took pity on my burning foot and offered me her slippers. Despite my protests, she got me to wear it.

Several things have changed for better, yet several things still lag behind. And several things have changed for worse - simplicity of the life is lost. I would not want the world to be exactly as it was then, still I do feel nostalgic about certain things.

The main temples of mother goddess that are visited by multitude of devotees during Navratri are the *shaktipithas.* One belief is that Lord Vishnu had to cut the body of Sati into fifty-two pieces to stop the destruction by Shiva who was perturbed by her death. The main temples are therefore where these pieces of her body were believed to have fallen. The nine nights are dedicated to the three main goddesses of Hinduism - Parvati, Lakshmi and Sarasvati.

The first three nights are dedicated to the goddess of action and energy. Her different manifestations Kumari, Parvati and Kali are worshipped during these days. They represent the three natures/ stages of womanhood - the innocent virgin young girl, caring wife/ mother and the angry old woman. Lakshmi is worshipped for the next three days in her various aspects as the goddesses of peace, plenty, fulfillment and bliss. Saraswati, the goddess of knowledge is worshipped during the final three days of the Navratri.

In various parts of India, the 'Ram-Leela' is performed during Navratri. Ram-Leela is a stage enaction of the *Ramayana*, the mythological book on Lord Rama. The day after Navratri, i.e. 'Dassera' (tenth day) or 'Vijayadashmi' is observed . It is believed that on this day, Lord Rama had killed the demon Ravana. So, on Vijayadashmi, effigies of Ravana are burnt all over India. It marks the victory of good over evil.

As the case with most festivals today, lots has been added and changed. It has also been seriously commercialised. So today it is a festival of religious, devotional, cultural and recreational activities. People enjoy this period's festivities by dancing them away to the blare of loud music and scant attention is given to the spiritual aspect of the festival. The Hindus of Gujarat perform their traditional dances 'Garba' & 'Dandiya-Raas' during Navratri. The women-folk, dresses in traditional clothing, dance in a circle, singing 'Garbas' (traditional songs and dance). 'Dandiya-Raas' (rhythmic dance with sticks) is played with 'dandiyas' (wooden sticks). Beautifully decorated 'mandaps' (stages) are set up for playing garba & dandiya and the mood is quite colourful.

In West Bengal, Navratri is celebrated as 'Durga-pooja' which is the most important festival in that part of India. Celebrations of Durga-pooja in Bengal are similar to celebration of Ganesh Chaturthi in Maharashtra. Idols of Goddess Durga are worshipped for nine days in beautifully decorated 'pandaals'. It is a public festival. On the tenth day, the 'Visarjan' or immersion of idols in the sea is performed.

This festival is a great holiday of the year, shared by Christians, Muslims and Hindus alike. It is connected with the autumnal equinox. Nominally, they commemorate the victory of Goddess Durga, wife of Lord Shiva over a buffalo headed demon (Mahisasur). The form under which she is adored is that of an image with ten arms and a weapon in each hand, her right leg resting on a lion and her left on the buffalo demon. This image is worshipped for nine days following on the sixteen sraddhas of the Pitri Paksh and then cast into the water.

According to Chandi Purana, Mahisasur, the buffalo headed demon, by his austere meditation compelled Brahma to grant him the boon of invincibility. Brahma announced that the demon would die at the hands of a woman. Deeming this an impossibility, Mahisasur terrorized earth and heaven. Vishnu and Shiva were enraged. Goddess Durga was created to massacre Mahisasur. On the advice of Brahma, Rama of Ayodhya, undertook an elaborate and dedicated worship of devi Goddess Durga. At the climax of the pooja, one out of 108 lotus flowers for pooja, was found missing. Rama offered to pluck out his eye to make up the missing flower. The goddess appeared and granted him victory over demon king Ravana. The victory day is thus celebrated as Dussehara and as Goddess Durga pooja, both festivals on the same day (Vijaya Dashmi). This festival creates a conviction that evil has been vanquished and a benevolent deity Trinayani Goddess Durga (Three eyed Goddess Durga) smiles upon the world. In this dew fresh season, the human soul bursts into celebrations.

Goddess Durga pooja or Nava Ratra (nine nights), commencing on the 1st and ending on the 10th day of the light half of Ashwin (September-October) are celebrated in various parts of India, specially Bengal. In Assam, the great festivity to invoke the blessings of Goddess Durga, the Mother goddess in her most benign and protective aspects, is celebrated with great I ceremony. Illumination, beautifully painted clay images of the deity, dances and plays, keep thousands entertained over the pooja holidays, until, the images are taken iri procession and immersed in the great river. ~ In Tripura, at Agartala, this festival of the mother goddess Goddess Durga in her benign and protective form, it celebrated as in Bengal. It is celebrated for four days with great enthusiasm and ends when images of the goddess are taken out in procession and immersed in the river.

In Imphal, this festival is known as Kwak Yatra when goddess Goddess Durga is propitiated with pomp and ceremony. Animal sacrifice used to be an obligatory requirement of Goddess Durga pooja (worship of warrior goddess Goddess Durga). This practice is now defunct all over India. At the poojas, now, symbolic slashing of pumpkins and sugarcane, is done. Formally pooja begins with the dawn recitation from the Chandi Puran on Mahalaya. The creation of Mahisasurmardine in these days is broadcast resoundingly over AIR and Doordarshan at 5 a.m. on shasti, the next day the goddess is invoked in bodhan ceremony. From saptami onwards, for three days, fasting worshippers offer pushpanjali.

On dashami, it all ends with the aforementioned sindoor khela and baran or aarti of the devi. Then, in a crescendo of shouting and dancing, the image is carried by bullock carts or trucks to the nearest river or pond and immersed. The worshippers return to the pooja pandal for shantijal, without which no religious ceremony is complete. Cultural activities during Goddess Durga pooja consist of Jatras, plays, songs and variety programmes to cater to needs of the modern public.

Night entertainments are norm. Show of films and videos on the occasion, has beeb discarded. The common people, in great distress have inevitable been drawn towards the source of life and enei the universal mother, Shakti Durga, who had delivered earth from Mahisasur, is worshipped increasingly to insp courage for the struggle against forces of evil. Devi Durga appears once in a year, to share her force and hearten her devotees to endure another year, till she descends from Kailash again.

During Winter the popular DASSARA festival is celebrated. It lasts for ten days. Like everybody else, Indians love celebrations and festivals. Most of the festivals in India are linked to the agricultural calendar. Many are actually harvest festivals or those signifying a change in the season. Each region has its own local festivals, besides the all India ones. One important festival celebrated all over India is Dasara or Dussehra. It is also called Nava ratri or nine nights festival.

The origin of this festival is not clearly known, but it would appear its roots reach back to staggeringly ancient times. It is essentially a mother goddess celebration.Traces of this festival are seen all the world over although they may be hidden under some other layers. Essentially it is a sort of thanksgiving to Nature in various forms.

The colour of Rajas is red, represented by that aspect of mother Durga we worship as goddess Lakshmi. She wears red. Rajas is of the nature of activity, passion and ambition, the source of thirst for physical enjoyment. Rajas binds fast one by attachment to action. (Gita Ch.14. Verse 7.)

The Rajasic person runs after power, position, name, fame and comforts, and involves himself in endless activities to acquire material wealth.

When we worship goddess Lakshmi for spiritual wealth, she bestows on her devotees the inexhaustible divine wealth or Daivi Sampat (which is described in the Gita, Ch.16, Verses 1,2

and 3). Divine wealth or the wealth of 26 divine qualities, brings with it material prosperity as well.

Tamas is black, represented by that aspect of mother Durga we worship as goddess Kali. She is sometimes depicted in dark blue.

Tamas is born of ignorance, deluding all embodied beings. Tamas binds fast in heedlessness, sleep, indolence, laziness (Gita Ch.14 Verse 8). Tamas is that binding force with a tendency to lethargy (lack of energy, vitality), sloth and foolish actions. It causes non-discrimination or delusion. It binds one who associates the Self with the body. A tamasic person acts under the compulsion of the body. He has no power of judgment. His actions are not guided by reasons. His senses are dull.

These are all baser animal qualities, the lower diabolical nature in man.We pray to mother Kali, as Durga the terrible, as supreme power and force, to destroy all our impurities, our vices, our defects. She is to fight and annihilate these demons. This is the 'strength' aspect of shakti as mentioned in the Upanishad. Mother Kali is the power that guides and protects the devotee's spiritual practice from its many dangers and pitfalls. Mother Kali represents the ferocious and destructive aspect of TIME.

In contrast with creative force in nature, this power is ever active disintegrating forms and structures. It drives heavenly bodies back into their nebulous state.

In the Kenopanishad, part three, (Yaksha Prashna), 12th Mantra, the Divine Mother is described as a woman wondrously fair, daughter of the snowy mountain Himavat, her name Hemavati or Uma.

She is the energy aspect of the Lord. Her other name is Durga. This cosmic energy or shakti is the omnipotent power of the Lord. We call her Durga, the Divine Mother.

Lower states of ignorance and egoism are typified by or personified as demons with such names as Dhumralochan, Chanda and Munda, which should be destroyed by the sudden burst of energy and rough handling. Dumralochan (the smoky-eyed, a person whose understanding is clouded by ignorance) stands for the grosser state of ignorance and egoism. Munda means the low. Munda is the low profile of our egoism. Chanda means fierce. Chanda is the more horrible and fierce side of it. Shumbha and Nishumbha signify more enlightened aspects of egoism. Shumbh means to shine.

Mahishasur stands for ignorance and stubborn egoism. Raktabij represents the more subtle states of desire which multiply endlessly to create more problems.

The following are the regular features of this festival:

A special ritualistic worship of the Mother Durga; this includes the recitation of Durga Saptashati or Devi Mahatmaya.

Recitation of Lalaitha Sahasrnama or Durga Sahasranama (Laksharchana 100,000 times too repeat the name of the Divine Mother) Devotees are exhorted to do the maximum number of Japa of the Navaarna Mantra AIM HREEM KLEEM CHAAMUNDAAYAI VICHHE or the Mantra JAI SHRI DURGA.

Some devotees observe fasting with milk and fruits only on all these nine days or at least three days. Visiting Temples and participating in-group chanting and seeking the blessings of the Divine Mother is the common feature in all these nine days.

Let us celebrate Dasara in the right spirit by making honest efforts to destroy the demon

Ego, the ten headed i.e. passion, pride ,anger ,greed, infatuations, lust, hatred, jealousy, selfishness and crookedness) and radiate peace and love wherever we go, and get the blessings of the Divine Mother.

Three aspects of the eternal smother has been depicted in this Devi Sapta Shloki —The Goddess Lakshmi represents Iccha shakti (wealth) Goddess Saraswati represents Jnana Shakti (knowledge) and Goddess Kali represent Kriya Shakti (strength). All three merge in one form as Durga.

The glory of Durga is described in Markendeya Purana,. It is known as Devi Mahatmyam or Durga Sapta sati (700 Mantras). Allegorical representation of the constant war going on within all of us— between our divine and demonic natures. In the Saptasati legend every dominant passion and vice has its special Demon representative. Shumbha is the embodiment of Lust, Nishumbha is Greed and Mashishasura represents Anger.

We celebrate Victory of Good over the evil. Durga sapta shloki (the seven mantras) is the essence of the Durga Sapta sati (seven hundred mantras). It is very powerful to achieve Health, wealth and education...

DIWALI

This is perhaps the most well-known of the Indian festivals: it is celebrated throughout India, as well as in Indian communities throughout the diaspora. It usually takes place eighteen days after Dusshera. It is colloquially known as the "festival of lights", for the common practice is to light small oil lamps (called *diyas*) and place them around the home, in courtyards, verandahs, and gardens, as well as on roof-tops and outer walls. In urban areas, especially, candles are substituted for diyas; and among the nouveau riche, neon lights are made to substitute for candles. The celebration of the festival is invariably accompanied by the exchange of sweets and the explosion of fireworks. As with other Indian festivals, Diwali signifies many different things to people across the country. In north India, Diwali celebrates Rama's homecoming, that is his return to Ayodhya after the defeat of Ravana and his coronation as king; in Gujarat, the festival honors Lakshmi, the goddess of wealth; and in Bengal, it is associated with the goddess Kali. Everywhere, it signifies the renewal of life, and accordingly it is common to wear new clothes on the day of the festival; similarly, it heralds the approach of winter and the beginning of the sowing season.

Diwali (also called Deepavali) is a major Hindu festival. Known as the "Festival of Lights," it symbolises the victory of good over evil, and lamps are lit as a sign of celebration and hope for mankind. Celebrations focus on lights and lamps, particularly traditional diyas (as illustrated). Fireworks are associated with the festival in some regions of the country.

Deepavali is celebrated for five consecutive days in the Hindu month of Ashwayuja. It usually occurs in October/November, and is one of the most popular and eagerly awaited festivals of India. Hindus, Jains and Sikhs alike regard it as a celebration of life and use the occasion to strengthen family and social relationships. For Jains it is one of the most important festivals, and beginning of the Jain year. It is also a significant festival for the Sikh faith.

Dates in Various Calendars: The date of Diwali is based on the Hindu calendar, which has solar sidereal years and lunar months. Although the festival is worshipped on exactly the same set of days across India, it falls in different months depending on the version of the Hindu calendar being used in the given region.

The *Amanta* ("ending on the no-moon") version of the Hindu Calendar has been adopted as the Indian national calendar. According to this calendar, which is prevalent in southern India and Maharashtra, Deepavali falls in the middle of the month of Ashwayuja. According to the *Purnimanta* ("ending on the full-moon") version prevalent in northern India, the 5-day celebration is spread over the last three days of the month of Ashwayuja and the first two days of the new month of Kartika. According to this calendar, the festival of Deepavali marks the new year's day of this calendar and is therefore an especially significant festival. Diwali is also known as festival of lights. Shown here is the view of Jaipur city on Diwali days.

The festival marks the victory of good over evil. The Sanskrit word Deepavali means array of lights that stands for victory of brightness over darkness. As the knowledge of Sanskrit diminished, the name was popularly modified to Diwali, especially in northern India. On the day of Diwali, many wear new clothes, share sweets and light firecrackers. The North Indian business community usually starts their financial new year on Diwali and new account books are opened on this day.

Hindus find cause to celebrate this festival for different reasons:

- As per sacred texts, according to Skandha Purana, the goddess Shakti observed 21 days of austerity starting from ashtami of shukla paksha (waxing period of moon) to get half part of the body of Lord Shiva. This vrata is known as kedhara vrata. Deepavali is the completion day of this austerity. This is the day Lord Shiva accepted Shakti into the left half of the form and appeared as Ardhanarishvara. The ardent devotees observe this 21 days vrata by making a kalasha with 21 threads on it and 21 types of offerings for 35 days. The final day is celebrated as kedhara gauri vrata.
- Diwali also celebrates the return of the Lord Rama, King of Ayodhya, his wife Sita and brother Lakshmana to Ayodhya from a war in which he killed the demon king Ravana. It is believed that the people lit oil lamps along the way to light their path in the darkness. In North India, the festival is held on the final day of the Vikram calendar. The following day marks the beginning of the North Indian new year, and is called Annakut.
- It commemorates the killing of Narakasura, an evil demon who created havoc, by Lord Krishna's wife Sathyabhama. This happened in the Dwapara Yuga during this time of Lord Krishna's avatar. In another version, the demon was killed by Lord Krishna himself. In South India, Diwali does not coincide with the beginning of a new year as

South Indians follow a different calendar, the Shalivahana calendar.

- In Bhavishyottara and Bramhavaivarta Purana, Diwali is associated with the Daitya king Bali, who is allowed to return to earth once a year.

The Five days of Diwali: Diwali is celebrated over five days in most of North India. All the days except Diwali are named using the designation in the Indian calendar. A lunar half-month is 15 days. Diwali as a new-moon day, marks the last day of a 15-day period. Diwali has emerged as one of the most famous Hindu festivals. An integral part of Diwali decorations, Rangoli is a colorful pattern drawn on the floor.

1. *Dhan-trayodashi* or *Dhan teras*: Dhan means "wealth" and Trayodashi means "13th day". Thus, as the name implies, this day falls on the 13th day of the first half of the lunar month. It is an auspicious day for shopping.
2. *Naraka Chaturdasi*: *Narak* means 'of a new era of Light and Knowledge'. *Chaturdasi* implies fourteenth day.
3. *Diwali*: the actual day of Diwali, is celebrated on the third day of the festival, when the moon completely wanes and total darkness sets in the night sky.
4. *Varsha-pratipada* or *Padwa*: Beginning of the New Year (Kartikadi Vikram). Pratipada means the first.
5. *Bhayiduj* (also Bhayyaduj, Bhaubeej or Bhayitika) — on this day, brothers and sisters meet to express their love and affection for each other.

The celebrations vary in different regions:

- In Southern India, *naraka chaturdashii* is the main day, with firecrackers at dawn.
- The main festival is on *Amavasya* evening with *Lakshmi Puja* which is followed by lighting of oil lamps around the house.

Diwali in Sikhism: Every year, thousands of Sikhs and Hindus celebrate Diwali at the Golden Temple in Amritsar, India. Sikhs also celebrate Diwali to commemorate the laying of the foundation stone for the Golden Temple in 1577. It is also known as Bandi Chhorh Divas. The Mughal emperor Jahangir arrested the Sikh

Guru Hargobind and imprisoned him in Gwalior. Later Jehangir relented and released the Guru. The Guru asked that 52 rulers imprisoned with him should also be released. To the joy of the Sikhs the Guru returned to Amritsar on Diwali and it prompted the followers to celebrate the day with joy and happiness.

On Diwali the Sikhs illuminate their Gurdwaras and homesare with Deewé (earthen oil lamps) or candles. Early in the morning, Sikh pilgrims take a dip in the sacred tank while reciting Japji Sahib, and then pray at the Golden Temple. Circumambulation of the tank is done.

Diwali in Jainism: Lord Mahavira, the last of the Jain Tirthankaras, attained Nirvana on this day at Pavapuri. According to Jain tradition the chief disciple of Mahavira, Ganadhar Gautam Swami also attained complete knowledge on this very day, thus making Diwali a really special occasion for the Jains to celebrate.

Diwali is first mentioned in Jain books as the date of the nirvana of Lord Mahavira. The oldest use of the word "Diwali/ Dipavali" occurs in Harivamsha-Purana written by Acharya Jinasena, composed in Shaka Samvat 705. The sample of text containing the word Diwali is below:

The way Jains celebrate Diwali is different in many respects. There is a note of asceticism in whatever the Jains do, and the celebration of Diwali is not an exception. The Jains celebrate Diwali during the month of Kartik for three days. During this period, among the Shvetambaras, devoted Jains observe fasting and chant the Uttaradhyayan Sutra, which contain the final pravachans of Lord Mahavira, and meditate upon him.

Vira Nirvana Samvat: The Jain year starts with Pratipada following Diwali. Vira Nirvana Samvat 2532 starts with Diwali 2005. The Jain businessmen traditionally started their accounting year from Diwali.

Diwali in Other Parts of the World: Diwali is celebrated in various parts of the world, in countries such as Britain, The Netherlands, Suriname, Canada, Guyana, Mauritius, Fiji, Japan, Indonesia, Malaysia, Myanmar, Nepal, Singapore, Sri Lanka, South Africa, Trinidad and Tobago, Thailand, United Arab Emirates, Australia, much of Africa, and the United States. With more and more Indians now migrating to various parts of the world, the number of countries where Diwali is celebrated has been gradually increasing. While in some countries it is celebrated mainly by Indian expatriates, in others it has become part of the general local culture. In most of these countries Diwali is celebrated on the same lines as described in this article with some minor variations. Some important variations are worth mentioning.

In Malaysia, Diwali is known as "Hari Deepavali," and is celebrated during the seventh month of the Hindu solar calendar. It is a federal public holiday. In many respects it resembles the traditions followed in the Indian subcontinent.

In Nepal, Diwali is known as *Tihar* and celebrated during the October/November period. Here, though the festival is celebrated for five days, the traditions vary from those followed in India. On the first day, cows are given offerings, in appreciation of the food they have given and agricultural work they have performed. On the second day, dogs and all living animals are revered and offered special food. On the third day, celebrations follow the same pattern as in India, with lights and lamps and much social activity. On the fourth day Yama, the Lord of Death, is worshipped and appeased. On the fifth and final day, brothers and sisters meet and exchange pleasantries.

Diwali is celebrated in the Caribbean Islands as well. Especially in Trinidad and Tobago, Diwali is marked as a special occasion and celebrated with much fanfare. It is observed as a national holiday in this part of the world and some Ministers of the Government also take part in the celebrations publicly.

Economics of Diwali: Diwali is an annual stimulus for the Indian economy. Indians purchase gold, gifts, decorations, crackers and household appliances during this festival. Companies offer huge discounts during the Diwali season to attract customers, which helps the economy and also helps the poor. It also helps the community in hunger since this festival shares it food. It also brings tourists to the country.

Since Diwali period also marks school holidays in most parts of India, many Bollywood movies are released during this period. This Diwali which leads us into Truth and Light is celebrated on a nation-wide scale on Amavasya- the 15th day of the dark fortnight of the Hindu month of Ashwin (Aasho) (October / November) every year. It symbolises that age-old culture of our country which teaches us to vanquish ignorance that subdues humanity and to drive away darkness that engulfs the light of knowledge. Diwali, the festival of lights even to-day in this modern world projects the rich and glorious past of our country and teaches us to uphold the true values of life.

The word "Diwali" is the corruption of the Sanskrit word "Deepavali" - Deepa meaning light and Avali, meaning a row. It means a row of lights and indeed illumination forms its main attraction. Every home - lowly or mightly - the hut of the poor or the mansion of the rich - is alit with the orange glow of twinkling diyas-small earthen lamps - to welcome Lakshmi, Goddess of wealth and prosperity. Multi-coloured Rangoli designs, floral decorations and fireworks lend picturesness and grandeur to this festival which heralds joy, mirth and happiness in the ensuring year.

This festival is celebrated on a grand scale in almost all the regions of India and is looked upon mainly as the beginning of New Year. As such the blessings of Lakshmi, the celestial consort of Lord Vishnu are invoked with prayers. Even countries like Gkyena, Thailand, Trinidad, Siam and Malaya celebrate this festival but in their own ways.

This Diwali festival, it is surmised dates back to that period when perhaps history was not written, and in its progress through centuries it lighted path of thousands to attain the ultimate good and complete ecstasy.

Diwali or more aptly Deepavali is very enthusiastically celebrated for five continuous days and each day has its significance with a number of myths, legends and beliefs.

The *First day* is called *DHANTERAS* or *DHANTRAYODASHI* which falls on the thirteenth day of the month of Ashwin. The word "Dhan" means wealth. As such this day of the five-day Diwali festival has a great importance for the rich mercantile community of Western India. Houses and Business premises are renovated and decorated. Entrances are made colourful with lovely traditional motifs of Rangoli designs to welcome the Goddess of wealth and prosperity. To indicate her long-awaited arrival, small footprints are drawn with rice flour and vermilion powder all over the houses. Lamps are kept burning all through the nights. Believing this day to be auspicious women purchase some gold or silver or at least one or two new utensils. "Lakshmi-Puja" is performed in the evenings when tiny diyas of clay are lighted to drive away the shadows of evil spirits. "Bhajans"-devotional songs- in praise of Goddess Laxmi are sung and "Naivedya" of traditional sweets is offered to the Goddess. There is a peculiar custom in Maharashtra to lightly pound dry coriander seeds with jaggery and offer as Naivedya.

In villages cattles are adorned and worshipped by farmers as they form the main source of their income. In south cows are offered special veneration as they are supposed to be the incarnation of Goddess Lakshmi and therefore they are adorned and worshipped on this day.

A very interesting story about this day is of the sixteen year old son of King Hima. As per his horoscope he was doomed to die by a snake-bite on the fourth day of his marriage. On that particular fourth day of his marriage his young wife did not allow him to sleep. She laid all the ornaments and lots of gold and silver coins in a big heap at the entrance of her husband's boudoir and lighted innumerable lamps all over the place. And she went on telling stories and singing songs. When Yam, the god of Death arrived there in the guise of a Serpent his eyes got blinded by that dazzle of those brilliant lights and he could not enter the Prince's chamber. So he climbed on top of the heap of the ornaments and coins and sat there whole night listening to the melodious songs. In the morning he quietly went away. Thus the young wife saved her husband from the clutches of death. Since then this day of Dhanteras came to be known as the day of "YAMADEEPDAAN" and lamps are kept burning throughout the night in reverential adoration to Yam, the god of Death.

The *Second day* is called *NARKA-CHATURDASHI* or *CHOTI DIWALI* which falls on the fourteenth day of the month of Ashwin. The story goes that the demon king Narakasur ruler of Pragjyotishpur (a province to the South of Nepal) after defeating

Lord Indra had snatched away the magnificent earrings of Aditi, the Mother Goddess and imprisoned sixteen thousand daughters of the gods and saints in his harem. On the day previous to Narakachaturdashi, Lord Krishna killed the demon and liberated the imprisoned damsels and also recovered those precious earrings of Aditi. As a symbol of that victory Lord Krishna smeared his forehead with the demon king's blood. Krishna returned home in the very early morning of the Narakachaturdashi day. The womenfolk massaged scented oil to his body and gave him a good bath to wash away the filth from his body. Since then the custom of taking bath before sunrise on this day has become a traditional practice specially in Maharashtra.

In South India that victory of the divine over the mundane is celebrated in a very peculiar way. People wake up before sunrise prepare blood by mixing Kumkum in oil and after breaking a bitter fruit that represents the head of the demon King that was smashed by Krishna, apply that mixture on their foreheads. Then they have an oil bath using sandalwood paste.

In Maharashtra also, traditional early baths with oil and "Uptan" (paste) of gram flour and fragrant powders are a must. All through the ritual of baths, deafening sounds of crackers and fireworks are there in order that the children enjoy bathing. Afterwards steamed vermiceli with milk and sugar or puffed rice with curd is served.

Another legend is about King Bali of the nether world mighty power had become a threat to the gods. In order to curb his powers Lord Vishnu in the guise of a Batu Waman- a small boy- visited him and begged him to give him only that much land which he could cover with his three steps. Known for his philanthropy King Bali proudly granted him his wish. That very moment that small boy transformed himself into the all-powerful Lord Vishnu. With his first step Lord Vishnu covered the entire heaven and with the second step the earth and asked Bali where to keep his third step. Bali offered his head. Putting his foot on his head Vishnu pushed him down to the underworld. At the same time for his generosity Lord Vishnu gave him the lamp of knowledge and allowed him to return to earth once a year to light millions of lamps to dispel the darkness and ignorance and spread the radiance of love and wisdom. Diwali is a five day Hindu festival which occurs on the fifteenth day of Kartika. Diwali means "rows of lighted lamps" and the celebration is often referred to as the Festival of Lights. During this time, homes are thoroughly cleaned and windows are opened to welcome Laksmi, goddess of wealth. Candles and lamps are lit as a greeting to Laksmi. Gifts are exchanged and festive meals are prepared during Diwali. The celebration means as much to Hindus as Christmas does to Christians.

Because there are many regions in India, there are many manifestations of the Diwali festival. In at least one area, the festival begins with Dhanteras, a day set aside to worship Laksmi. In the Indian culture, wealth is not viewed as a corruptive power. Instead, a wealthy person is considered to have been rewarded for good deeds of a past life.

The *Third day* of the festival of Diwali is the most important day of LAKSHMI-PUJA which is entirely devoted to the propitiation of Goddess Lakshmi. This day is also known by the name of "CHOPADA-PUJA". On this very day sun enters his second course and passes Libra which is represented by the balance or scale. Hence, this design of Libra is believed to have suggested the balancing of account books and their closing. Despite the fact that this day falls on an amavasya day it is regarded as the most auspicious.

The day of Lakshmi-Puja falls on the dark night of Amavasya. The strains of joyous sounds of bells and drums float from the temples as man is invoking Goddess Lakshmi in a wondrous holy "pouring-in" of his heart. All of a sudden that impenetrable darkness is pierced by innumerable rays of light for just a moment and the next moment a blaze of light descends down to earth from heaven as golden-footed Deep-Lakshmi alights on earth in all her celestial glory amidst chantings of Vedic hymns. A living luminance of Universal Motherhood envelopes the entire world in that blessed moment of fulfillment of a long-awaited dream of the mortal. A sublime light of knowledge dawns upon humanity and devotion of man finally conquers ignorance. This self enlightenment is expressed through the twinkling lamps that illuminate the palaces of the wealthy as well as the lowly abodes of the poor. It is believed that on this day Lakshmi walks through the green fields and loiters through the bye-lanes and showers her blessings on man for plenty and prosperity. When the sun sets in the evening and ceremonial worship is finished all the home-made sweets are offered to the goddess as "NAIVEDYA" and distributed as "PRASAD". Feasts are arranged and gifts are exchanged on this day gaily dressed men, women and children go to temples and fairs, visit friends and relatives. Everything is gay, gold and glitter!

One of the most curious customs which characterises this festival of Diwali is the indulgence of gambling, specially on a large scale in North India. It is believed that goddess Parvati played dice with her husband, Lord Shiv on this day and she decreed that whosoever gambled on Diwali night would prosper throughout the ensuring year. This tradition of playing cards-flush and rummy with stakes on this particular day continues even to-day.

On this auspicious day Lord Shri Krishna around whom revolved the entire story of our great epic Mahabharat and the philosopher, who preached Karmayog through his Geeta to Arjun on the battlefield of Kurukshetra, discarded his body.

Bhagwan, Mahavir, the Jain prophet also attained "Nirvan" on this day.

Swami Ramtirth, the beloved "Ram Badshah" of millions of Indians was not only born on this day and took "Sanyas" but also took "Samadhi" on this day.

Swami Dayanand Saraswati, founder of Arya Samaj in 1875 in Mumbai, with his superb yogic powers greed his soul from his body and mingled with divinity on this auspicious day of Diwali.

We kindle innumerable lights on this day to immortalise the sacred memories of those great men who lived to brighten the lives of millions of their fellow beings.

One very interesting story about this Diwali day is from Kathopanishad of a small boy called Nichiketa who believed that Yam, the god of Death was as black as the dark night of amavasya. But when he met Yam in person he was puzzled seeing Yam's calm countenance and dignified stature. Yam explained to Nichiketa on this Diwali day of amavasya that by only passing through the darkness of death, man sees the light of highest wisdom and then only his soul can escape from the bondage of his mortal frame to mingle with the Supreme Power without whose will not an at ton moves in the world. And then Nichiketa realised the importance of worldly life and significance of death. Nichiketa's all doubts were set at rest and he whole-heartedly participated in Diwali celebrations.

The *Fourth day* is PADWA or VARSHAPRATIPADA which marks the coronation of King Vikramaditya and Vikaram-Samvat was started from this Padwa day.

Govardhan-Puja is also performed in the North on this day. As per Vishnu-Puran the people of Gokul used to celebrate a festival in honour of Lord Indira and worshipped him after the end of every monsoon season but one particular year the young Krishna stopped them from offering prayers to Lord Indra who in terrific anger sent a deluge to submerge Gokul. But Krishna saved his Gokul by lifting up the Govardhan mountain and holding it over the people as an umbrella.

Govardhan is a small hillock in Braj, near Mathura and on this day of Diwali people of Punjab, Haryana, Uttar Pradesh and Bihar build cowdung, hillocks, decorate them with flowers and then worship them.

This day is also observed as Annakoot meaning mountain of food. In temples specially in Mathura and Nathadwara, the deities are given milkbath, dressed in shining attires with ornaments of dazzling diamonds, pearls, rubies and other precious stones. After the prayers and traditional worship innumerable varieties of delicious sweets are ceremoniously raised in the form of a mountain before the deities as "Bhog" and then the devotees approach the Mountain of Food and take Prasad from it.

Goddess Lakshmi is worshipped in every Hindu household and her blessings sought for success and happiness. This day is looked upon as the most auspicious day to start any new venture. In many Hindu homes it is a custom for the wife to put the red tilak on the forehead of her husband, garland him and do his "Aarathi" with a prayer for his long life. In appreciation of all the tender care that the wife showers on him, the husband gives her a costly gift. This Gudi Padwa is symbolic of love and devotion between the wife and husband. On this day newly-married daughters with their husbands are invited for special meals and given presents. In olden days brothers went to fetch their sisters from their in-laws home for this important day.

The *Fifth and final day* of Diwali Festival is known by the name of "BHAYYA-DUJ" in the Hindi-speaking belt "BHAV-BIJ" in the Marathi-speaking communities and in Nepal by the name of "BHAI-TIKA". As the legend goes Yamraj, the God of Death visited his sister Yami on this particular day. She put the auspicious tilak on his forehead, garlanded him and led him with special dishes and both of them together ate the sweets, talked and enjoyed themselves to their heart's content, while parting Yamraj gave her a special gift as a token of his love and in return Yami also gave him a lovely gift which she had made with her own hands. That day Yamraj announced that anyone who receives tilak from his sister will never be thrown. That is why this day of Bhayyaduj is also known by the name of "YAMA-DWITIYA" Since then this day is being observed as a symbol of love between sisters and brothers. It became also imperative for the brother to go to his sister's house to celebrate Bhayyaduj.

In today's world when pressing everyday problems are teaming as under all the tender words of personal relationships, the celebrating of this day has its own importance in continuing to maintain the love between brothers and sisters for it is the day of food-sharing, gift-giving and reaching out to the inner most depths of the hearts.

Diwali on the whole has always been the festival with more social than religious connotations. It is a personal, people-oriented festival when enmities are forgotten, families and friends meet, enjoy and establish a word of closeness.

As a festival of light and beauty it encourages artistic expressions through home-decorations stage-plays, elocution competitions singing and dancing programmes, making gift items and making delectable sweets thereby discovering new talents of younger people. As a result innumerable communities with varying cultures and customs mingle together to make Diwali celebrations a very happy occasion for all.

History of Diwali: India is a land of festivals. Diwali, the Festival of Lights, is celebrated with fervor and gaiety. The festival is celebrated by young and old, rich and poor, throughout the country to dispel darkness and light up their lives. The festival symbolizes unity in diversity as every state celebrates it in its own special way. The celebration of the four-day festival commences on Aswayuja Bahula Chaturdasi and concludes on Kartika Shudda Vijiya. The first day of the festival Naraka Chaturdasi marks the vanquishing of the demon Naraka by Lord Krishna and his wife Satyabhama. 'Puranas' have it that Naraka, son of Bhudevi, acquired immense power from a blessing given by Lord Brahma after a severe penance. He soon unleashed a reign of terror in the kingdom of Kamarupa, harassing celestial beings with his invincible might. Unable to bear the tyranny of the demon, the celestial beings pleaded with Lord Krishna to save them from his torture. But Naraka could not be easily killed as he had a boon that he would face death only at the hands of his mother Bhudevi. So, Krishna asks his wife Satyabhama, the reincarnation of Bhudevi, to be his charioteer in the battle with Naraka. When Krishna feigns unconsciousness after being hit by an arrow of Naraka, Satyabhama takes the bow and aims the arrow at Naraka, killing him instantly. Later Lord Krishna reminds her of the boon she had sought as Bhudevi.

The slaying of Naraka by Sathyabhama could also be taken to interpret that parents should not hesitate to punish their children when they stray on to the wrong path. The message of Naraka Chaturdasi is that the good of the society should always prevail over one's own personal bonds. The second day is Amavasya when Lakshmi puja is performed. It is believed that on this day Goddess Lakshmi would be in her benevolent mood and fulfill the wishes of her devotees. One version says that it was on this day that Goddess Lakshmi emerged from Kshira Sagara (Ocean of Milk) when the Gods and demons were churning the sagara (ocean) for nectar (Amrit) The other version is that when Lord Vishnu in the guise of Vamana, sought three feet of land from the generous demon king Bali, the latter had to surrender his head as Vamana had conquered the earth and the sky in two strides. Lord Vishnu banishes Bali into the Pathala Loka (netherland) by keeping his third stride on Bali's head. Later, pleased by his generosity, Lord Vishnu grants him a boon and he in turn requests the Lord to guard his palace at Pathala Loka. Meanwhile, the Goddess is unable to bear the separation and her grief affects the functioning of the entire universe. Brahma and Lord Shiva offer themselves as guards and plead with Bali to relieve Vishnu. So, on the Amavasya day, Lord Vishnu returns to his abode and Goddess Lakshmi is delighted. It is believed that those who worship Goddess Lakshmi on this day would be bestowed with all the riches.

The third day is "Kartika Shudda Padyami." On this day Bali would come out of Pathala Loka and rule Bhuloka as per the boon given by Lord Vishnu. Hence, it is also known as "Bali Padyami". The fourth day is referred to as "Yama Dvitiya." On this day, sisters invite their brothers to their homes. However, in the northern part of India it is celebrated as the return of Ram along with Sita and Lakshman from his 14 years of exile after killing Ravana. To commemorate his return to Ayodhya, his subjects illuminated the kingdom and burst crackers. For the Gujaratis, Marwaris and other business community Diwali marks the worship of Goddess Lakshmi and also the beginning of the new financial year. For Bengalis, it is the time to worship Goddess Kali or Durga. The Goddess Durga continued her "Vilaya Tandava" even after killing demon Mahishasura.

Significance of Diwali: Deepavali is a festival where people from all age groups participate. They give expression to their happiness by lighting earthen 'diyas' (lamps), decorating the houses, bursting firecrackers and inviting near and dear ones to their households for partaking in a sumptuous feast. The lighting of lamps is a way of paying obeisance to god for attainment of health, wealth, knowledge, peace, valor and fame. It is one time in the whole year that children volunteer to leave their beds long before the day begins. In fact, the traditional oil bath at 3 a.m, is the only chore that stands between them and the pre-dawn adventures. They emerge, scrubbed clean to get into their festive attire, and light up little oil lamps, candles and scented sticks(agarbathis), the wherewithal for setting alight crackers and sparklers. Who shall set off the first chain of crackers that go boom, bang and vroom? and who is the owner of the 10-minute 'banger' that steals the thunder from your little chain of needle-sized crackers? Does the boy next door have more crackers than me? Competition is stiff, and even the little girl in silk frocks and their finery are watching out for the best sparklers and flowerpots, the rockets and Vishnuchakras, which light-up the night sky like a thousand stars. Grown-ups are the soul of generosity. Festive bonhomie abounds.

Diwali is the one Hindu festival that unites the whole of India. It is traditionally known as the "festival of lights", for the common practice is to light small oil lamps (called diyas) and place them around the home, in courtyards, gardens, verandahs, on the walls built around the home and also on the roof tops. In cities, especially, candles are substituted for diyas; and among the riches, candles are made to substitute for fashionable and classy neon lights. The celebration of the festival is customarily accompanied by the exchange of sweets and the explosion of fireworks. Diwali is an occasion for cheerfulness and togetherness. This is an occasion for young and the old, men and women, rich and poor - for everyone to celebrate. Irrespective of their religious and economic background, the festival is celebrated throughout the country to ward off the darkness and welcome light into life as light is always associated with hope for the future Diwali is celebrated 20 days after Dussera, on Amavasya - the 15th day of the dark fortnight of the Hindu month of Ashwin (Aasho) (Oct/ Nov) every year. Diwali celebrates Rama's homecoming, that is his return to Ayodhya after the defeat of Ravana and his coronation as king The legend related to the festival is that King Dashratha had three wives namely Kaushalaya, Keykayee and Sumitra and four sons Rama, Bharat, Laxmana and Shatrughan. Rama was the son of Queen Kaushalaya and Bharat was the son of Queen Keykayee. Keykayee wanted Bharat to be the next King of Ayodhya, while King Dasharatha wanted Rama, his eldest son to be the King. But Keykayee made full use of the two wishes King Dasharatha had promised. Keykayee asked for sending Rama to exile for the period of fourteen years and to crown Bharat as the king, though Bharat refused to accept the kingship. During that time Lord Rama fought and won fierce battle in the southern part of the Indian subcontinent, killing the king of Demons, Ravana who had forcibly taken away his wife Sita. Diwali marks his victorious return to his kingdom along with Hanuman, the Vanar who helped him in achieving success.

The legend states it took 20 days for Rama to return to his kingdom after defeating Ravana. As with other Indian festivals, Diwali signifies many different things to people across the country. In north India, Diwali celebrates Rama's homecoming from fourteen years of exile that is his return to Ayodhya after defeating Ravana and his coronation as king; in Gujarat, the festival is celebrated to honor goddess Lakshmi, the goddess of wealth; and in Bengal, it is related with the goddess Kali. But everywhere, it is celebrated with the same sprit and signifies the renewal of life. Diwali is one of the most celebrated festivities in the Indian culture. Uniting all members of the community, young and old, rich or poor, the lighting of the lamps represents a way of paying obeisance to God for attainment of health, wealth, knowledge, peace and valoured fame People give expressions to their happiness by lighting earthen diyas and decorating the houses to welcome Lakshmi- the Goddess of wealth and prosperity, bursting fire crackers and inviting the near and dear ones to their households for partaking in the luxurious feast. The lighting of lamps is a way of paying obeisance to God for attainment of health, wealth, knowledge, peace and fame and it also signifies goodness. It is also marked as the beginning of the Hindu New Year and as a brand new beginning for all. Diwali is celebrated for five days, each day having it's own significance, rituals and myths

The Jain communities of India celebrate Diwali as a New Year's Day. Lord Mahavira, the founder of Jainism, attained his Nirvana on the day of Diwali.

Sikhs celebrate Diwali to express joy at the return of the sixth Guru to Amritsar in 1620; Emperor Jahangir had imprisoned him along with 52 Hindu kings. The Guru was granted freedom but refused to leave until the kings were also released.

Diwali is by far the most enthusiastically enjoyed festival in India. People of different nationalities, races, religions and backgrounds come together to share their joys generating a feeling of universal brotherhood and inter-religious harmony. Diwali, literally a garland of lamps, is an apt description of this festival of lights. Tradition maintains that lamps are lit to keep alive the memory of Prince *Rama's* return to Ayodhya after conquering the tyrant *Ravana*, the ruler of Lanka, who had abducted his consort *Sita*. The heroic deeds of Rama are recounted in the Hindu epic *Ramayan* and Diwali symbolizes the victory of virtue over vice. Rama, we are told had gladly accepted an exile in the forest to keep his step-mother happy and save his father from embarassment. He is considered the epitome of a dutiful son and a responsible ruler. Another myth traces the origins of the festival to the annual 'inspection tours' of Lakshmi, the Hindu goddess of wealth and prosperity. The faithful believe that on this day Lakshmi goes around visiting her devotees and sets up residence in the house she finds best spruced up and most hospitable. Diwali is an occasion for spring cleaning, painting the walls, decorating the floor with attractive designs wrought in coloured powder or paste made with rice.

The ritual traditionally associated with Diwali is gambling. Friends get together to indulge in games of chance, dice or cards. The 'addicts' seek legitimacy for their unusual pastime by referring to the celestial game of dice played by the great lord *Shiva* with his companion *Parvati* - a scene superbly sculpted at *Kailash* temple, *Ellora*. Others rationalise that this is just to remind oneself of the fickleness of lady luck and to inculcate a sense of balance in our pursuit of material success.

The children can be seen bursting fire crackers and lighting candles or earthen lamps. This is a time of generously exchanging sweets with neighbours and friends. Puffed rice and sugar candy are the favourite fares.

Rangoli: Rangoli is one of the most popular art among Indian women, which is mainly painted on the ground in front of their houses using different color powders. This art can be predominantly seen during the tamil month of MAARKAZHI in Tamil Nadu, India. The MAARKAZHI month falls between December 15th and January 15th in western calendar. According to Hindu mythology, during this month the Goddess ANDAL prayed to the Lord THIRUMAL to marry her. It was said that her wish came true. So, this month is said to be so auspicious for unmarried girls to pray to god to have a spouse of their dreams. During this month unmarried girls arise before the Sun rise to paint beautiful rangolis to welcome the Lord THIRUMAL and they sing THIRUPPAVAI, praises of the Lord THIRUMAL which was said to be sung by the Goddess ANDAL.

CHHATH

The Chhath festival of sunworship is celebrated mainly in Bihar, Eastern UP and other parts of India where large of Bhojpuri speaking populace is present. It is a festival in which mothers pray for long and healthy life of their children. The Mothers observes fast for the full day and in the evening when moon rises she gives worships moon. Again in the morning mother worships Rising SUN by standing in the river water or pond.

Chhath Puja is an Indian thanksgiving festival dedicated to the Sun God. During the celebrations of Chhath Puja, people gather on the banks of the River Ganges to bathe in its sacred water, pray and make ritual offerings to the Sun God. Chhath Puja is a highly elaborate festival noted for its impressive display of colorful costumes, music, singing and extravagant rituals. When *Chhath* Puja takes place, sometime during the months of October and November, immediately following the six-day festival of lights known as Diwali. Chhath Puja lasts for one night and one day.

Chhath Puja Celebrated: Chhath Puja is celebrated mainly in the northern regions of the Indian state of Bihar. The festival takes place, on the banks of the River Ganges, in people's homes and at the Sun Temple of Baragaon, two kilometers outside Nalanda, in Bihar. Chhath Puja is also celebrated in Varanasi in the state of Uttar Pradesh.

- On the day before the festival of Chhath Puja, it is customary for participants to gather on the riverbanks and cleanse themselves, briefly, in the water of the River Ganges.
- After cleansing, a token amount of sacred water is retained for use as offerings during the festival of Chhath Puja.
- Before Chhath Puja, people fast throughout the day and into the early evening.
- The fast is followed by worship in the home. Festive fare consisting of freshly harvested rice, puris (a local bread

type delicacy), and fruit such as bananas, coconuts and grapefruit are then served to the family.

- On the second day of Chhath Puja a strict 24-hour fast is observed; not even water is consumed.
- Cooking utensils are purified by the senior women of the household, as part of the ritual preparation of offerings for the main part of the celebration of Chhath Puja.
- At sunset, worshippers proceed to the riverbank bearing their offerings in baskets held high to avoid the impure touch of human hands.
- The participants then pay homage to the Sun God, at the precise moment of the setting sun.
- Further celebrations take place at nightfall under temporary canopies made from sugar cane stalks where offerings are laid out as a tribute to the god of fire.
- Well before sunrise, when the sky is pitch black, worshippers return to the riverbank to pray to the rising sun; this ritual is considered the focal point of the ceremony of Chhath Puja.

Chath Puja: Useful Terms

- Surya: The sun (the Sun God is worshipped during the festival of Chhath Puja).
- Chhath: In the context of Chhath Puja, Chhath refers to the number six and the importance of this date on the Indian festival calendar
- Puja: Various interpretations exist of the word "puja," including worship with offerings, especially of flowers, and ritual anointment with sandalwood paste. Puja is the combination of the Sanskrit words for sin and birth.
- Prasad: Ritual offerings.
- Puris: This deep-fried bread, made from wheat flour, is traditionally offered at the festival of Chhath Puja.
- Thekuwa: This is a wheat-based cake served during the festival of Chhath Puja. **Bihar** is a state in India and a center for Buddhist worship. Bihar is famous, worldwide, as the starting point for the "Buddhist pilgrimage circuit."

The name "Bihar" derives from the word "vihara," meaning "Buddhist monastery." Apart from the festival of Chhath Puja, Bihar is also associated with the lavish celebration of other major Indian festivals including Diwali, Ramnavami, Dussehra and Holi.

KARWA CHAUTH

The fast of Karwa Chauth is kept 9 days before Diwali. It falls on the fourth day of the Kartik month by the Hindu calendar (fourth day of the waning moon or the dark fortnight).

Karwa Chauth is considered one of the most important fasts observed by the married Hindu women. On this day the women pray for the welfare and long life of their husbands. The festival is followed mainly in the northern parts of the country.

Married women eat food early in the morning, before sunrise. They are not supposed to eat or even drink water during the day. In the evening the ladies listen to the Karwa Chauth Katha (the legend). The fast is over after the moonrise.

The Puja Process: The pooja preparations start a day in advance. Married women buy the shringar or the traditional adornments and the other pooja items like the karwa, matthi, heena etc. Early in the morning they prepare food and have it before sunrise. The morning passes by in other festive activities like decorating hand and feet with heena, decorating the pooja thali and meeting friends and relatives.

In the late afternoon women gather at a common place like temple or a garden or someones' place who has arranged the pooja. An elderly lady or the pujarin narrates the legend of Karwa Chouth.

The essentials of this gathering and listening of the Karwa chauth story, a special mud pot, that is considered a symbol of lord Ganesha, a metal urn filled with water, flowers, idols of Ambika Gaur Mata, Goddess Parwati and some fruits, mathi and food grains. A part of this is offered to the deities and the storyteller.

Earlier an idol of Gaur Mata was made using earth and cowdung. Now just an idol of Goddess Parwati is kept. Every one lights an earthen lamp in their thalis while listening to the Karwa story. Sindoor, incense sticks and rice are also kept in the thali. At this time the women wear heavy saris or chunries in red , pink or other bridal colors, and adorn themselves with all other symbols of a married women like, nose pin, tika, bindi, chonp, bangles, earrings etc.

Once the moon rises, the women see its reflection in a thali of water, or through a dupatta or a sieve. They offer water to the moon and seek blessings. They pray for the safety, prosperity and long life of their husbands. This marks the end of the day long fast.

Karwa Chauth falls about nine days before Diwali. It is the most important fast observed by Hindu women of North India. On this day married Hindu women offer prayers seeking the welfare, prosperity, and a long life of their husbands.The fast is very difficult to observe as it starts before sunrise and ends only after offering prayers and worshipping the moon, which usually rises at about 8.45 p.m. No food or water is to be taken after 4 a.m. or after sunrise. The fast is broken once the moon is sighted and special rituals and prayers marking the day have been offered.

In the evening women dress up in special clothes, usually red or pink coloured and apply *bindis* on their foreheads. New brides wear their bridal outfits and others wear outfits woven with gold. Bangles and other jewellery are worn and special henna patterns are applied on the hands. The fasting women in a neighbourhood usually gather in a group and narrate mythological stories illustrating the importance of fasting on Karwa Chauth. After the moon rises, the women try to spot its reflection in water. Then they pray for their husband's safety and long life, and finally break their fast.

Karwa Chauth falls about nine days before Diwali. It is the most important fast observed by Hindu women of North India. On this day married Hindu women offer prayers seeking the welfare, prosperity, and a long life of their husbands.The fast is very difficult to observe as it starts before sunrise and ends only after offering prayers and worshipping the moon, which usually rises at about 8.45 p.m. No food or water is to be taken after 4 a.m. or after sunrise. The fast is broken once the moon is sighted and special rituals and prayers marking the day have been offered.

In the evening women dress up in special clothes, usually red or pink coloured and apply *bindis* on their foreheads. New brides wear their bridal outfits and others wear outfits woven with gold. Bangles and other jewellery are worn and special henna patterns are applied on the hands. The fasting women in a neighbourhood usually gather in a group and narrate mythological stories illustrating the importance of fasting on Karwa Chauth. After the moon rises, the women try to spot its reflection in water. Then they pray for their husband's safety and long life, and finally break their fast.

'Karwa Chauth' is a ritual of fasting observed by married Hindu women seeking the longevity, well-being and prosperity of their husbands. It is popular amongst married women in the northern and western parts of India, especially, Haryana, Punjab, Rajasthan, Uttar Pradesh and Gujarat.

This festival comes 9 days before Diwali on 'kartik ki chauth', i.e., on the fourth day of the new moon immediately after Dusshera, in the month of 'Karthik' (October-November).

The term 'Chauth' means the 'fourth day' and 'Karwa' is an earthen pot with a spout - a symbol of peace and prosperity - that is necessary for the rituals. Hence the name 'Karwa Chauth'.

The Fast: It is the most important and difficult fast observed by married Hindu women. (Unmarried women, widows, and spinsters are barred from observing this fast.) It begins before sunrise and ends only after offering prayers and worshipping the moon at night. No food or water can be taken after sunrise. The fast is broken once the moon is sighted and rituals of the day have been performed. At night when the moon appears, women break their fast after offering water to the moon. In the evening, women dress up in special clothes, usually a red or pink sari or 'lehenga-choli' with gold woven 'zari' patterns. New brides often wear their bridal costume. All deck up in jewelry and wear 'mehendi' or henna patterns especially on the hands. Decorative 'bindis' on the forehead are a must for all women taking part in this celebration. Fasting women from all over the neighborhood gather in a group and narrate mythological stories that underscore the significance of Karwa Chauth. And, of couse, all wives expect lavish gifts from their husbands!

The fast of Karwa Chawth truly sets the merry tone of the fun and frolic, festivity and feasting that come in good measure during Diwali — the biggest festival of the Hindus. In India, a marriage is considered to be a bond of a lifetime. This marital bond is considered very sacred. Karwa Chauth festival falls about nine days before diwali on the Kartik ki Chauth some time in October or November. It is the most important fast observed by the women of North India. A woman keeps such a fast for the well-being of her husband, who becomes her protector after she leaves her parents home. Her husband provides her with food, shelter, clothing, respectability, comfort and happiness.

It is said that in a village, seven brothers and one sister was staying with their parents (money lender). The sister was youngest among them. That's why everybody adored her. When she was 10 or 12 years of age they married her. After marriage on first karwa chauth, she came to her mother's house. Her mother-in-law affectionately sent sargai for her. She put mehndi on her hands along with her mother and bhabhis (brother's wife) and did sargai in the morning before sunrise and kept nirjal fast (without taking water).

By the evening the brothers got worried that how can their small sister live without food and water till night. They consulted among themselves and decided that we will create artificial moon for our sister. Two brothers went to the forest and burnt cowdung coal. The other two brothers went home and said let's go sister the moon has risen. All her bhabhis (brother's wife's) kept quite. Sister said "let's go Bhabhi the moon has risen, lets worship the moon and offer ark (water is offered to the moon) to it. All the Bhabhi said "So early only your moon could have risen, You go."

She was not only young but also simple hearted, she really thought everyone's moon rises separately.

She hurriedly took the pooja material to the terrace. There in the forest one brother was standing with a sieve in front of the cowdung coalfire, so from distance she thought that the moon is rising from behind bushes. She offered her worship and ark to the moon .As soon as she started eating Puya's, she received a message from her in laws that her husband has become seriously ill suddenly.

On hearing this, the Girl's father and brothers along with her rushed to her in law's house. There her husband was seriously ill. Every body was worried. Hakim (auyarvedic Dr.), Doctors were called but nobody could understand the illness.

Then the family enquired from priests and Astrologers. They told them that this has happened because the girl has eaten puya's, after seeing the artificial moon. Now the only solution is that till the next year karwa chauth, the girl take good care of her husband, then keep fast on Karwa Chauth and exchange karwa with Gaur Maata and make her say "le suhaagan karwa le","de suhagaan karwa de". Then her husband will be well and will live long. On hearing this, the girl decided to take good care of her husband for one year.

Next year Karwa chauth arrived, her mother sent sargai for her. As per the tradition, she did sargai and kept fast. Her mother also sent material for baya, karwa and money. In the evening, all married ladies dressed up wore chunari, making preparation for the pooja, she waited to exchange karwa with Gaur Maata. When the first Gaur Maata arrived. The girl held her feet and pleaded her:

" O'Gaur Maata, Please exchange karwa with me."

After lot of pleading Gaur Maata sat with her and said

"Sister of seven brothers karwa le",

"Jo bhukhi naa reh sake (who can't stay hungry) karwa le",

"Jo payasi naa reh sake (who can't stay thirsty) karwa le",

"Jo Chalni meh chaand dakhe (One who see moon in sieve) karwa le."

She begged her again and again to say "Le Suhaagan Karwa Le" Gaur Maata said, "I won't say this. My other sisters will come, you make them say." And after saying this, she went away. After some time 2nd Gaur Maata came and she also went away saying what the earlier one had said. In this way they came one by one when the ninth Gaur Maara came, the girl was worried. When she begged her again and again and held her feet, then Gaur Maata said," when my youngest sister will come, you ask her , I will not say. My sister is scary looking but good at heart, don't let her go, make her say it." After some time 10th Gaur maata came. She had dark complexion, had big teeth, horrible face and was wearing lot of jewelry. When she heard the small girl pleadings, she sat down with her to exchange karwa and like other Gaur Maata's said

"Sister of seven brothers karwa le",

"Jo bhukhi naa reh sake (who can't stay hungry) karwa le",

"Jo payasi naa reh sake (who can't stay thirsty) karwa le",

"Jo Chalni meh chaand dakhe (One who see moon in sieve) karwa le."

The girl fell on her feet and said "O' Mother please forgive my mistakes, Please say "Le suhaagan karwa le". If you will say this , my husband will live. I will always worship you. Please bless me. On girls repeated pleading, Gaur Maata felt pity for her and said-Let it be so and said "Le suhaagan karwa le" and the girl said "de suhaagan karwa de". Then, the same thing was repeated by both of them in reverse order. When they said this ten times Girls husband was well again. Everybody touched Gaur Maata's feet".

Karva Chauth is a Hindu festival celebrated in Punjab, Rajasthan, Uttar Pradesh and Gujarat. On this day married women keep a fast for the welfare, prosperity, longevity and well being of their husbands.

This festival comes 9 days before Diwali on 'kartik ki chauth', the fourth day of the dark moon. In Karva Chauth, karva (karuaa) means a clay pot, and chauth (from char meaning four) corresponds to the fourth. Specifically, in this case Chauth (signifying the day of Karva Chauth festival) is the fourth night (day) after the Full Moon in Kartik month (of Hindu calendar) following the Autumnal Equinox.It is believed that a Pati-Vrata (devoted) woman has the power to confront the God of Death, Yama. A lady called Veeravati broke her fast and her husband died. She preserved the body of her husband and he came back to life the next Karva Chauth.

The story of Karva is well known. Her husband was caught by a crocodile. Karva bound the crocodile with a cotton yarn. She then asked Yama to send the crocodile to hell. Yama refused. Karva threatened to curse Yama. Yama, afraid of being cursed by

Pati-vrat wife, sent the crocodile to hell. Karva and her husband enjoyed many years of wedded bliss. The fact that Yama was afraid of being cursed by a devoted wife showed the power a good faithful woman. There is great festivity on this day. Early in the morning, before sunrise, the women bathe, wear new clothes and eat a meal of select grains and fruit. For the rest of the day, they abstain from food and even water, though the more strict rules of observance are not always kept.

They pray to Shiva and Parvati, hoping that their own married lives will be as successful as that of the divine couple. In every neighbourhood, women gather together in the afternoon to perform a puja and to recite the story of 'Karva Chauth'. Most women are dressed in beautiful red or pink clothes and traditional jewelry. Moonrise is eagerly awaited. Once the moon is sighted, women gather on the terrace and pray for their husband and family's welfare, an elderly woman in the house narrates the story of Karva Chauth, and all the fasting women end their fast with a sip of water. It is a day of celebration, decoration and exchanging the Karwa Chauth gifts. On this occasion, the woman keeping the fast receives lots of gifts from all family members and friends.

Traditional karwa chauth gift include that of 'sargi' given by Mother-in-laws that consists of various types of sweetmeats, and sometime clothes and 'Baya' given by parents of their son-in-law. This Baya contains few Mathris, Almonds, and some gifts. This is one Indian festival, which has great significance and also brings the family together.

Origin: Karva Chauth originated as a social and seasonal festival, but somewhere down the line the festival deviated from its original form. The word Karva Chauth, is composed of Karva- meaning a clay pot - and Chauth (from char meaning four) corresponding to the fourth day after the Full Moon in Kartik month (of Hindu calendar) following the Autumnal Equinox.This time of the year is just after the harvest of Kharif (monsoon) crops and people are usually in a festive mood. They like to remember and meet their relatives and friends, and exchange gifts with them. Diwali is a similar seasonal festival - in addition to having religious significance - that is nine days after Karva Chauth.

The idea behind Karwa Chauth is very sweet and noble. In olden days girls were married at a very early age and used to go and live with their in-laws in other (often very remote) villages. Everyone would be a stranger there for the new bride. If she had any problems with her husband or in-laws, she would have no one to talk to or seek support from. Modes of communication/ transport were not very developed and hence it was not easy for her to approach her parents and relatives.Thus the custom started that, at the time of marriage, when bride would reach her in-laws, she would befriend another woman (of similar age) there who would be her friend (kangan-saheli) or sister (dharam-behn) for life. It would be like god-friends or god-sisters. Their friendship would be sanctified through a small Hindu ceremony right during the marriage. Once the bride and this woman had become god-friends or god-sisters, they would remain so throughout their lives.. They would also treat each other like real sisters. During any difficulty later in life, involving even the husband or in-laws, these women would be able to confidently talk or seek help from each other.

Thus Karva Chauth started as a festival to celebrate this friendship (relationship) between the once-brides and their god-friends (god-sisters). Praying and fasting for the sake of husband came later and is secondary. It was probably added, along with other mythical tales, to enhance the festival. In any case, husband would always be associated with this festival, because the day on which this holy friendship between two god-sisters started was essentially the day of bride's marriage to him. Thus praying and fasting for husband by his wife during a celebration of her relationship with the god-friend would be quite logical.

Karva Chauth is a fast undertaken by married Hindu women who offer prayers seeking the welfare, prosperity, well-being, and longevity of their husbands. Karva Chauth falls about nine days before diwali on the Kartik ki Chauth some time in October or November. It is the most important fast observed by the women of North India.

A woman keeps such a fast for the well-being of her husband, who becomes her protector after she leaves her parents home. Her husband provides her with food, shelter, clothing, respectability, comfort and happiness. This is indeed a very tough fast to observe as it starts before sunrise and ends after worshipping the moon, which usually rises at about 8.45 p.m. No food or water is to be taken after 4 a.m. or after sunrise. Nowadays, this fast is kept even in modern educated homes, becoming a symbol of the sentiment that a woman has for her husband.

A sari (in the baya) is a must for the first Karva Chauth of a girl. One thing to be taken care of is that the baya reaches the girl's in-laws home, where the girl has gone during the course of the day, before the evening. The baya is given to the mother-in-law after the manasna. If the mother-in-law is not present, then the eldest lady in the house is presented with the baya. Sometimes, the elder one chooses to take only the perishable items, and leaves cash and clothes for the mother-in-law.

The preparation for the puja should be started at about 4 or 5 p.m. Someone older, who is willing, or the housewife herself as the situation demands, prepares a suitable place in the puja room, in case it is a big room which can accommodate all the women who have been invited for the baya; otherwise the best place is a verandah or the open courtyard, since generally the weather is not cold during this season. The puja place is decorated with kharia matti, which has been soaked in water two to three hours earlier, and takes a semi-liquid form. A chowk like in any other puja - is decorated on the floor.

This whole chowk should be placed against a wall on one side, where a similarly decorated patta is kept, on which the Gaur Mata is seated. The Gaur Mata used to be made with cowdung in the shape of a human figure, just about two inches tall.

Nowadays, a picture or an idol of Parvati is placed on the patta.'just about an hour or so before moonrise, those who have observed the vrat, dress up again in their chunris or in red or pink clothes with chonp and bindi on their foreheads. Everyone now gathers around the place where a carpet or durrie is spread over the leaving space for the puja items.

The baya of individual is kept on a thaali, over the karva, with a little water and seven pieces of pua in it (seven broken from one bigpua). The karva itself is dee with kharia, aipun and a little roli..A strand of (red thread) of any thickness is tied around the part of the karva. The top cover is also decorated in the thaali is placed on the cover. The women sit facing the and one elder member (there is no taboo on widow the family narrates the story and does the chanting , each woman doing the puja. This is known as man which means to give away and never take back. First of all, roll teeka is applied on the forehead of Gaur before the start of the puja. All the women doing puja also apply roli teeka on their foreheads and parting (known as maang).

Everyone does pujan by dipping the third finger of the right hand in water sprinkling it with the help of the thumb three time the deity; the same procedure has to be repeated aipun and roli and, lastly, the rice is showered. depicts the bathing of the deity, decoration with a putting of the teeka with roli and, lastly, worship the deity with rice.

Karva Chauth and its Social Significance: A few days before Karva Chauth, married women would buy new karvas (spherical clay pots) 7"-9" in diameter and 2-3 litres capacity and paint them on the outside with beautiful designs. Inside (filling the karva half to three-quarters), they would put bangles and ribbons, home-made candy and sweets (rice krispees etc.), make-up items (mascara etc.), and small clothes (e.g. handkerchief). The women (god-friends and god-sisters) would then visit each other on the day of Karva Chauth or immediately afterwards, and exchange these karvas.

Season-wise, soon after the harvest, it is an excellent time to enjoy festivities, meet one another and exchange gifts. During the time of Karva Chauth, parents also used to send gifts (e.g., grains, food items and new clothes) to married daughters and their children. Such gifts from parents to married daughters (and their children) are given also for *Ser* (the festival occurring in spring around Vernal Equinox after harvest of winter crops).

BIHU FESTIVAL

The breathtaking hills and valleys of Assam come alive with the sound of Bihu thrice a year. A festival that marks the change of season, Bihu is accompanied both by prayer and great rejoicing. One of the seven northeastern states of India (which are also known as the Seven Sisters), Assam is renowned for its picturesque landscape, exotic fauna and fun-loving people.

Origin: Originating in the pre-Aryan days around 3500 B.C., the festival of Bihu used to last for a whole month, though nowadays work pressure has reduced it to a week. A no holds barred dancing session is the most intriguing part of the festival and symbolises the fertility rites of the original inhabitants of the hilly regions of the northeast in India.

The farmers fancied that the erotic content of the songs would sexually arouse the earth's body, leading to an abundant harvest. Bihag Bihu or Rangoli Bihu, the first of the three Bihus, is celebrated in the month of April on the dates coinciding with the *sankranti, chait* or *baisak* (13, 14 and 15 April).

Festival Celebration During The Assamese New Year: According to the solar calendar that the Assamese follow, the New Year usually falls on 14th April. Brilliantly-coloured flowers and luxuriant foliage dress the whole of Assam in all the hues of the rainbow during the month of April. An abundance of *kopoful* (orchids), mostly purple in colour, in unusual shapes and sizes dot the trees, and the *bhebel* creepers are in full bloom creating an enchanting kaleidoscope of colours. No one can fault the Assamese his choice of seasons for the Bihu festivals.

The vivid attire of the Assamese youth and the colourful accessories like kopoful adorning the hair of the young lasses blend with the hues of nature, spreading joy and good cheer. The day is marked with dancing, though restricted exclusively to men, who participate with unbridled enthusiasm and energy. But the winds of change have blown through this remote state also. Surrendering to contemporary trends, youngsters gather in the town centre and learn the steps from an old hand much in demand on this day.

Gomacha Weaving for Dance: Assamese women are experts at weaving the *gomacha,* a towel with intricately woven designs, ceremonially presented as *any bihu* (bihu presents) to the men of the family. A young girl too may gift these beautiful souvenirs to her beau as a token of love. Young lads love to flaunt their prizes by tying them around their waist or as headbands while dancing. But things start warming up as the approach. Now a few words about the bihu dals. They are wandering minstrels who come visiting through the week, dancing and singing devotional songs (hosari) in praise of Lord Krishna (the black god of the Hindus), invoking his blessings for health, wealth and happiness.

They sing to the accompaniment of an eclectic collection of musical instruments like the dhol (drum), pepa (made of buffalo horn), gogona (made from bamboo and held between the teeth) and small cymbals. Bihu dals along with other groups gather in open grounds called bihu tolis where dancing competitions and beauty pageants are held, and the winners get to see their names in print in the local newspapers.

Garur Bihu: The first day or garur bihu also called uraka falls on the day of sankranti and is devoted to the cow that is considered to be a sacred animal in India. The rationale behind the worshipping of cows is very simple. They are the greatest assets of a farmer because not only do they produce milk but also help plough fields, transport men, crop and so on. A lot of tender, loving care is showered on cows on this day, starting with bathing them in the pond.

The horns and hooves are brushed with whisks made from deegloti or makheatr (lilsoca salocrfolea). A mixture of twigs, turmeric and moong dal (pulses) acts as a disinfectant, and is applied as a paste. A hearty meal of gourd and brinjal is fed to the cows after which their foreheads are marked with vermilion. As the night falls, the tired but satiated cows are led back to their sheds and thoroughly cleansed. Only then does the household sit down for a sumptuous meal of assorted preparations of chirwa (flat rice) and a mind-boggling array of sweets. The following day is welcomed as manuhor bihu or the bihu of human beings. The Assamese celebrate their New Year on this day. A lavish feast called bihu kabo loi is laid out for the day and married daughters along with other relatives are invited to partake of the meal.

On this day, delicacies such as pitha (made from rice and coconut), laddoo (made from shredded coconut) and til laddoo (made from sesame seed) are prepared. of course, no festival in India is complete without buying new clothes and Bihu is no exception. Everyone receives gomachas as presents from the ladies of the house. Women look very graceful in their new mekhele chadar, woven with the golden-coloured muga silk that is indigenous to Assam. The chic look is completed with the accessories like gumkham bracelets made from an alloy of silver and gold nuggets found in the rivers.

Gabhori Bihu: Gabhori bihu falls on the third day of the festival and is earmarked as the day for young ladies. The fair maidens of Assam look gorgeous in their muga silk wear and ornate gumkham bracelets.

The orchids adorning the hair of the ladies add a whimsical touch to the formality of the outfit. Swaying to the beat of the toka (drum) and gogona (made from bamboo held between the teeth), the women dance the night away under the gentle breeze of banyan trees. Couplets are created spontaneously. Starting with a slow tempo, the rhythm builds up to a crescendo. Once the merrymaking is over, it is customary to present fermented betel leaves over a gomacha to the dancers.

On the final day, the festivities end on a religious note wherein families inscribe a mantra (religious hymn of the Hindus) on the leaves of *nahar pat* (Indian ironwood tree). Through this mantra, Lord Shiva (the Destroyer in the Holy Hindu Trinity of Creator-Preserver-Destroyer) is invoked to protect everyone against disease, storms and rain, and to bring peace and prosperity in the forthcoming year.

Kati Bihu: The second bihu named kati bihu or kangali bihu is held in the month of *kartik* (September or October). But there is a world of difference in the celebration of this bihu from the former. Slowly but surely, winter is approaching, heralding the season for sowing seeds.

This is a solemn occasion as people worship the deities for a rich harvest. The young learn to value hard work so that they do not squander money away. Predictably enough, this bihu is dedicated to the worship of none other than Goddess Lakshmi who is the dispenser of wealth to mortals.

As night falls, lamps are lit in the paddy fields where farmers have toiled through the day. At the end of a hard day's work, all the members of a family pray to the benign Goddess for the well-being of their crop and cattle. Sacred to the Hindus, the *tulsi* (basil) tree is planted or pruned in the courtyard of each household. Water is poured over the plant with great reverence after puja is performed every day.

The medicinal properties of tulsi are well known the world over; the age-old recipe of tulsi leaves mixed with a few grains of black pepper and *misri* (sugar in the form of crystals) is a surefire way to stay in good health.

Magh Bihu: The Magh bihu that generally falls on 14th January on the sankranti of the month, is the third bihu that calls for a grand celebration in Assamese homes. This is again a joyous occasion as the granaries are stocked with the recently harvested crop.

Seven days of non-stop fun and frolic mark this festival. But the best thing about this bihu is the elaborate and sumptious cuisine that is prepared. This grand feast known as *bhog* is held on the night of the first day of the festival that is also called *uruka*.

Khel Dhemali-(Fun Games): If you are an outdoor person who enjoys sports of all kinds, Assam is the place to be in at this time of the year. Everyone indulges in *khel dhemali* (fun and games). Each village holds its share of fights between various creatures, big and small including cockfights and buffalo fights, for the entertainment of the locals. An inexpensive way to have fun, though the poor animals might beg to differ. The chilly winters offer the best excuse to light bonfires in the great outdoors and dance around them with gay abandon. All this is reminiscent of the festivals of Lohri in Punjab, *Pongal* in Tamil Nadu and Goopi in Andhra Pradesh, which is not surprising as sankranti is a time for festivals all over India.

3

THE MUSLIM FESTIVALS

MUHARRAM

Muharram is the first month of the Islamic calendar. It is one of the four sanctified months of the year. Fighting in this month is looked down upon and is often put to the side in respect for Islam. Since the Islamic calendar is lunar, Muharram moves from year to year when compared to the Gregorian calendar.

The first day of Muharram is the start of the Islamic New Year. The Festival of Muharram takes place during this month in which Shia Muslims especially commemorate the Battle of Karbala. The commemoration reaches its climax on the tenth day of Muharram, known as Ashurah.

This day is related to the time of Moses when he crossed the Red Sea escaping from the Pharaoh. Sunni Muslims often fast on this sacred day. Later, in the month of Ramadan it is recommended to fast so the day of Ashura is optional.

This month of Muharram also has traditions which have no support from Islamic teachings. For example, the celebration of the Muslim new year, and the partying and card giving, etc, associated with it is considered to be a bidah and even haraam to some.

Muharram is so called because it was unlawful to fight during this month; the word is derived from the word 'haram' meaning forbidden. It is held to be the most sacred of all the months. This months is most sacred to the Shi'a community and the fast on the first ten days of the month to commemorate the slaying of Hussain, a grandson of Muhammed, by the Sunnis. The tenth day is called

Ashura, meaning, 'the tenth', and it is a day of voluntary fasting. The Sunnis also fast on the tenth day because they believe that Adam and Eve, heaven and hell, life and death, fate and the pen were created on this day.

The Remembrance of Muharram is an important period of mourning in the Shiaite branch of Islam.

A banner (*aalam*) being carried in a procession during the Remembrance of Muharram in Bahrain. For the duration of the remembrance, it is customary for mosques to provide free meals (*nazar*) on certain nights of the month to all people. These meals are viewed as being special and holy, as they have been consecrated in the name of Husayn, and thus partaking of them is considered an act of communion with God, Husayn, and humanity. In Trinidad and Tobago all ethnic and religious communities participate in the event, locally known as "Hosay".

Many of the events associated with the remembrance take place in congregation halls known as "Hussainia".

The Tenth of Muharram and Ashurah: The Islamic year begins with Muharram ul Haram, the first month of the Hijri Calendar. While followers of other religions spend their opening month in worthless merriment, the first month of Islam teaches us lessons of admonition, good counselling, knowledge of Allah Ta'ala, sacrifice, selflessness, patience and seeking the pleasure of Allah Ta'ala.

The tenth day of Muharram (Ashurah) has many distinctive qualities and features. Allah Ta'ala created the heavens and the earth on this blessed day. On this day He gave His infinite blessings and bounties to many of His Prophets and delivered them from the clutches of their enemies.

Allah Ta'ala created Hazrat Adam (Alaihis-Salam) in this month, pardoned him of his mistake, and Hazrat Noah's (Alaihis-Salam) Ark landed successfully on Mount Judi, and he saved Hazrat Ibrahim (Alaihis-Salam) from fire and rescued Hazrat Musa (Alaihis-Salam) from Pharaoh.

On the first of Muharram offer 2 rakats Nafl prayer. In each rakat after Surah Fateha recite Surah Ikhlas 3 times. After the Salam pray to Allah Ta'ala for all your needs and desires. From the blessing of this prayer, Allah Ta'ala will appoint an angel for such a person. The angel will guide him or her to do only good deeds and prevent them in engaging in sinful acts.

On the eve of "Ashurah" offer 100 rakats Nafl. In each rakat recite Surah Ikhlas 3 times after Surah Fateha. After Salam recite first 'Kalimah' 100 times. Allah Ta'ala will forgive all the sins of such a person.

Dua-e-Ashurah - An Insurance for a Year's Life: Hazrat Imam Zainul Abidain (Radi Allah Anhu) reports that who ever recites this dua on the tenth of Muharram, any time after sunrise and before sunset, or listens to its recitation from someone else, Allah Ta'ala will certainly make it an insurance for a years' life for him, by keeping death away from him. However, if one is to become the victim of death in that year, they will by some strange coincidence not remember to recite it.

Nafl Salat for the Eve of Ashurah: On the eve of Ashurah offer 4 rakats Nafl Salat as follows: In every rakat after Surah Fateha recite "Ayetul Kursi" once and Surah Ikhlas 3 times. After completing this Namaz recite Surah Ikhlas 100 times. Allah Ta'ala will purify such a person of all their sins and grant them endless bounties and blessings in paradise.

The Fast of Ashurah: On the 9th and 10th of Muharram, one should fast. If it is not possible to fast on both days, then every effort should be made to fast on the 10th day of Muharram, as there is great reward for this fast. (Muslim Shareef).

The following are some of the desirable acts one should do on the day of Ashurah:

1. To observe fast on this day.
2. To give as much charity as you can afford.
3. To perform Nafl Salat prayers.
4. To recite Surah Ikhlas 1000 times.
5. To visit and be in the company of pious Ulema.
6. To place a hand of affection on an orphan's head.
7. To give generously to one's relatives.
8. To put surma in one's eyes.
9. To take a bath.

10. To cut one's nails.
11. To visit the sick.
12. To establish friendly ties with one's enemies.
13. To recite Dua-e- Ashurah
14. To visit the shrines of Awliyas and the graves of Muslims.

Hazrat Abdullah bin Masood (Radi Allah Anhu), a Companion of the Holy Prophet Muhammad (Sall Allahu Alaihi wa Sallam) reports the following saying of the Messenger of Allah Ta'ala, "Whosoever prepares ample food and drink for his family on this sacred day and delights in feeding them generously, Allah Ta'ala will increase His provisions for that year and place much blessings and good therein."

Imam Hussain (Radi Allah Anhu) and his companions were martyred on the tenth of this month.

Like any month in the Islámic Calendar there are in this first Islamic month, many anniversaries which are celebrated every where in the world.

Muharram festival commemorates the martyrdom of Hazrat Imam Hussain, the grandson of the Holy Prophet (peace be upon him). This festival starts at the 1st day of Muharram and lasts for 10 days until 10th of Muharram. Muharram is the first month of Islamic calendar.

During this month, while on a journey, Hazrat Imam Hussain, his family members and a number of his followers were surrounded by the forces of Yazid, the Muslim ruler of the time. During the siege, they were deprived of food and water and many of them were put to death. The incident happened at a place called Karbala in Iraq in 61st year after Hijra. This dispute was result of a disagreement among Muslims on the question of succession after the demise of Hazrat Ali, the fourth caliph.

Some sects of Muslims hold meetings where speeches are made on the happenings of Karbala and on the lives of martyrs. The Shias, however, observe this festival in a different fasion. As Muharram, the first month of the Muslim year, approaches, they put on black clothes, as black is regarded as a color of mourning. Majalis (assemblies) are held every day during the first nine days where shia orators relate the incident of the martyrdom of Hazrat Imam Hussain and his party in a great detail. On the 10th day of Muharram, large processions are formed and the devoted followers parade the streets holding banners and carrying models of the mausoleum of Hazrat Imam Hussain and his people, who fell at Karbala. They show their grief and sorrow by inflicting wounds on their own bodies with sharp metal tied to chain with which they scourge themselves. This is done in order to depict the sufferings of the martyrs. It is a sad occasion and everyone in the procession chants "Ya Hussain", with loud wails of lamentation. Generally a white horse beautifully decorated for the occasion, is also included in the procession, to mark the empty mount of Hazrat Imam Husain after his martyrdom.

During these first ten days of Muharram, drinking posts are also set up temporarily by the Shia community where water and juices are served to all, free of charge.

The 1st of Muharram is New Year's Day, and with it marks the beginning of the Islamic (Hijri) Calendar. Its real significance lies in the major turning point in the course of Islam. As told in the Noble Qur'ân: "Verily the number of months with Allah is twelve months (in a year), so was it ordained by Allah on the Day when He created the heavens and the earth; of them four are Sacred. That is the right religion, so wrong not yourselves therein ...".

Today itself, as we usher in the new year, many of us take the time to at least briefly reflect on the major lessons in the past year and anticipate new experiences in the fresh year of 1422 Hijrah. This is also the day that we should be reminded of the Prophet's last pilgrimage and the message that he wants us to carry in our hearts.

The prophet offered the noon and afternoon prayers in Arafah along with 100,000 worshippers, and the victory of Islaam over blasphemy became decisive and final. Thereafter, the Prophet mounted his camel, and delivered the historical sermon. In it, he had said: "... All mankind is from Adam and Eve, an Arab has no superiority over a non-Arab nor a non-Arab has any superiority over an Arab, also a white has no superiority over black nor a black has any superiority over white except by piety and good action. Learn that every Muslim is a brother to every Muslim and that the Muslims constitute one brotherhood. Nothing shall be legitimate to a Muslim which belongs to a fellow Muslim unless it was given freely and willingly. Do not, therefore, do injustice to yourselves...".

The Period of mourning is observed in the first month of the Islamic calendar, and it commemorates the death of Hazrat Imam Hussain in the battle of Karbala. Muharram means 'respected'. It is the first month of the Islamic calendar.The first ten days of this month are observed as a period of mourning by Muslims, particularly by those belonging to the Shiah sect, in memory of the tragedy of 680 AD. Hazrat Imam Hussain, the grandson of Muhammad the Prophet was killed in the battle of Karbala. This event, called Muharram, is named after the month in which it took place. The tenth day, called Ashura, is observed as the day for a public expression of their grief and is the most important day of the month.

During the pre-Islamic period in the Arabian penninsula, fighting was prohibited in four months of the year.These months, of which Muharram was one, were considered sacred. This period of inactivity was a necessity in heavily decorated replicas of the tomb of the Imam and his family are made for Muharram the era of warring tribes. The tradition was maintained even after the advent of Islam, though provisions to accommodate and accept war in special situations, like a threat to the sovereignty of an empire, were introduced. The gory battle of Karbala was fought against this law and tradition of Islam. The inhabitants on the banks of rivers Euphrates and Tigris were traditional rivals. Their animosity was contained to some extent by Muhammad. But when his son-in-law Hazrat Ali was the Caliph, the old enmity re-surfaced. Hazrat Ali had two descendants, Hazrat Imam Hussain and Hazrat Imam Hassan. Hussain was the ruler of the part of the empire known today as Iran. The other part in modern Iraq was ruled by the Umayyads. Hussain was called upon by the Shiahs of Kufa, a small town in the Umayyad kingdom, to accept their allegiance and claim his place as the leader of the Islamic community. This was against the wishes of the ruler of Kufa, Yazid, who instructed his governor, Ibn-e-Ziad to take appropriate action. Meanwhile, in response to the call of the Shiahs, Hussain accompanied by his family members, headed for Kufa. When they reached Karbala, enroute to Kufa, the forces of the governor surrounded them and their 70 men. Hussain, his family and his troops were tortured and killed, and Hussain's head was severed and presented to the king. They received no help from the Shiahs of Kufa. This happened on the tenth day of Muharram and it was called Ashura.

To commemorate this tragedy, the 40 days starting from the first day of Muharram to Chehalum, are observedas a period of mourning by the Shiahs. During this period, women foresake alladornments, even their bangles. All kinds of celebration like marriage are disallowed during this period. Shiah Muslims are celibate for these 40 days. The first 10 days however, are the most important and are passionately observed asa period of mourning. During the first nine days of the month, majlish (enacted grief-stricken scenes from the battle of Karbala) are organised in Shiah mosques. Huge Shiah crowds wearing black assemble at imambaras, where plaintive verses in memory of Imam Hussain are recited.

These nine days are also spent in making Taziahs. On Ashura, the most important day, processions with Taziahs are taken out in commemoration of the sad event. The procession also includes a well-decorated horse, representing the horse of Imam Hussain. Emotional plays, enacting scenes from the battle of Karbala, are performed by bare-chested Shiah men. They strike their body with chains while some walk with bare feeton burning coals. Crying "hai Hussain hum na rahe", meaning 'Oh Hussain, we were not there', they express their anguish at their in ability to have prevented him from being tortured. By beating themselves, the Shiahs relive the pain Hussain suffered and thus express their sorrow. They also distribute water, soft drinks and fruit juices to passers-by in an effort to quench the thirst of the six-month old son of Hazrat Imam Hussain and many others who are believed to have died asking for water. The Taziah processions from allover the town terminate at the Karbala of the city. Most old habitations with a Muslim tradition have a specially marked place to represent the original Karbala.

The Taziahs are buried there. Sometimes they are dismantled so that they can be used again. Often they are immersed in a river. According to a popular belief among the Shiahs, the mud on the grave of Hazrat Imam Hussain turns blood red on Ashura. Muharram is also a time for making vows. People pledge their promises to the Taziah of Hussain. They can do this in two ways. The first is by sending milk,a soft drink, dates or refined sugar to the craftsman who is making the Taziahs.

The craftsman recites the Al-Fatiha breaks a coconut and distributesits water with the soft drink or milk in small cups to those present. The second method of making a vow is by performing an act of penance or self-torture before the Taziah. This is generally practiced by woman who volunteer to stand and watch over the Taziahs for a night or more. They go to the place where it is built, and accompany it through its route to the Karbala. This commitment is performed on the ninth night of the month of Muharram. Some people offer to roll on the ground for a certain distance in front of the Taziah as thanksgiving for favours that have been granted or for wish fulfillment. Though the 10 days of Muharram are a period of mourning for the Sunni sect too, they do not indulge in passion plays and nor do they cry out Hussain Hussain because their tradition stipulates grieving in silence. They keep a two-day roja on the ninth and tenth of the month, wear only black clothes and read the Namaz and AlFatiha five times a day.

Contrary to popular belief, Muharram is not a particular day, but the name of a month that marks the beginning of the year according to the Islamic calendar. Muharram is one of four months that have been designated as holy according to the Islamic calendar, the other three being – Dhul-Qa'adah, Dhul-Hijjah and Rajab.

Fasting in the Month of Muharram : Fasting is advocated in the month of Muharram. The Prophet is believed to have said: "The best fasts after the fasts of Ramadan are those of the month of Muharram." Although the fasts of the month of Muharram are not obligatory, yet one who fasts in these days out of his own will is entitled to a great reward by Allah Almighty. Fasting on the tenth day of Muharram, called Ashura, is particularly important, as it supposed to lead to great rewards. A person does not have to fast for the whole month. On the contrary, each fast during this month has merit.

Muharram – an Auspicious Time : The month of Muharram is also associated with many auspicious events in Islamic history. Allah is supposed to have created the heavens and the earth on this blessed day. On this day He give His infinite blessings and bounties to many of His Prophets and delivered them from the clutches of their enemies.

Allah created Hazrat Adam in this month and pardoned him of his mistake. Hazrat Noah's Ark landed successfully on Mount Judi during this time centuries ago. God is also said to have saved Hazrat Ibrahim from fire and rescued Hazrat Musa from the Pharaoh during the month of Muharram.

You must be wondering what there is to mourn about then? The tenth day of Muharram or Ashura is of supreme importance for Shia Muslims as they celebrate the death anniversary of Hussain, the grandson of the Prophet Muhammad.

The Tragedy at Kerbala : In the month of Muharram many centuries ago, (approximately October 20th 680 A.D.), an event took place in Iraq at a place known as Kerbala on the bank of the river Euphrates.

A large army, which had been mobilised by the Umayyad regime, besieged a group of persons numbering less than a hundred and put them under pressure to pay allegiance to the Caliph of the time and submit to his authority. The Caliph was a man much taken with earthly pleasures that deviated from the Islamic way of life. The small group resisted and a severe battle took place in which they were all killed. The leader of the small band of men who were martyred in Kerbala was none other than Imam Husain, the grandson of the Holy Prophet. Imam Husain's martyrdom at Kerbala represents a conscious confrontation with anti-Islamic forces and a courageous resistance for a sacred cause. The tragedy was that the one who stood up to defend Islam was cut down in so cruel a manner. It is for this reason that the death of Imam Husain is mourned annually in the Muslim world.

The Observances: "Among the Shias in India the following ceremonies are common, although considerable differences in detail may be observed according to regions. As soon as the new moon appears, people assemble in the imam bara (lit, enclosure of imam), a permanent meeting place built in stone or, as mostly in southern India, they assemble in the 'ashur khanah (lit, ten-day house), a temporary structure. There they recite thefatihah over some sherbat (sweetened, cool drink), rice or sugar in Husain's name. The cool drink is meant to remind the faithful of the terrible thirst Husain and his family and retinue had to suffer. Food and drink are later distributed to the public, especially to the poor. In some places a pit is dug in which a fire is lighted every evening of the festival, and young and old people fence across it with sticks or swords. Or they run around it calling out: Ya'Ali! Ya'Ali! Shah Hasan! Shah Husain! Dulha! Hae Dost! Rahiyo! Oh 'Ali! (Noble Hasan! Noble Husain! Bride-groom! Friend! Stay! Stay!)

"The'ashur khanah is usually draped with black cloth on which texts of the Quran are written. The imam bara, too, will be decorated. Inside are placed the tazian-s or tabuts, wooden structures covered with silver paper, coloured paper and tinsel fringes. They are made with imagination and artistic sense and are meant to represent Husain's mausoleum, erected on the plains of Karbala, or else the Prophet's tomb at Medina or even the Taj Mahal of Agra. Nearby are placed imitations of articles which Husain is supposed to have used at Karbala, e.g., a turban of gold, a sword, a shield, a bow and arrow. There are also'alam-s or standards of different shapes, each one having its own special name and history. Often the 'a lam has the form of a human hand (panjab) fixed on top of the pole. This is the popular emblem representing the five members of the prophet's family: Muhammad, Fatima, 'Au, Hasan and Husain."

Processions and Other Ceremonies: "From the seventh to the tenth of Muharram processions are held to commemorate the martyrdom of Hasan's son, Qasim, who was slain shortly after his wedding, as well as the martyrdom of Husain. Along with the procession goes a white horse (duldul or dhu'l-janah) which represents the horse on which Husain rode, or it refers to the bridal horse of Qasim, who was married to Husain's favourite daughter Fatimat-us-sughra (as distinguished from Fatimah, the daughter of Muhammad), just before the battle of Karbala. With this in mind the people shout at intervals: Bride-groom! Bridegroom! On the eighth day a lance or spear is carried to represent Husain's head, which was carried on the point of a javelin by order of Yazid. In addition to these representations ta 'ziya h-s or tabut-s and standards of Hasan, Husain and Qasim are carried. All the time people beat their breasts, saying: Hasan, Husain! Sometimes the pro-cession halts, and then a group of men and boys, naked from the waist, beat themselves with a bundle of sharp blades so that the blood streams down their backs or, forming a large group, they beat their breasts in a uniform rhythm crying all together: Ya Hasan! Ya Husain! The tenth day is 'ashara 'ashurah . On this day the tabut-s or ta 'ziah-s are either stripped and thrown into the water, or they are taken to a ground set apart for this purpose (called Karbala) and literally buried in specially dug graves.

On the evening of the twelfth day people sit up all night, reading the Quran and reciting marsiyah-s and verses in honour of Husain. On the thirtieth day a quantity of food is cooked and, after saying the fatihah over it, it is given to the poor. With this act of charity the Muharram celebrations end."

The Memory of Karbala: Husain was the second son of Ali ibn Abu Talib and Fatimah bint Muhammad, the last Prophet. He was born in the 4th year after the hijra. His older brother, Hasan was named as the successor to his father, after Ali was murdered in the mosque in Kufah, Iraq. After Ali's death, people pledged their allegiance to Hasan as the khalifa (successor). Soon after he took office, however, Mu'awiyah, who had fought with Ali over the caliphate, formed an army to attack Hasan. In the interests of peace and unity, Hasan handed over the position of khalifa to Mu'awiyah who ruled until his death and passing of the caliphate to his son, Yazid.

Mu'awiyah, who was the son of Abu Sufyan (the arch enemy of Islam until he accepted Islam after the Muslims returned to Makkah), was not well liked among the "religious" Muslims. They disliked his son, Yazid, even more. Yazid's open disregard for Islamic law (shariah) and practices made many Muslims cringe at the thought of him taking the caliphate. Mu'awiyah, however, who insisted on turning the caliphate into a monarchy, pushed people to pledge allegiance to his son. On his deathbed, Mu'awiyah told Yazid not to try to force Imam Husayn to give allegiance to him because this would cause too much trouble. Soon after, in 60 A.H., Mu'awiyah died.

Little time passed before Yazid made it clear to his governors in Madinah that they were to force Imam Husayn to pledge allegiance to him or send Imam Husayn's head to him in Damascus. Representatives of Yazid came to Husayn in Madinah and asked for his allegiance. Imam Husayn asked for some time before he made his decision. In the meantime, he was able to move his family to Makkah where they were protected by the Sacred Precincts, Masjid-al-Haraam. It is forbidden in Islam to harm anything within these precincts.

Many people in the Ummah at that time who were already dissatisfied with the caliphate began to send letters to Imam Husayn urging him to join them in the city of Kufah in Iraq. They swore to defend him to the death and gave their allegiance to him. To investigate the situation, Imam Husayn sent his cousin, Muslim ibn Aqil to Kufah. After discussing the situation with the people of Kufah, he was killed and beheaded by supporters of Yazid on Wednesday, 9th of Dhul-Hijja, the Day of Arafat, in the year 60 A.H. (680).

It was the time of pilgrimage in Makkah, and Imam Husayn had begun to perform the pilgrimage rites. When he learned that some of Yazid's men had come dressed as pilgrims to kill him in Makkah, he gathered his people together to leave for Iraq. He did not want his blood to be spilled within the sacred precincts and to have the sacred rite of Hajj dishonored by that violence. Thus, he, some members of his family, and a group of followers set out towards Kufah on 8th of Dhul-Hijjah.

As the Imam approached Iraq, he was informed that many of the people who had voiced their support for him had turned and now supported the reign of Yazid, possibly to save their own lives. It was then that many of his representatives, including Muslim Ibn Aqil were abused and killed.

As he and his followers marched closer to Iraq, a person that he met along the way who learned where he was going urged and pleaded with him not to continue his journey towards Kufah, but the Imam replied:

"Servant of God," he answered, "wise decisions are not hidden from me. yet the commands of God, the Exalted, cannot be resisted. By God, (my enemies) will not leave me till they have torn the very heart from the depths of my guts. If they do that, God will cause them to be dominated and humiliated until they become the most humiliated of the factions among nations."

Before the Imam and his followers were able to reach Kufah, Yazid's army surrounded them about 44 miles outside of Kufah in a desert called Karbala. At this point, Yazid's army cut off Imam Husayn's water supply, and his followers began to suffer from extreme thirst. Among these people were members of the Prophet's family, companions, and some women and children.

As the days passed in the month of Muharram, the first month of the new year on the Islamic calendar, Yazid's army, numbering 30,000, closed the circle around Imam Husayn's followers who were suffering from dehydration.

On the tenth day of Muharram, called Ashura, Imam Husayn and his followers went out with less than 100 people to meet the army of 30,000.

Ali Zayn al Abidin, son of Imam Husayn, peace be upon them, reported:

When the cavalry began to approach al-Husayn, he raised his hands and said:

"O God, it is You in Whom I trust amid all grief. You are my hope amid all violence. You are my trust and provision in everything that happens to me, (no matter) how much the heart may seem to weaken in it, trickery may seem to diminish (my hope) in it, the friend may seem to desert (me) in it, and the enemy may seem to rejoice in it. It comes upon me through You and when I complain to You of it, it is because of my desire for You, You alone. You have comforted me in (everything) and have revealed its (significance to me). You are the Master of all grace, the Possessor of all goodness and the Ultimate Resort of all desire."

The Imam and his followers fought all day and fell to their deaths fighting in the cause of Allah. That day, all who fought were martyred. Among them were two children of Imam Hasan, and Imam Husayn's five year old child.

"When the Imam himself was ready to fight, he saw his six-month-old baby was dying from thirst. The Imam brought his infant near to the enemy and demanded some water for baby, saying: You want me but not this baby so take him and give him some water. The words of the Imam had not been finished that the thirst of the baby was quenched by a deadly poisoned arrow from the enemy which pinned the baby's neck to the arm of his father. The Imam threw some of his blood toward the sky saying: "O' Lord! Your Husayn has offered whatever You have given him. Bless me by acceptance of this sacrifice." Finally Imam came to the field and fought for a long time and was finally martyred. The army of Yazid having killed Imam Husayn, cut his head and raised it on a lance.

"The army of the enemy, after ending the war, burned the tents of the women and children accompanying the Imam and his companions, and plundered those helpless women. They decapitated the bodies of the martyrs, denuded them and threw them to the ground without burial. Then they moved women and children along with the heads of the martyrs to Kufah. They took with them the daughters and sisters of al-Husayn, peace be on him, together with 'Ali b. al-Husayn, peace be on him. The latter was still sick with a dysentery and was almost on the point of death. The bodies of the martyrs were under the sunshine for three days till a tribe passing that place found them and performed the burial.

"The event of Karbala, the capture of women and children of the Household of Prophet, their being taken as prisoners from town to town, and the speeches made by Zaynab, the daughter of Ali, who was one of the prisoners, became a scandal for the Umayyad Kingdom. Such abuse of the Household of Prophet nullified the propaganda which Muawiyah had built up for years. The scandal reached to the extent that Yazid denounced the actions of his agents in public. That was exactly what Imam Husain wanted to do, otherwise he would not bring women and children with him and sacrifice some, and let the rest to become captives. That was the only way to make a wave in order to awaken the

Muslim nation. "The event of Karbala was a major factor in the overthrow of Umayyad kingdom though its effect was delayed. Among its immediate results were the revolts and rebellions combined with bloody wars which continued for twelve years. During those riots none of the important elements in Karbala could escape revenge and punishment, including Yazid.

The Fast of Aashoorah The tenth day of this sacred month, Muharram is known as Aashoorah. It is one of the most important and blessed days of Allah in the Islaamic calendar. Some ulamaa (scholars) are of the opinion that before the fasts of Ramadhaan were made compulsory, the fast of the day of Aashoorah was compulsory upon the ummah. This is stated in a hadeeth reported by Aaishah radhiyallahu anha that the Holy Prophet sallallahu alayhi wasallam ordered the observance of the fast of Aashoorah. However, when the fast of Ramadhaan became compulsory, then whosoever wished, kept this fast and whosoever desired did not observe this fast. Bukhari Vol.1 Page 268 But, nevertheless the Prophet sallallahu alayhi wasallam continued to fast this day and encouraged his Companions to do the same.

Ibne Abbas radhiyallahu anhu says: I did not see Rasulullah sallallahu alayhi wasallam anxiously await the fast of any day, which he gave preference to over other days, but this day, the day of Aashoorah. Bukhari Vol.1 Page 268 Humayd Ibne Abdur Rahamaan narrates that he heard Muaawiyah Ibne Abi Sufyaan radhiyallahu anhu on the day of 'Aashoorah, during the year he performed hajj, saying on the pulpit: "O the people of Madinah! Where are your ulamaa (scholars)? I heard Rasullullah sallallahu alayhi wasallam saying: This is the day of 'Aashoorah. Allah has not enjoined its fasting on you but I am fasting it. Whosoever wish, keep (this) fast and whosoever desires do not observe (this fast)." Bukhari Vol.1 Page 268. In another hadeeth, Ibne Abbas raahiyallahu anhu narrates that the Holy Prophet sallallaha alayhi wasallam came to Madinah and found the Jews fasting on the day of 'Aashoorah. Hence the Holy Prophet sallallahu alayhi wasallam inquired of them, "What is (the significance of) this day on which you fast?"

They replied, "This is a great day. On this day Allah saved Moosa and his people and drowned Fir'awn and his nation. Thus

Moosa alayhis salaam fasted on this day as a token of thanksgiving, therefore we too fast on this day." The Messenger of Allah sallallahu alayhi wasallam said, "We are more worthy of Moosa and nearer to him than you." Thereafter, the Holy Prophet sallallahu alayhi wasallam fasted on this day and ordered (his Companions) that a fast be kept on this day. Muharram is observed by the Shia community of Muslims in commemoration of the martyrdom of Prophet Mohammed's grandson, Imam Hussain, who was killed in the Battle of Karbala in AD 680. The prophet's son-in-law Ali, and Ali's elder son Hassan, are also remembered during this period as having suffered and died for righteous causes.

The word muharram also means respect. The first ten days of the month are observed as a period of mourning. After the death of the Prophet Mohammed, the Quran was considered the final word. The Prophet had named no successor. One faction of his followers believed that succession should remain within Mohammed's family, while another disagreed. After a long dispute, Abu Bakr, a loyal follower of Mohammed, was elected his successor. His reign was peaceful, as was that of his successors.

However, during the reign of Ali, the Prophet's son-in-law, there was opposition from the masses. Ali was assassinated and his elder son Hassan was poisoned. His younger son Hussain, his family and his troops, were tortured and killed, and Hussain's head was severed and presented to the king.

The killing of Hussain happened on the tenth day of month of Muharram, and the event was called Ashura. It is now observed as a day for public expression of grief. These circumstances divided the Muslim community into the Shias and the Sunnis. The Shias consider Ali, Hassan and Hussain the rightful successors of Prophet Mohammed and mourn their death during Muharram.

The Shias observe the entire month as a period of mass mourning. There is no celebration or expression of joy of any kind. Women are expected to forsake all adornments. Public enactments of grief, depicting scenes from the Battle of Karbala, are carried out in Shia mosques on the first ten days.

The Shias in India observe certain ceremonies in common, though the details differ considerably. As soon as the new moon appears, people clad in black assemble and recite plaintive verses over sweetened cold drink, in memory of Imam Hussain.

The cool drink is meant to remind people of the terrible thirst Hussain and his family had to suffer. Food and drink are later distributed to the public, especially to the poor. The first nine days are also spent in making bamboo and paper replicas of the martyr's tomb. On Ashura, the tenth day, decorated taziyas, or tombs embellished with precious metals, are carried through the city streets. A horse is led in procession in memory of Hussain's horse, Dul Dul.

Wrestlers and dancers enact scenes depicting the Battle of Karbala. Bare-chested Shia men strike their body with chains or walk barefoot over burning coal while uttering cries of anguish for the torture that Hussain suffered. Apart from reliving his suffering, it is also an expression of the people's inability to save Hussain from the brutalities.

Muharram or the 'sacred month' is the first month of the Islamic or Hegira calendar. The Hadith instructs to observe fasting on the 9th and 10th of this month. Fasting on *Ashura* (the 10th of Muharram) was a *faraz* (obligatory) until fasting in ramadan was made faraz. Both in pre-Islamic times as well as at the time of the Prophet *Muhammad* (Sm), it was *haram* (forbidden) to be in war in this month. Muslims of the Shiah group observe the first ten days of the month as a period of mourning for the death of Imam Husain (R), the grandson of Hazrat Muhammad (Sm). The tenth day of Muharram is called Ashura. Imam Husain (R) was killed on this day at the hands of the troops of Yazid, the son of Muawiyah, the Umaiyya caliph. Shiahs take out processions with tazia, the replica of the tomb of Imam Husain (R) and they show their grief by clapping on their chests or flagellating themselves with knives or chains. The mourning continues for forty days till the first ten days of the next month Safar. Muharram had been observed since the 10th century. In Bengal also it has been observed for the last few centuries.

The centre of observances of Muharram in Dhaka is the *Husaini* dalan Imambara. As mark of mourning, Shiahs dress in black for at least ten days of Muharram. During this time, they refrain from merrymaking, listening to music, or seeing plays or movies. They also do not arrange weddings during this month. Keeping in mind that Imam Husain (R) and his followers suffered from unavailability of water, some Shiahs refrain from eating fish. During these first ten days of the month, *majlis* (mourning assemblies), are held at the imambaras, separately for men and women.

The story of the martyrdom of Hazrat Husain (R) is told and *marsiyas* (elegies) are sung or recited in the assemblies. At the end of the service, food is distributed to the people. On the seventh of Muharram, *shirni* (special offerings) are made and the people pray for Allah's blessings. Food and fruits in large quantities and varieties are distributed on the occasion. Those who pray for Allah's blessings, pick out a food item, and make a *manat*, or promise, not to eat that food for a year. In case the prayer is deemed accepted, they promise to offer shirni the next year. Along with the shirni, some also offer silver *panja*, the model of an open palm with five fingers that represent the five holy figures, the Prophet Muhammad (Sm), his daughter Fatima (R), his son-in-law Ali (R), and his two grandsons Hassan (R) and Husain (R).Muharram processions were common in Bengal in the 18th century. Horses and elephants were also used in the processions. Processions nowadays are much smaller. In Dhaka, the procession begins at Husaini Dalan and, after winding its way through the streets, terminates at a place designated Karbala on the banks of the Dhanmandi Lake.

The replica of *Duldul*, the horse of Imam Husain (R) and the flags in the procession show a symbolic presence of Imam Husain (R). Also latikhela (stick fights) are organised to remind of the battle between the troops of Imam Husain (R) and Yazid. As with other festivals in Bangladesh, Muharram has become an occasion for fairs at various places.

ID-UL-ZUHA

Also called Bakrid, Id-ul-Zuha, is a festival of great rejoice. Special prayers and exchange of greetings and gifts marked the Id-ul-Zuha (Bakrid), the festival of sacrifice, celebrated with traditional fervour and gaiety in India. Id-ul-Zuha is a reminder of Prophet Ibrahim's readiness to sacrifice his son for God's sake.

It also marks the completion of Haj (pilgrimage to Mecca). On this day, special 'Dua' is recited by thousands of muslims for peace and prosperity.

It is a commemoration of Hazrat Ibrahim's great test of obedience to Allah, who ordered him to sacrifice the person dearest to him. Ibrahim decided to sacrifice his son Ismail, at Mina, near Mecca. As the great religious leader was on the point of applying the sword to the throat of his dear son, it was revealed to him that the exercise was merely a test of his faith in Allah, and that he could sacrifice a ram instead. On Bakrid, the Muslims go to the mosques in the morning to offer prayers to Allah. and then sacrifice the animal at home. Bakr means 'sheep', and on Bakrid, the affluent sacrifice one animal per member of the family, and distribute two-thirds of the meat among the poor. A full-grown camel, cow, goat or sheep, free from any disease, is sacrificed. Bakrid is also a day for feasting and visiting friends to say Id Mubarak.

It is one of the grandest Muslim festivals, and is also known as *Bakrid*. It fails on the 10th day of the Muslim month Zil-Hijja. There is an interesting story about the celebration. Once Hazrat Ibrahim was ordered by Allah in a dream to sacrifice his dearest thing. To Ibrahim his son was the dearest, So, he decided to sacrifice his son on the altar of Allah. He sought the permission of the members of the family and blindfolded himself so that at the time of sacrifice his love for the son may not deter him from the act. He struck with his sword, but when he removed the fold from his eyes, to his great pleasure and surprise, he found that he had sacrificed a ram instead of his son. Since, then a ram, or goat or a camel is sacrificed and distributed among the neighbours and relatives.

The sacrifice of a ram or goat also symbolizes that man's position in the creation is far more high than any beast, and any sacrifice, however great, is a small thing for the sake of religion and Allah. The sacrificial ram or goat is reared with great care and is kept quite healthy and fat And the man who does the sacrifice must. be a man of a character and deeply religious.

This Muslim festival of sacrifice, Id-ul-Zuha (Arabic) or Bakrid in India is celebrated all over the country. On this day Muslims sacrifice a goat or Bakr (Urdu) to commemorate the sacrifice of Prophet Ibrahim, who willingly agreed to kill his son at the behest of God.

According to Islamic belief, to test Ibrahim's faith, Allah commanded him to sacrifice his son Ismail. He agreed to do it but found his paternal feelings hard to suppress. So he blind - folded himself before putting Ismail on the altar at the mount of Mina near Mecca. When he removed his bandage after performing the act, he saw his son standing in front of him, alive. On the altar lay a slaughtered lamb. This festival coincides with the Haj pilgrimage in Mecca.

Prayers are offered in the mosques and the sacrificial meat is then distributed after the Id prayers. Special delicacies are prepared and served among family and friends on the occasion.

Bakr-Id: The feast of Bakr-Id is an occasion to give and to sacrifice. It is a day to thank the Almighty for one's good fortune and to share it with the less fortunate brethren.

Legend has it that Allah commanded Hazrat Ibrahim (Abraham) to sacrifice his son Ismail on Mount Mina near Mecca. Ibrahim, unable to see himself kill his son, blindfolded himself and carried out the pronouncement of God. When he took off the blindfold, a lamb lay slaughtered on the altar and his son stood there unharmed.

Ibrahim understood then that this willingness on Ibrahim's part to give up his only son was what God sought, and not the sacrifice of human flesh and blood. The legend ascertains that all God requires of man is a surrender of his will and self. Like Ibrahim, who willingly surrenders his beloved son to God, a true follower of Islam is expected to sacrifice something that is dear to him.

The animal sacrifices made during Bakr-Id are mainly to provide food to the poor and to commemorate the noble act of Ibrahim. This spirit of sacrifice is what truly underlines the spirit of Bakr-Id. Incidentally, the day also coincides with the day when the holy Quran was declared complete. Bakr-Id is celebrated from the tenth to the twelfth day in the Islamic month of Dhul Hijjah. Every year, while pilgrims to the Mount of Mina make animal sacrifices as part of the pilgrimage rituals, Muslims the world over celebrate Bakr-Id in a similar fashion.

Every true Muslim who possesses wealth equal to or more than 400 grams of gold or is capable of affording two square meals a day, is expected to sacrifice an animal. A goat (also called bakri, hence Bakr-Id), sheep, camel or any other four-legged animal is slaughtered during one of the three days of the festival, and the meat is distributed. The sacrificial offering is divided in three parts - one for the self, another for friends, and the third, most importantly, for the needy. The sacrifice can be offered at any time before the afternoon of the third day.

Festivities mark the first day, when people wear new clothes, offer prayers at the mosque, and greet friends and relatives. Special prayers are offered on all three days. It is said that the celebrations are carried on over three days to ensure that the entire Muslim community partakes in the noble of act of giving and sharing.

Bakr-Id is celebrated all over India with much fervour, as it is in the rest of Islamic world. The name Bakr-Id, however, is most popular in India. In Arabic, the feast is usually referred to as Id-ul-Azha or Id-ul-Zuha.

Besides Hinduism, India is also the home of innumerable other faiths and the religious and cultural diversity of this nation is manifested in the large number of non-Hindu festivals.

The sizeable Muslim communities have their Ids in common with Muslims across the world. *Id-ul-Fitr, Id-ul-Zuha* and *Id-i-Milad* are the three festive occasions widely celebrated by Muslims in India.

Id is celebrated with great enthusiasm all over the country, and one can see Muslims of all age groups and from all stratas of society attired in new clothes, visiting mosques to offer *namaaz.*

The tombs of many Sufi saints attract devotees of all religious persuasions, especially during the urs or death anniversaries. The best known urs are centred at tombs in towns like Ajmer, Delhi, Manakpur, Nagore and Dongri.

The Id-ul-Azha commemorates the ordeal of Hazrat Ibrahim, who had been put to a terrible test by God when he was asked to sacrifice whatever was dearest to him and he decided to sacrifice the life of his son. As he was on the point of applying the sword to his son's throat, it was revealed to him that this was meant only to test his faith, and it was enough, if instead he sacrifices only a ram in the name of *Allah*. This is celebrated on the tenth day of *Zilhijja*, when the *Haj* celebrations at Mecca are rounded off by the sacrifice of goats or camels. In India, too, goats and sheep are sacrificed all over the country and prayers are offered.

ID-UL-FITR (RAMZAN ID)

Coming with the new moon, this festival marks the end of Ramzan, the ninth month of the Muslim year. It was during this month that the holy Koran was revealed. Muslims keep a fast every day during this month and on the completion of the period, which is decided by the appearance of the new moon, Id-ul-Fitr is celebrated with great eclat. Prayers are offered in mosques and *Idgahs* and elaborate festivities are held.

ID-I-MILAD (BARAH-WAFAT)

The Prophet was born on the twelfth day of *Rabi-ul-Awwal*, the third month of the Muslim year. His death anniversary also falls on the same day, the word *'barah'* standing for the twelve days of the Prophet's sickness. During these days, sermons are delivered in mosques by learned men, focusing on the life and noble deeds of the Prophet.

In some parts of the country, a ceremony known as *sandal* rite is performed over the symbolic footprints of the Prophet engraved in stone. A representation of *'buraq'*, a horse on which the Prophet is believed to have ascended to heaven, is kept near the footprints and anointed with sandal paste or scented powder, and the house and casket containing these are elaborately decorated. Elegies or *'marsiyas'* are sung in memory of the last days of the Prophet. The 12th day or the *Urs* proper is observed quietly, in prayers and alms giving

Id-uz-Zuha or Id-ud-Dhua popularly caller Bakri Id or Id Ebaqr ia a day of thanksgiving to God by means of sacrificing some animal like a goat, sheep, camel or bull. This month of the year which is considered propitious for pilgrimage to Mecca.

Id-ul-Zuha or Id-ud-Duha are essential muslim festivals when thousands gather at mosques all over the country to offer prayers.

Id-ul-Fitr popularly known as Id is a festival celebrated on the first day of Shawwal, the tenth month of the Hijmi year since the time of Prophet Mohammed. Fitr means breaking the fast of refraining from fasting, while Id means happiness. The festical thus marks the end of the fast during the preceding month of Ramzan. Muslims regard this month as one of the great bounty from God.

Id-ul-Zuha, the festival of sacrifice popularly known as Bakr Id, is celebrated by Muslims in April/May. It marks the end of Ramzan, the month of fasting. Bakr Id celebrates the devotion of Prophet Abraham (Hazrat Ibrahim), who was willing to sacrifice his only son Ishmael at the behest of God.

On this day Muslims sacrifice a goat (bakr in Urdu) to commemorate Hazrat Ibrahim's sacrifice. Two-thirds of the meat is kept by the family and one-third is distributed to the poor after Id prayers. The day is marked with family get-togethers, exchange of gifts and feasting on specially prepared delicacies like biryani, kebabs and kulfi. Id coincides with the Haj pilgrimage at Mecca

JAMSHED NAVROZ

Over 3000 years ago, Shah Jamshed of the Peshadian dynasty ascended the throne on the Spring Equinox. His descendants, the Parsi community, celebrate it as the New Year, the dawn of a new day (Navroz literally means "new day"). It is celebrated, even today, with prayers and feasting.

In homes, a special spread, Haft-Sinn - the seven S's - is prepared. Seven is considered to be a lucky number and the spread contains seven items that begin with "s" in farsi: sabzeh (home grown sprouts), samanou (wheat germ), sib (apples), sonbol (hyacinth), senjed (sorb tree berry), seer (garlic), somagh (sumac).

The table also holds seven foods beginning with 'sh' in Persian, sharab (wine), shakkar (sugar), shir (milk), shirinberej (sweet meat), shirin (sweet), shira (syrup) and shahad (honey); a copy of the Gathas (scriptures); a lit lamp; a mirror; a bowl of water with live fish; a shallow earthenware plate with sprouted wheat or beans (for prosperity); flowers (for colour); a gold or silver coin (for wealth); painted eggs (for productivity); and sweets and rosewater in bowls (for sweetness and happiness). These are meant to symbolize creation and to welcome spring.

Visitors to the house are first led to this table. They are asked to smile into the mirror, so that they may smile throughout the year. They are asked to look at the coin, so that they may have wealth the whole year round. They are sprinkled with rosewater so that they stay fragrant and healthy. After that, they are led to another table for a meal.

4

THE SIKH FESTIVALS

BAISAKHI

The Mughal Emperor, Aurangzeb, installed himself as the Emperor of India in 1657. To achieve his aim he had annihilated almost all his family opposition. Immediately after consolidating his power he embarked on a policy of religious persecution and set upon the process of Islamization of India. The Brahmins were his primary target. He levied unethical religious taxes against Hindus, and shut their temples and places of learning. He had been convinced by his clerics that once the Brahmins accepted Islam the others would follow. The Brahmins, particularly the inhabitants of Kashmir, looked for some dynamic leadership to fight this subversion.

The Brahmins of Kashmir approached Guru Tegh Bahadur (1621-1675), the ninth in the line of Sikh Gurus, who was on the throne of the Sikh religion. They asked him for guidance on combatting the atrocities committed by the Mughal Emperor. At the time of their meeting, Guru Tegh Bahadur's nine year old son, Gobind Rai, was sitting beside him. As Guru Tegh Bahadur went into a deep state of contemplation, his young son asked the reason of his repose. Guru Tegh Bahadur said that the matter was of vital importance; the world is aggrieved by oppression; and no brave man had yet come forward who was willing to sacrifice his life to free the earth from the burden of' Aurangzeb's persecution of Hindus. Young Gobind Rai replied: "For that purpose who is more worthy than thou who art at once generous and brave." So after entrusting the Guruship to Gobind Rai, Guru Tegh Bahadur proceeded towards Delhi, the seat of the Mughal Empire.

Upon reaching Delhi, the Guru and his loyal attendants were immediately imprisoned by Aurangzeb. While in prison, Guru Tegh Bahadur foresaw the beginning of his ecclesiastic journey. To test his son's courage and capability to carry on the Guru's mission, he wrote him saying, "My strength is exhausted, I am in chains and I can make not any efforts. Says Nanak, God alone is now my refuge. He will help me as He did his Saints." In reply young Guru Gobind Rai wrote: "I have regained my Power, my bonds are broken and all options are open unto me. Nanak, everything is in Thine hands. It is only Thou who can assist Thyself."

Guru Teg Bahadur offered his life for the freedom of conscience and conviction of anyone belonging to a faith other than his own. His spirit of sacrifice and courage was kindled into the heart of Gobind Rai.

Hundreds of people gathered around the place where Guru Tegh Bahadur was martyred in Delhi. The executioner abandoned the Guru's body in the open. No one came forward openly to claim the body to perform religious rites. Even ardent disciples withdrew unrecognized. Taking advantage of the stormy weather that followed the execution, two persons covertly took the body of Guru Tegh Bahadur for cremation. This cowardice fomented in Gobind Rai an urge to endow his Sikhs with a distinct identity.

With the criteria of courage and strength to sacrifice, Gobind Rai became the tenth Sikh Guru. He wanted to instill these principles in his downtrodden followers. He wanted to uplift their morale to combat the evil forces of injustice, tyranny, and oppression.

He was 33 years old when he had Divine inspiration to actuate his designs. Every year at the time of Baisakhi (springtime), thousands of devotees would come to Anandpur to pay their obeisance and seek the Guru's blessings. In early 1699, months before Baisakhi Day, Guru Gobind Rai sent special edicts to congregants far and wide that that year the Baisakhi was going to be a unique affair. He asked them not to cut any of their hair—to come with unshorn hair under their turbans and chunis, and for the men to come with full beards.

On Baisakhi Day, March 30, 1699, hundreds of thousands of people gathered around his divine temporal seat at Anandpur Sahib. The Guru addressed the congregants with a most stirring oration on his divine mission of restoring their faith and preserving the Sikh religion. After his inspirational discourse, he flashed his unsheathed sword and said that every great deed was preceded by equally great sacrifice: He demanded one head for oblation. After some trepidation one person offered himself. The Guru took him inside a tent. A little later he reappeared with his sword dripping with blood, and asked for another head. One by one four more earnest devotees offered their heads. Every time the Guru took a person inside the tent, he came out with a bloodied sword in his hand.

Thinking their Guru to have gone berserk, the congregants started to disperse. Then the Guru emerged with all five men dressed piously in white. He baptized the five in a new and unique ceremony called *pahul,* what Sikhs today know as the baptism ceremony called *Amrit*. Then the Guru asked those five baptized Sikhs to baptize him as well. He then proclaimed that the *Panj Pyare* — the Five Beloved Ones — would be the embodiment of the Guru himself: "Where there are Panj Pyare, there am I. When the Five meet, they are the holiest of the holy."

He said whenever and wherever five baptized (*Amritdhari*) Sikhs come together, the Guru would be present. All those who receive Amrit from five baptized Sikhs will be infused with the spirit of courage and strength to sacrifice. Thus with these principles he established *Panth Khalsa,* the Order of the Pure Ones.

At the same time the Guru gave his new Khalsa a unique, indisputable, and distinct identity. The Guru gave the gift of *bana,* the distinctive Sikh clothing and headwear. He also offered five emblems of purity and courage. These symbols, worn by all baptized Sikhs of both sexes, are popularly known today as Five Ks: *Kesh,* unshorn hair; *Kangha,* the wooden comb; *Karra,* the iron (or steel) bracelet; *Kirpan,* the sword; and *Kachera,* the underwear. By being identifiable, no Sikh could never hide behind cowardice again.

Political tyranny was not the only circumstance that was lowering peoples' morale. Discriminatory class distinctions (—the

Indian "caste" system—) promoted by Brahmins and Mullahs were also responsible for the peoples' sense of degradation. The Guru wanted to eliminate the anomalies caused by the caste system. The constitution of the *Panj Pyare* was the living example of his dream: both the high and low castes were amalgamated into one. Among the original *Panj Pyare*, there was one *Khatri*, shopkeeper; one *Jat*, farmer; one *Chhimba*, washer-man; one *Ghumar*, water-carrier; and one *Nai*, a barber. The Guru gave the surname of *Singh* (Lion) to every Sikh and also took the name for himself. From Guru Gobind Rai he became Guru Gobind Singh. He also pronounced that all Sikh women embody royalty, and gave them the surname *Kaur* (Princess). With the distinct Khalsa identity and consciousness of purity Guru Gobind Singh gave all Sikhs the opporunity to live lives of courage, sacrifice, and equality.

The birth of the Khalsa is celebrated by Sikhs every Baisakhi Day on April 13. Baisakhi 1999 marks the 300th anniversary of Guru Gobind Singh's gift of Panth Khalsa to all Sikhs everywhere.

Vaisakhi (known as Baisakhi) marks the beginning of the new Spring year and the end of the harvest in India. Vaisakhi falls in the Nanakshahi calendar (neither in the Amantha- nor in the Purnimantha-calendar) on the first day of Vaisakh and marks the sun entering Mesha Rasi (this fact is called Mesha Sankranti). Vaisakhi is therefore determined by the sun and not the moon. It usually falls on April 13, falling on April 14 once every thirty-six years. It coincides with 'Rongali Bihu' in Assam, 'Naba Barsha' in Bengal, Puthandu in Tamil Nadu, 'Pooram Vishu' in Kerala, and the Sinhala/Tamil new year festival in Sri Lanka.

At the Vaisakhi festival of 1699, at Keshgarh Sahib near Anandpur, Guru Gobind Singh, the Tenth Guru of the Sikhs founded the Akal Khalsa (Community of the Pure). Guru Gobind Singh, had organised for followers from all over India to meet him at the Vasakhi Fair in Anandpur.

Guru Gobind Singh emerged from a tent with a sword, and asked for people to give their lives for their faith. A young Sikh volunteered, followed the Guru into a tent. Shortly after, the Guru reappeared alone with his sword covered with blood, and asked for a second volunteer. A second Sikh stepped forward and again the Guru took him into the tent, and re-appeared alone, his sword covered in more blood. This was repeated for a third, fourth and fifth volunteer.

The crowd became very unnerved, as many believed that the Guru had killed the five Sikhs. He soon came out of the tent again, this time followed by all five Sikhs who were alive and well and dressed in turbans and other symbols that have since become symbols of Sikh identity. He called the five Sikhs the Panj Pyare - the beloved five.

Then the Guru put water in a bowl for sprinkling over the five in a simple initiation ceremony. He said prayers as he stirred the water with a short steel sword; symbolising the need for strength. The Guru's wife, Mata Sundri, then came forward and placed some sugar crystals into the holy water or amrit as a reminder that strength must always be balanced by sweetness of temperament. After completing his prayers, the Guru then sprinkled the amrit over the five.

He declared them to be the first members of a new community of equals, to be called the Khalsa, meaning "pure". These "saint soldiers" were to dedicate their lives to the service of others and the pursuit of justice for people of all faiths. The Panj Pyare were asked to wear five distinctive symbols of their new identity, The Five Ks.

In a move to end social divisions the five dropped their surnames - then linked to caste or occupation - and took the common name *Singh*, meaning "lion", a reminder of the need for courage. At the same time, the Guru gave Sikh women the name or title *Kaur*, meaning "princess", to emphasise dignity and complete equality.

The Guru then knelt before the five and asked them to initiate him. Hence, the Khalsa became a community in which master and disciple were equal.

For Sikhs, this seasonal festival also has great importance as the founding of the (Soldiers of the Timeless One) at Anandpur Sahib, the famous Golden Temple of Amritsar, India. The Akal Khalsa played an important role in resistance against Mughal rule. This act of total surrender of one's life to the service of the AKAL (God), the Timeless One, and at the feet of Guru Gobind

Singh created the Sikh religion. For many centuries after that, the first male child of many Hindu families in Punjab was ordained as a Sikh.

Vaisakhi used to fall on the 13th of April, but due to a change in the calendar it now falls on the 14th of April, once in 36 years.

Celebrations: To mark the celebrations, devotees, irrespective of their religion, throng gurdwaras- the Sikh place of worship - and temples in different parts of the area. The celebrations start early as devotees, with flowers and offerings in their hands, proceed towards the gurdwaras and temples before dawn. Processions through towns are also common.

Baisakhi is one of the major festivals of Sikhs and is celebrated with lot of enthusiasm and gaiety in the state of Punjab and all throughout the world where there is a significant Sikh population. For the large farming community of Punjab, Baisakhi Festival marks the time for harvest of rabi crops and they celebrate the day by performing joyful bhangra and gidda dance. For the Sikh community, Baisakhi Festival has tremendous religious significance as it was on a Baisakhi Day in 1699, that Guru Gobind Singh, the tenth Sikh Guru laid the foundation of Panth Khalsa-the Order of the Pure Ones. Date of Baisakhi Festival falls on the first day of Vaisakh month (April-May) according to Nanakshahi or Sikh Calendar. For this reason, Baisakhi is also popularly known as Vaisakhi. According to English calendar, the date of Baisakhi corresponds to April 13 every year and April 14 once in every 36 years. This difference in Baisakhi dates is due to the fact that day of Baisakhi is reckoned according to solar calendar and not the lunar calendar. The auspicious date of Baisakhi is celebrated all over India under different names and different set of rituals and celebrations. Baisakhi date coincides with 'Rongali Bihu' in Assam, 'Naba Barsha' in Bengal, Puthandu in Tamil Nadu and 'Pooram Vishu' in Kerala.Baisakhi CelebrationsPeople of Punjab celebrate the festival of Baisakhi with exuberance and devotion. As the festival has tremendous importance in Sikh religion, major activities of the day are organized in Gurdwaras. People wake up early to prepare for the day. Many also take bath in the holy river to mark the auspicious occasion. After getting ready people pay a visit to their neighbourdood gurdwara and take part in the special prayer meeting organized for the day. At the end of the Baisakhi ardas, congregates receive specially prepared Kara prasad or sweetened semolina. This is followed by a guru ka langar or community lunch. Later, during the day people of Sikh faith take out a Baisakhi procession under the leadership of Panj piaras. The procession moves through the major localities of the city amidst the rendition of devotional songs by the participating men, women and children. Mock duels, bhangra and gidda performances make the procession joyous and colourful. Celebrations by Farmers. For the large farming community of Punjab and Haryana, Baisakhi marks a New Year's time as it is time to harvest rabi crop. On Baisakhi, farmers thank god for the bountiful crop and pray for good times ahead. People buy new clothes and make merry by singing, dancing and enjoying the best of festive food. Cries of "Jatta aai Baisakhi", rent the skies as gaily men and women break into the bhangra and gidda dance to express their joy. Everyday farming scenes of sowing, harvesting, winnowing and gathering of crops are expressed through zestful movements of the body to the accompaniment of ballads and dhol music. In several villages of Punjab Baisakhi Fairs are organized where besides other recreational activities, wrestling bouts are also held.

Legends of Baisakhi: There are various legends associated with the colourful and vibrant festival of Baisakhi. A study of these interesting legends of Baisakhi reveal that the day of Baisakhi is significant not just for Sikhs but also for Hindus and Buddhists alike. Besides, it is joyous to note that as a harvest festival, people of all communities in Punjab celebrate Baisakhi in a harmonious manner.

Baisakhi Festival marks the time for the harvest of Rabi crops and is therefore celebrated with utmost joy and enthusiasm in the state of Punjab where agriculture is the predominant occupation of the people. To celebrate the occasion, people dress themselves gaily and perform the joyful bhangra and giddha dance on the tune of the dhol. Farmers in Punjab celebrate Baisakhi Festival to hilt by feasting and merrymaking before they hit on tiring but joyful task of harvesting from the next day. As a harvest festival, Baisakhi is also celebrated by different names and with different rituals in several regions of India. *Regional celebrations of Baisakhi* are marked as Rongali Bihu in Assam, Naba Barsha in Bengal, Puthandu in Tamil Nadu, Vishu in Kerala and Vaishakha in Bihar. The day of Baisakhi marks the birth of Khalsa Panth and therefore holds tremendous significance for the Sikhs. It was on the *Baisakhi Day* meeting organized at Anandpur Sahib, in 1699, that the tenth Guru of Sikhs, Guru Gobind Sigh laid the foundation of Khalsa Panth and called on the Sikhs to sacrifice themselves for their community. Besides, it was on the Baisakhi Day that Guru Gobind Singh administered amrit (nectar) to his first batch of five disciples, the *Panj Piaras* making them Singhs, a martial community. After the Baisakhi Day in 1699 the tradition of gurus was discontinued, and the Granth Sahib - the Holy book of the Sikhs was declared the eternal guide of the Sikhs. According to a popular legend in Sikhism, it was on the day of Baisakhi in 1567 that Guru Amar Das had first institutionalized Baisakhi as one of the special days when all Sikhs would gather to receive the guru's blessings at Goindwal. Martyrdom *of Guru Arjan Dev Yet* another legend related to Baisakhi, says that on the day of Baisakhi Guru Arjan Dev was martyred by the Muslim rulers. It is said that in an act of barbaric cruelty Muslim rulers threw the Guru alive into a cauldron of boiling oil. *Foundation of Arya Samaj* The day of Baisakhi Festival is also important for the Hindus as it on this day in 1875 that Swami Dayanand Saraswati founded the Arya Samaj - a reformed sect of Hindus who are devoted to the Vedas for spiritual guidance and have discarded idol worship. *Attainment of Nirvana by Gautam Buddha For* the Buddhist, the day of Baisakhi Festival is significant, as according to a popular legend it was on this auspicious day that Gautam Buddha attained enlightenment or Nirvana under the Mahabodhi tree in the town of Gaya. For this reason, the day of Baisakhi is celebrated as *Buddha Purnima* is several parts of the country.

Baisakhi Day or Vaisakhi Day of March 30th, 1699 is of significant importance for the Sikhs. It was on this day that Guru Gobind Singh - the Tenth Guru of the Sikhs founded the Akal Khalsa (Community of the Pure) at a ceremony organized at Keshgarh Sahib near Anandpur. The Akal Khalsa played a significant role in resistance against Mughal rule. Every year on April 13 Sikhs celebrate with pomp and gusto the birth of the Khalsa Panth. In the year 1667 Aurungzeb, the Mughal Emperor installed himself as the Emperor of India after annihilating almost all his family opposition. Immediately after gaining power, Aurungzeb embarked on a policy of religious persecution and started the process of Islamization of India. Brahmins became the prime targets of Aurungzeb in this regard as his clerics made him convinced that once the Brahmins accepted Islam the others would follow. Pursuing his agenda, Aurungzeb levied unethical religious taxes against Hindus and shut their temples and places of learning. The Brahmins, particularly those of Kashmir, desperately felt the need for a dynamic leadership to fight this subversion by the Mughal Emperor. They approached Guru Tegh Bahadur (1621-1675), the ninth in the line of Sikh Gurus, who was on the throne of the Sikh religion and asked him for guidance on the issue. During this meeting, Guru Tegh Bahadur's nine-year-old son, Gobind Rai, was sitting beside him. Finding Guru Tegh Bahadur under deep contemplation, the young son asked the reason of his repose.

The Guru explained the situation to the child and said the world is aggrieved by oppression and no brave man had yet come forward to willingly sacrifice his life to free the earth from the burden of Aurangzeb's persecution of Hindus. To this young Gobind Rai replied, *"For that purpose who is more worthy than thou who art at once generous and brave."* Pleased with his son's reply, Guru Tegh Bahadur entrusted the Guruship to Gobind Rai and proceeded towards Delhi, the seat of the Mughal Empire. Just as they reached Delhi, the mighty Aurangzeb imprisoned the Guru and his loyal attendants. Foreseeing his ecclesiastic journey during imprisonment, Guru Tegh Bahadur thought of testing his son's courage and capability to carry on the Guru's mission. In a letter to Gobind Rai, the Guru wrote, *"My strength is exhausted, I am in chains and I can make not any efforts. Says Nanak, God alone is now my refuge. He will help me as He did his Saints."* In his reply young Guru Gobind Rai wrote, *"I have regained my Power, my bonds are broken and all options are open unto me. Nanak, everything is in Thine hands. It is only Thou who can assist Thyself."* Later, Guru Tegh Bahadur was martyred in Delhi in the presence of hundreds of people. The executioner abandoned the Guru's body in the open. But no one dared to come forward to claim the body to perform religious rites. Even the ardent disciples withdrew unrecognized.

It was only when the stormy weather occurred, that two persons took advantage of the situation and covertly took the body of Guru Tegh Bahadur for cremation. This cowardice of Sikhs incited in Gobind Rai an urge to endow his Sikhs with a distinct identity. With the desire to instill courage and strength to sacrifice among his fellow men, Gobind Rai became the tenth Sikh Guru. At the age of 33, Guru Gobind had Divine inspiration to actuate his designs. The Guru found the occasion of Baisakhi could serve his purpose, as every year thousands of devotees would come to Anandpur at the time of Baisakhi (springtime) to pay their obeisance and seek the Guru's blessings. Early in the year 1699, months before Baisakhi Day, Guru Gobind Rai sent special edicts to congregates far and wide that that year the Baisakhi was going to be a unique affair. He asked them not to cut any of their hair and to come with unshorn hair under their turbans and chunis. Besides, men were asked to come with full beards.

The Baisakhi Day of March 30, 1699 at the call of the Guru, thousands of people gathered at the Anandpur Sahib, the famous Golden Temple of Amritsar, India on the Vaisakhi Day, March 30, 1699. To instill courage in the fellow men, Guru Gobind made a powerful oration and revealed to them his divine mission of restoring amongst Sikhs and preserving the Sikh religion. At the end of his speech, the Guru flashed his unsheathed sword and said that every great deed was preceded by equally great sacrifice and demanded one head for oblation. To the Guru's call, Daya Ram, a Khatri of Lahore offered himself. The Guru took him inside a tent. A little later he reappeared with his sword dripping with blood, and asked for another head. One by one four more earnest devotees - Daram Das - a Jat of Delhi, Mohkam Chand - a washerman of Dwarka (Gujarat), Himmat - a cook of Jagannath (Orissa) and Sahib Chand - a barber of Bidar (Karnataka) offered their heads. Every time the Guru took a person inside the tent, he came out with a bloodied sword in his hand. Astonished with their Guru's behavior and believing him to have gone berserk, people started to disperse. Shortly after, Guru Gobind emerged with all five men dressed piously in white. He baptized the five in a new and unique ceremony called *'Khande di Pahul'* (the double-edged Sword Amrit), what Sikhs today call *Amrit*. After this, the Guru asked the five baptized Sikhs to baptize him as well. They were then knighted as *Singhs,* as the Five beloved ones, the first members of the new community of equals, to be called the Khalsa, meaning "pure". Guru Gobind proclaimed that the *Panj Pyare or the Five Beloved Ones* would be the embodiment of the Guru himself, "Where there are Panj Pyare, there am I. When the Five meet, they are the holiest of the holy." These "saint soldiers" were to dedicate their lives to the service of others and the pursuit of justice for people of all faiths. The Guru also said whenever and wherever the five baptized or *Amritdhari Sikhs* comes together, the Guru would be present. All those who receive Amrit from five baptized Sikhs will be infused with the spirit of courage and strength to sacrifice. Thus with these principles, *Guru Gobind established Panth Khalsa, the Order of the Pure Ones.* The Guru also gave his new Khalsa a unique, indisputable, and distinct identity. The Guru gave the gift of *bana,* the distinctive Sikh clothing and headwear. He also offered five emblems of purity and courage.

Apart from fighting the political tyranny, Guru Gobind also sought to eliminate social discriminations in the name of caste with the establishment of Khalsa Panth. The Panj Piyaras set by the Guru amalgamated people of low and high caste into one as it consisted of people of different strata of the society. To further do away with the system of caste discrimination and to give to all Sikhs an opportunity to live lives of courage, sacrifice, and equality, the Guru gave the surname of Singh (Lion) to every Sikh and also took the name for himself. From Guru Gobind Rai, he became Guru Gobind Singh. He also pronounced that all Sikh women embody royalty, and gave them the surname *Kaur* (Princess).

Joyful festival of Baisakhi is celebrated with lot of charm and gusto in the vibrant state of Punjab. People perform set Baisakhi customs and traditions for the day with sincerity and devotion. Since Baisakhi is celebrated as the birth of Guru Gobind Singh - the Tenth Sikh Guru and the foundation day of Khalsa Panth, major activities for the festival are centred on gurdwaras - the Sikh place of worship. As a harvest festival Baisakhi is celebrated in open fields with energetic bhangra and gidda dance by gaily dressed men and women of Punjab. *Baisakhi Rituals at Gurudwaras* People following Sikh faith wake up early in the morning on a Baisakhi day and pay visit to gurdwaras to attend special prayer meetings. While most Sikhs strive to visit the revered Golden Temple or Anandpur Sahib, where the Khalsa was pronounced, those who are unable to do so visit their neighborhood gurdwara.At a gurdwara, the Guru Granth Sahib, the holy book of Sikhs is ceremonially taken out and is given a symbolical bath with milk and water. After these simple rituals, Guru Granth Sahib is placed on its throne with care.

The book is then read out to the followers gathered in the gurdwara.Just as on a *Baisakhi Day* ceremony held in 1699 under the guidance of Guru Gobind Singh where Panch Pyaras or the Five beloved ones chanted verses, five priests going by that name chant verses recited by the five originals. Similarly, just as Guru Gobind Singh Ji had used amrita prepared in an iron vessel to bless the panch pyare, even to this date amrit or holy nectar is prepared in an iron vessel and is distributed amongst all gathered after the chanting of sacred verses. As a tradition, devotees sip amrita five times and take a vow to work for the brotherhood, the Khalsa Panth. Religious songs (kirtans) are sung after the amrit is drunk for the spiritual upliftment of those gathered. At noon, after the Baisakhi ardas, the Karah Prasad or sweetened semolina is offered to the guru for his blessings. It is then distributed to the congregation.

The ceremony culminates with a special guru-ka-langar or the community lunch. People sit in rows with their heads covered as volunteers serve them with vegetarian meal. Later, during the Baisakhi day, sacred Guru Granth Sahib is taken out in a procession. At the head of the procession are the Panj Piaras, symbolizing the journey made by the five fearless devotees from their homes to Anandpur, to be baptised by Guru Gobind Singh. *Baisakhi processions* are attended by men, women and children alike with faith and enthusiasm. The procession moves through major localities of the city and is welcomed by citizens and members of social and cultural societies. Colourful bhangra and gidda dance apart from mock duels are performed during Baisakhi processions. Another fascinating part of Baisakhi celebrations is the accompaniment of drummers, bands playing religious times, devotees singing religious songs and men swinging swords. Loud Sikh chants of 'Bole so nihal', 'Deg teg fateh' and rhythmic chants of *'Sat nam'* and *'Wahe guru'* ring out from the middle of the singing and drumming. Some men may wear the headgear (bana) of Guru Nanak, others that of Guru Gobind Singh.In their discourse at the end of the ceremony, Sikh religious leaders strive to promote the feeling of charity amongst people, especially children in honor of Guru Gobind Singh. In some places, especially Punjab, such processions are taken out even before Baisakhi. *Celebrations in the Fields.* Since Baisakhi is also celebrated as a harvest festival, farmers in Punjab celebrate Baisakhi with energetic performance of bhangra and gidda dance. Men and women clad themselves in their traditional Bhangra dress and dance to the beat of dhol in a joyful festive atmosphere.

Vibrant Festival of Baisakhi is considered to be an extremely important festival in India for number of reasons. Apart from being important for the farmers as a harvest festival, the festival is of prime importance in Sikhism as a foundation day of Khalsa Panth. Besides, auspicious Baisakhi day is of importance for astrological reasons too !! Astrological Significance of Baisakhi The festival of Baisakhi falls on April 13 every year and April 14 once in every 36 years. Change in date is because of the fact that date of Baisakhi is reckoned according to the solar calendar. Astrologically, the date of Baisakhi is significant as marks sun's entry into Mesh Rashi. For this very reason, many people also know Baisakhi as Mesha Sankranti.

The auspicious date of Baisakhi is celebrated all over India under different names and rituals. It is celebrated as 'Rongali Bihu' in Assam, 'Naba Barsha' in Bengal, 'Puthandu' in Tamil Nadu, 'Pooram Vishu' in Kerala and 'Vaishakha' in the state of Bihar. Significance of Baisakhi for Farmers For the agriculturally rich state of Punjab and Haryana, Baisakhi marks the time for harvest of Rabi (winter) crops and is therefore extremely significant for the farmers. Baisakhi Festival is also celebrated as a Thanksgiving Day festival in these states. After waking up early and dressing themselves in new clothes, farmers visit temples and gurdwaras to express gratitude to God for the good harvest and seek blessing for ensuing agriculture season. Farmers also celebrate Baisakhi by performing energetic bhangra and gidda dance and participating in Baisakhi Fairs. Significance of Baisakhi in

SikhismBaisakhi is of major importance for the people following Sikh faith. As it was on a Baisakhi Day, in the year 1699 that the Tenth Guru of Sikhs, Guru Gobind Singh founded Khalsa Panth or the Order of Pure Ones and gave a unique identity to Sikhs. On the same day the guru administered amrit (nectar) to his first batch of five disciples making them Singhs, a martial community. By doing so, he eliminated the differences of high and low and established that all human beings were equal.Sikhs celebrate Baisakhi by participating in special prayer meetings organized at gurdwaras. They also carry out joyful Baisakhi processions to mark the day.Significance of Baisakhi in Other Religions The day of Baisakhi is of significance for the Hindus as it was on this day in 1875 that Swami Dayanand Saraswati founded the Arya Samaj - a reformed sect of Hindus who are devoted to the Vedas for spiritual guidance and have discarded idol worship. Besides, Baisakhi day is of relevance for the Buddhists as Gautama Buddha attained enlightenment and Nirvana on this auspicious day.

Baisakhi marks the arrival of the harvesting season. The festival always falls on April 14 and marks the beginning of the solar year. Just before the festival the farmer returns home with his bumper crop, the fruit of his whole year's hard labour.

This festival is in celebration to thank God for good harvest for the year and coming year also. Early morning of Baiskhai, people take dip in holy rivers. Cries of "Jatta aai Baisakhi" rent the skies as the people of Punjab attired in their best clothes break into the Bhangra dance to express their joy.

The dancers and drummers challenge each other to continue the dance. The scenes of sowing, harvesting, winnowing and gathering of crops are expressed through zestful movements of the body to the accompaniment of ballads. Both men and women, celebrate the day with Bhangra and Gidda.

Fairs are organized at various places in Punjab, where besides other recreational activities, wrestling bouts are also held. The occasion is celebrated with great gusto at Talwandi Sabo, where Guru Gobind Singh stayed for nine months and completed the recompilation of the Guru Granth Sahib. The Sikhs celebrate this day by visiting gurudwaras and distributing kada prasad. Processions led by the Panj Piaras or the five religious men are taken out. Kirtans and recital of passages from the Granth Sahib are also organized in gurdwaras, where people line up to receive the delicious prasad and perform kar sewa-that is, offering help in the daily chores of the gurdwara. The most sacred pilgrimage centres is Amritsar, where Golden Temple is situated. Relatives and friends are welcomed and offered lassi and sweets. This festival brings bright hopes for the future.

Baisakhi, also spelled Vaisakhi, is the festival which celebrates Sikh New Year and the founding of the Sikh community, known as the Khalsa.The story of the foundation of the Khalsa started with the martyrdom of Guru Teg Bahadur, the 9th Guru, who was publicly beheaded by Mughul rulers for protecting freedom of worship for both Sikhs and Hindus.The son of Guru Teg Bahadur, who was called Guru Gobind Singh, became the next Guru. He stated that Sikhs should always be prepared to stand up for their beliefs, whatever the cost. In 1699, Sikhs from all over the Punjab gathered together to celebrate the Hindu harvest festival of Baisakhi. Guru Gobind Singh came out of a tent carrying a sword and requested that anyone prepared to give his life come forward. A young Sikh came forward and disappeared into the tent with the Guru. Then the Guru reappeared alone with his sword covered in blood and asked for another volunteer. This was repeated another four times until a total of five Sikhs had gone into the tent with him. Everyone present was very worried until eventually all five emerged from the tent alive, with Guru Gobind Singh, and wearing turbans. The five became known as the *Panj Piare*, or 'Beloved Five'. Guru Gobind Singh's wife mixed some amrit. The Guru said some prayers over the five and they were sprinkled with the amrit. This is how the Amrit ceremony came into being and these five Sikhs became the first members of the Khalsa.

India's rich and glorious civilization is mirrored in its innumerable festivals. These festivals mark the seasons which signal to man the time for work and the time for relaxation, the commencement of the agricultural cycle with sowing in spring, and its culmination with the harvesting of the golden grain. And then, of course, we have, in endless variations of legend and myth, the hallowed perceptions that there is an ever-renewed war of light and darkness, of the divine and the demoniac in the unceasing evolution of the world. Generally, the sites of these festivities are on the banks of the rivers which have their sacred import with myths and legends woven around their origin and names.

Baisakhi, marks the beginning of New Year, particularly in the northern part of India. It is among the few Indian festivals that has a fixed date. Baisakhi is always on April 13th. In Kerala, Baisakhi is called as "*Vishu*" and in Tamil Nadu, it is celebrated as "*Puthandu*".

Considered a holy day, the devout celebrate the Baisakhi with a dip in the holy rivers just around the break of dawn. It is on this day that Sun enters Aries, the first sign of Zodiac. This signifies ushering of the new year.

In Punjab (the land of Green Revolution) particularly and in the northern belt of India in general, farmers perform their own prayers and rejoice. For on this day, they commence cutting their harvest. The fields can be seen full of nature's bounty. Dressed in their typical folk attire, both men and women, celebrate the day with Bhangra and Gidda. Sweets are distributed, old enmities are forgiven and life is full of joy, merriment and everyone seems to belong.

Baisakhi, however, has had a new dimension added to it by Guru Gobind Singh. For it was on the day of Baisakhi in 1669, that he established the Khalsa Panth and gave a final impetus to the course of the earlier nine Gurus of Sikhism.

People perform *Kar Sewa* (physical labour to help in the daily chores of the gurudwara as a symbol of humility) in gurudwaras and listen to recitations from Guru Granth Sahib. Colourful processions, led by the Panj Piaras, are taken out. Children and youth demonstrate their skills in martial arts to the accompaniment of musical bands. The Granth Sahib, which was designated the eternal guru of Sikhs by Guru Gobind Singh, is also taken out in procession.

Children are taught to perform acts of charity on this auspicious occasion and are expected to continue to do so all through the year. Many Sikhs choose to be baptized into the Khalsa brotherhood on this day. The wrappings of the Nishan Sahib flag post at most gurdwaras are changed on Baisakhi.

There is a mood of celebration in the air and what better way to express joy than to break into a dance! Men perform the vigorous Bhangra dance with energetic steps to the beat of *dholak* (traditional drum) while women perform Gidda dance wit h great fervour and rhythmic steps. Though a community festival, Baisakhi is also celebrated in individual homes. Since it is a harvest festival, there is no fasting or special puja on this occasion. Houses are cleaned and freshly painted. Friends and relatives are invited for meals and a sumptuous feast is served. Meat and alcohol are part of the day's fare. Baskets of fruits and boxes of sweet are sent to the families of the married daughters.

Guru Amar Das had first institutionalized Baisakhi in 1567 as one of the special days when all Sikhs would gather to receive the guru's blessings at Goindwal. It was on this day in 1699 that the tenth Guru of the Sikhs, Guru Gobind Singh, founded the Khalsa Panth. He discontinued the tradition of Gurus in Sikhism by declaring the Granth Sahib to be the eternal Guru of all Sikhs. He asked his followers to be ready to lay down their lives to save others. Five volunteers of five different castes were made the Panj Piaras, who would lead the rest. They came from different places like Punjab, Uttar Pradesh, Andhra Pradesh and Bihar.

The first lesson on how to be a true Sikh was imparted to these people by Guru Gobind Singh, who asked them not to cut their hair or beard (*kesh*), to always carry a comb (*kangha*), a sword (*kirpan*) so that they would be always ready for battle, to wear an underwear (*kachcha*) and an iron bangle (*kada*). These are known as the five Ks and are mandatory for every Sikh. The Panj Piaras in turn baptized Guru Gobind Singh into the Khalsa brotherhood. On this day, Guru Arjan Dev was martyred by the then Muslim rulers. Again, on this day in 1875, Swami Dayanand Saraswati founded the Arya Samaj - a reformed sect of Hindus who are devoted to the Vedas for spiritual guidance and have discarded idol worship.

Fairs: A number of cattle fairs are organised at this time of the year. The villages wear a festive look and vendors selling ice cream, flossy sugar lollipops and chaat make a brisk business. Toys, handicrafts and mundane household goods are sold at these places.

On this memorable Baisakhi day (March 30 of A.D. 1699) , Guru Gobind Singh Sahib called a big meeting at Kesgarh Sahib near the City of Anandpur Sahib. Between fifty to eighty thousand Sikhs attended this meeting. When all were expecting to hear words of comfort and consolation from the lips of their Guru, they were perturbed to see him with a drawn sword in his hand and cried ' Is there anyone here who would lay down his life for Dharam?' There was a big silence, but the Guru went on repeating his demand. At the third call Daya Ram, a Khatri of Lahore, rose from his seat and offered himself. The Guru took him into an adjoining enclosure....(and soon after) came out with the (blood) dripping....(sword in hand) and flourshing it before the gathering, asked again, 'Is there any other Sikh here who will offer himself as a sacrifice (for the cause of dharma)?

At this Daram Das, a Jat of Delhi (Haryana side) came forward and was taken into the enclosure....(The Guru again came out with the blood-stained sword, and made his previous demand). In the same way three other men stood up, one after another, and offered themselves for the sacrifice. One was Mohkam Chand, a washerman of Dwarka (Gujarat State); another was Himmat, a cook of Jagannath (Orissa State); and the third was Sahib Chand, a barber of Bidar (Karnataka State). The Guru, after dressing the five in handsome clothes, brought them from the assembly.

These five were then administered 'Khande di Pahul' (the double-edged Sword Amrit). They were then knighted as Singhs, as the Five beloved ones, the first members of the Order of the Khalsa. The Guru then asked them to administer the Pahul to him in the same manner in which he had given the Pahul to them, and it was done so.

With the creation of Khalsa, the Khalsa created history and since the birth of Khalsa, the history of Punjab has been the history of Sikhs. Baisakhi played a significant role in this regard. In 1762, Ahmed Shah Abdali, with the sole purpose to destroy the entire Sikh nation, declared 'Jehad'(holy-war) against the Sikhs and all the Muslims of the Punjab rallied under this slogan. The Sikhs were surrounded near the village Kup in Ludhiana District. Chronicles mention that about twenty thousand Sikhs were martyred in a single day.

This event is known in the history of the Sikhs as "Ghallughara" (Bloody Carnage). After this, Ahmed Shah Abdali thought that he had crushed the entire Sikh nation, but was greatly disillusioned when after a few months heard that the Sikhs in large number are celebrating Baisakhi at Amritsar. In due course of time Baisakhi reminds every Sikh of his cultural and religious heritage. On Baisakhi day all the Sikhs used to assemble at Amritsar and decide their problems relating to politics and religion. This convention still goes on. The celebrations of Baisakhi are similar to the three-day schedule of the the celebrations of other Gurpurabs. It is generally celebrated on 13th April every year.

This also marks the beginning of a month long *Vaisakha* bathing. The pilgrimage to the holy shrine of Badrinath, in the Himalayas, also commences from this day. The charities done during Vaisakha month are believed to earn great religious merits and so people generously give money, grains and other things to the poor and needy and the *Brahmins*, and observe fast, chant the glories of the lord and practice such other pious activities.

The holy book of the Sikhs, 'Granth Sahib' is taken in a procession, led by the 'Panj Pyaras' (five senior Sikhs) who are symbolic of the original leaders. It was on this day that Guru Gobind Singh organised his first batch of five disciples making them Singhs, a martial community. Kirtans and recital of passages from the 'Granth Sahib' are also organized in gurdwaras, where people line up to receive the delicious Kada prasad (sweetened semolina) and perform kar sewa-that is, offering help in the daily chores of the gurdwara. The occasion is celebrated with great gusto at Talwandi Sabo, where Guru Gobind Singh stayed for nine months and completed the recompilation of the Guru Granth Sahib and in the Golden temple in Amritsar. On Baisakhi day, water is drawn from all the sacred rivers of India and poured in to the huge tank surrounding.

GURU GOVIND SINGH JAYANTI

Punjab, rightly claimed as the traditional sword-arm of Bharatvarsha, has valiantly borne the first brunt of all the pre-European aggressors on her. And one of the most luminous stars which rose in that north-western horizon and shed its lustre over the entire length and breadth of the country is undoubtedly Guru Govind Singh the tenth and the final Guru in the holy tradition initiated by that great saint Guru Nanak.Richly had Guru Govind Singh inherited the legacy of the fearless martyrdom of his father-Guru Tegh Bahadur. Guru Tegh Bahadur, with a view to instilling courage and confidence among the Kashmiri Hindus to withstand Aurangzeb's fanatical tyranny and threats to Islamize them, challenged the Moghal emperor to convert him first. And the great Guru preferred to have his head roll down in Chandni Chowk of Delhi rather than sacrifice his faith, Govind Singh was just a boy of nine years at that time. On coming to know of his father's terrible end he exclaimed: "He saved with his blood the honor of Hindu Dharma. Oh, what a remarkable act in this Kaliyuga! He preferred to give up his life, but not his faith!"

GURUPURB

Gurupurb is not a single festival or occasion. These are holy days and are associated with anniversaries of the many of the Sikh Guru's birth or death, martyrdom day and anniversary of the installation of the Adi Granth Sahib. People from Sikh religion celebrate Gurupurbs. Some Gurupurbs are local events celebrated only where the original event took place. Some are celebrated universally. Some of the important Gurpurab's are the birth anniversaries of Guru Nanak, the founder of Sikhism (Oct.-Nov.) and of Guru Gobind Singh, the last Guru (Dec.-Jan.).

Celebrations are done by reading of the holy verses in the Guru Granth Sahib and by holding processions where the 'Guru Granth Sahib' is carried in procession through the town. The holy book is placed on a van strewn with flowers and has a troop of five armed guards around it.

The Sadh Sangat of Sikh Dharma held its first celebration of Baisakhi in Los Angeles in April, 1970. In December of 1970, 84 Western Sikhs traveled on a yatra to India with Yogi Harbhajan Singh (later to have the titles of Siri Singh Sahib and Bhai Sahib bestowed on him at Akal Takhat Sahib), and in Amritsar, those 'new' Sikhs received Amrit from the Panj Piare at Akal Takhat Sahib. These were American youth in their early twenties, inspired to live as Khalsa as a result of their deep respect for and aspiration to live to the example of Siri Singh Sahib Bhai Sahib Harbhajan Singh Khalsa Yogiji, who had embarked upon his service of inspiring the youth of the West to the Khalsa life-style, as a step in the fulfillment of Guru Gobind Singh's prophesy that 960,000,000 we shall be. He was most humble in his approach to his service of Guru, as exemplified by his action at that moment when these 84 students came to cross the threshold of Akal Takhat Sahib to receive Amrit. He would not cross the threshold with them; "I have brought you this far. Now you go the remainder of the distance without me, as this is a relationship between you and Guru."

In June of 1973, the Siri Singh Sahib appointed Singh Sahib Dayal Singh as Head Granthee for Sikh Dharma and bestowed upon him the title of Bhai Sahib. Bhai Sahib Dayal Singh was only 17 years old at the time but he had a fervent love for the Guru and Gurbani. He was a constant sevadar, mowing lawns, cooking langar, sweeping the Gurdwara steps, placing fresh cut flowers in front of the Guru. Always full of love, smiles, and constant encouragement for everyone. With his incredible devotion he was one of the first persons to teach many Western Sikhs how to read Gurmukhi, how to recite their Banis, and how to do Prakash and Sukhasn seva and conduct a kirtan program. On Baisakhi Day, April 13, 1974 Sant Mihen Singh and his followers, while visiting Los Angeles, distributed Amrit to Western born Sikhs at Guru Ram Das Ashram and Bhai Sahib Dayal Singh served as one of the Panj Piare on that day, thus becoming the first Western born Sikh ever to administer Amrit. An Amrit Sanchar was held every year thereafter on Baisakhi in Los Angeles.

It was a great loss to the Panth Khalsa when Bhai Sahib Dayal Singh left for the heavenly abode resulting from a fatal car accident on September 22nd, 1975, just short of his 21st birthday, en route to New York, where he was to depart for India and a visit to the Golden Temple. Council of the Western Hemisphere began to hold its annual spring meetings the week of Baisakhi in Los Angeles. The Sadh Sangat would come to Los Angeles from all parts of the world where Sikh Centers were being established: Central and South America, Canada, Europe, Africa, and Asia. Under the direction and inspiration of Siri Singh Sahib Bhai Sahib

Harbhajan Singh Khalsa Yogiji, and with Guru as their constant guide, the Khalsa spirit among these new Sikhs grew and flourished. The Sadh Sangat continued to grow and by the early 1980s attendance at the Baisakhi kirtan program was large enough to require a bigger venue to accommodate the hundreds of people attending the Baisakhi Kirtan program.

The Siri Singh Sahib Ji inspired the sangat members of Sikh Dharma to invite all of the Gurdwaras of California to participate and join the celebration. He had a deep desire to see the Sikh community unified and working closely together. He inspired the sadh sangat of Guru Ram Das Ashram to extend invitations to all the Gurdwaras of California to participate in the Baisakhi celebration. Similarly, he encouraged everyone to participate in programs held by other Gurdwaras, not only here in Los Angeles, but throughout California and the world. In his wisdom, he deeply understood the cultural challenges, including acceptance of Westerners into the Punjabi culture and vice versa. One of his messages to Western Sikhs everywhere was that we should be grateful for the great devotion of all those Sikhs who have carried the Guru for 400 years and made huge sacrifices through the centuries, so that we can all enjoy the darshan of Siri Guru Granth Sahib today.

He also had a vision of Sikh Dharma being a Dharma beyond borders and nationality, which he referred to as "sarab dharma," a dharma that includes people of all races and cultures. Since the late 1980s, the Sikh Dharma Baisakhi Celebration has been held at the vast Los Angeles Convention Center, in collaboration with a network of Southern California Gurdwaras. The Baisakhi Gurupurb has been attended throughout the years by many dignitaries from India, including Gurcharan Singh Tohra, S. Tarlochan Singh, Jethadars of Akal Takhat, S.S. Professor Darshan Singh, S.S. Professor Manjit Singh, and many members of SGPC.

The programs have also been graced by some of the most well known Ragi Jethas, Bhai Harjinder Singh, Sant Anoop Singh, Master Darshan Singh, Bhai Hari Singh, Bhai Nirmal Singh, and many, many others. Each year the program has been attended by prominent Los Angeles, state of California and U.S. political dignitaries, including Lt. Governor Cruz Bustamante,

Congressman Howard Berman, Congresswoman Diane Watson, many L.A. county supervisors and council members and, most recently, then Los Angeles Mayor elect Antonio Villaraigosa (who donned a full turban for the occasion).

The idea of adding a Nagar Kirtan (Parade) to the Baisakhi Celebration had been percolating among the Guru Ram Das Ashram organizing committee for several years prior to 1997. This year celebrates the ninth year the Nagar Kirtan has been a joyful part of the Baisakhi Celebration and, thanks to the seva of many devoted Sikhs, it is one of the most inspiring traditions that we continue to cherish during Baisakhi. A lot of acknowledgement goes to all sangat members who make financial contributions to both the Kirtan Darbar and Nagar Kirtan.

Teachings Of Guru Nanak: He was not only the founder of the Sikh religion, he was a great poet, philosopher, humanist and a powerful social reformer, a teacher of mankind. Nanak said that one need not become a sanyasi sacrificing one's family, to please God. Those who practice devotion, whose mind is pure and who have sympathy, patience and honesty, are in no way inferior to a sanyasi. He considered that all human beings were highborn; no one was low.He stressed, "Do not ask someone's caste; those whose devotion is accepted by God are good people. God appreciates those who have conquered the 'I' and 'greed'. Nanak washes the feet of those who concentrate their minds on God, the source of truth".

Celebrations: The akhand path or the continuous reading of Granth Saheb, the sacred book of the Sikhs, begins three days before Guru Nanak Jayanti. The sacred scripture is read non-stop from beginning to end. The Akhand Path culminates on the day of the Guru Purab and the holy book is then taken out in a procession. It is beautifully decorated with flowers and carried on a float. Children participate in the procession and march to the tune of local band playing religious hymns. Five armed guards who are called the panj pyare lead the procession. At the head of the procession is the Nishan Saheb or the Sikh flag.

A few days before Guru Purab, people take out Prabhat Pheris or the early morning processions from the Gurdwaras. They go around their locality singing shabd or the religious hymns.**Langar**Later in the day, special kirtans are arranged in the Gurdwaras. The devotees attend langar or the common meals where everyone eats the same food irrespective of caste, class, or creed. Devotees offer their services for cooking food, cleaning the Gurdwara or carrying out other chores. This is called the Kar Seva. In the evening, the Gurdwaras are illuminated and people visit them in large numbers. People also illuminate their homes with candles and earthen lamps.

The 7th Day of bright half of MaargashiraPunjab, rightly claimed as the traditional sword-arm of Bharatvarsha, has valiantly borne the first brunt of all the pre-European aggressors on her. And one of the most luminous stars which rose in that north-western horizon and shed its lustre over the entire length and breadth of the country is undoubtedly Guru Govind Singh the tenth and the final Guru in the holy tradition initiated by that great saint Guru Nanak.Richly had Guru Govind Singh inherited the legacy of the fearless martyrdom of his father - Guru Tegh Bahadur.

Guru Tegh Bahadur, with a view to instilling courage and confidence among the Kashmiri Hindus to withstand Aurangzeb's fanatical tyranny and threats to Islamize them, challenged the Moghal emperor to convert him first. And the great Guru preferred to have his head roll down in Chandni Chowk of Delhi rather than sacrifice his faith, Govind Singh was just a boy of nine years at that time. On coming to know of his father's terrible end he exclaimed: "He saved with his blood the honor of Hindu Dharma. Oh, what a remarkable act in this Kaliyuga! He preferred to give up his life, but not his faith!"It is with such a fiery note of idealism that the young Govind Singh embarked upon his life-mission even from his infancy. As a child he had drunk deep at the fount of *Raamaayana*, *Mahaabhaarata* and *Puraanas*.

He was inspired with the heroic examples of Sri Rama, Sri Krishna, Bheema and Arjuna. He felt convinced that he too like those great forbears was born to vanquish the wicked and protect *Dharma*. He began preparing himself in a thorough-going fashion to play that historic role. He assimilated the spiritual truths enshrined in the *Vedas, Upanishads* and the *Bhagavad Geeta*. He became adept in Persian, Arabic and Punjabi languages just as in Samskrit and Hindi, and was a peerless poet as well.

As an archer he was unequalled in the whole of Hindusthan. No wonder, equipped as he was with such a rare combination of *brahmateja* and *kshaatrateja*, he wrote in his autobiographical poem *Vichitranaatak* that he was commanded by God to take birth to uphold the true path of *Dharma*.No catastrophe to his personal self or to his family members, however tragic, could shake his rock-like resolve to pursue his chosen mission.

When his two elderly sons, Ajit and Jujhar whom he had sent to lead the battle laid down their lives before his very eyes thus did the Guru offer prayers to God: "O Lord, I have surrendered to Thee what belonged to Thee." Later, when his two younger kids Jorawar and Phatte were bricked alive by the Moghals for refusing to succumb to Islam, and the heart-rending news reached the Guru, he simply lifted his hands in prayer and uttered the words: "These two, Thy trust, I have rendered unto Thee."

The Guru's mother, Gujjari Devi, from whom the two kids had been snatched away, broke her heart and died.The tone of the historic epistle which the Guru wrote some time later to Aurangzeb is evidence of the majestic equanimity and the supremely high moral posture he maintained even in the wake of such dire calamities: "I know you believe neither in God nor in your prophet, nor do you know the worth of an oath on Koran. Did your God ask you to tyrannise over others? Fie on your sovereignty and on your regard for God and religion! Fear God, who is the Master of earth and heaven and Whose vengeance is terrible. What if you have killed my four sons? By putting out a few sparks, you cannot quench the blazing fire. My protection is God than Whom there is no one higher."The Guru bore all the cruel blows of Fate with an invincible will and fortitude and pressed forward in rousing and organizing his countrymen in the cause of *Swadesh* and *Swadharma*. He moved from the north to the southern parts of the country contacting and trying to string together the various patriotic forces. Finally, in the south he found a great warrior turned into a yogi, Maadhav Daas by name, and charged him with the task of proceeding to Punjab to lead the struggle there.

Maadhav Daas, known in history as Bandaa Bairaagi, abided by the Guru's command and carried out the war of liberation with such remarkable ability and was crowned with such rare success - finally falling a martyr to the cause in the true tradition of the Gurus - that even to this day he stands as a glowing testimony to the magic touch of Guru Govind Singh.Finally the Guru himself, while in the south at Nanded, fell a martyr to the treacherous designs of the Moghals and embraced *Mahaasamaadhi* in the true tradition of *yogis*.Could such a string of stirring martyrdoms of all his four sons, his father, his mother and finally he, the great Guru himself, followed by that of his successor, ever go in vain?

The flames of those sacrificial offerings soon spread and inflamed millions of hearts. By the turn of the century, the vast areas of the strategic north-western region of Bharat right up to the Khybar Pass were freed from the foreign Islamic yoke and the tide of one thousand-year old invasions from that quarter turned back once and for all.The spirit of oneness and harmony which the Guru infused in the society has also made him a social reformer of the highest order. His vision encompassed the whole of Bharat, and his love embraced within itself the lowliest in the society.

The *Panch Pyaare*, the five self-sacrificing heroes of the *Khaalsa* whom he chose through a fiery ordeal on a a*Vaishaakha Pratipada*, were those drawn from distant parts of the country, right from Bidar in Karnataka, Jagannaath Puri in Orissa, Dwaraka in Gujarat to Delhi and Lahore. And three of them belonged to the so-called lower castes.The Guru's breadth of national vision could not brook any idea or gesture which would even remotely suggest an exclusive or a warped mind.

The *Khaalsa*, the Pure, were to be the devotees of *Akaal* - The Timeless Reality - in the true tradition of the Hindu *tapaswis*. The Guru had founded the creed for the achievement of all-round glory of Hindu society and Hindu Dharma. He thundered: *Sakala jagat me Khaalsa panth gajei* (may the creed of the pure and the dedicated flourish the world over) and *Jagai dharma Hindu sakala bandha bhajai*. (may the wickedness vanish and the Hindu dharma live for ever.)The five signs the Guru prescribed for the *Khaalsas* signified the highest virtues of heroic Hindu manhood; unshorn hair like that of the ancient sages and *kshatriyas* as a pledge of dedication, a comb to keep it clean, a steel bracelet indicating the universality of the Almighty, an underwear to denote chastity, and a steel dagger to remind him of his role as the defender of Faith.The Guru knew the potency of ancient Hindu epics and *Puraanas* and had organized a Poets' Council to translate the *Puraanas* into Hindi.

His own poetry composed in Hindi, in its Braj form, overflowed with the essence of *Raamaayana*, *Mahaabhaarata* and all the *Puraanic* legends and their Gods and Goddesses and radiated the lofty spiritual message of *Upanishads* and *Bhagavadgeeta*. *Sarvakaal* was to him the father and *Devi Mahaa Kaali* the mother.

The *Guru Granthsaheb* which he re-edited contained the hymns and couplets of saints of various regions. Neither the Sikhs nor the rest of Hindus ever considered themselves distinct or separate from each other. Right up to the recent times, every Hindu family used to nominate one of its boys as a Sikh. Blood relationship between the *Keshadhaaris* and non-*Keshadhaaris* continues undisturbed even to this day. Brother belonging to both sections living under a common paternal roof is not an uncommon sight even today.Rarely do we come across in the annals of human history a life of such all-round greatness as that of *Guru Govind Singh* - a *yogi* and a warrior-martyr, a poet and a social reformer, a national emancipator and a *dhaarmic* rejuvenator - all rolled into one supremely majestic personality commanding the reverence of his countrymen and even of his enemies.No better appreciation could be there of the inspiring legacy left behind to the entire nation by that great Guru than what Swami Vivekananda has observed: "Mark me, every one of you will have to be a Govind Singh, if you want to do good to your country.

You may see thousands of defects in your countrymen, but mark their Hindu blood. They are the first gods you will have to worship, even if they do everything to hurt you; even if every one of them sends out a curse to you, you send out to them words of love. If they drive you out, retire to die in silence like that mighty lion, Govind Singh. Such a man is worthy of the name of Hindu; such an idea ought to be before us always."

Bibliography

Ann Grodzins Gold, *Fruitful Journeys: The Ways of Rajasthani Pilgrims.* Berkeley: University of California Press, 1988.

Asim Roy, *The Islamic Syncretistic Tradition in Bengal.* Princeton: Princeton University Press, 1983.

Chakravarti, C.: *The Tantras: Studies on their Religion and Literature,* Punthi Pustak, Calcutta, 1963.

Chaturvedi, M.D.,: *Hinduism, The Eternal Religion,* Bharatiya Vidya Bhavan, Bombay, 1992.

Coomeraswamy, Ananda K.: *Buddha and the Gospel of Buddhism,* MacMillan, London, 1928.

De Bary: *Self and Society in Ming Thought,* Columbia University Press, New York, 1970.

Fadiman, James & Robert Frager: *Essential Sufism,* San Francisco, 1997.

Farquhar, J. N.: *A Primer of Hinduism,* Faber & Faber, London, 1912.

Gambhirananda, Swami: *Brahma Sutra Shamkar Bhasya,* Adavita Ashrama, Calcutta, 1977.

Hawley, John Stratton: *Songs of the Saints of India,* Oxford University Press, New York, 1988.

John, Elsner: *Pilgrimage: Past and Present in the World Religions,* Harvard University Press, Cambridge, 1995.

Jonathan P. Parry, *Death in Banaras.* Cambridge: Cambridge University Press, 1994.

Kantikar, Hemant: *Kalidasa's Abhijnana Shakuntala,* Popular Prakashan, Bombay, 1984.

Kinsley, David R., *Hinduism a Cultural Perspective,* Prentice-Hall, New Jersey, 1993.

Mearns, David J.: *Shiva's Other Children: Religion and Social Identity amongst Overseas Indians*, Sage, Walnut Creek, 1995.

Michael Gilsenan, *Recognizing Islam*. New York: Pantheon Books, 1982.

Michell, George: *The Hindu Temple: An Introduction to Its Meaning and Forms*, University of Chicago Press, Chicago, 1988.

Miller, Barbara Stoler: *The Bhagavad-Gita: Krishna's Counsel in Time of War*, Bantam, New York, 1986.

Philip Lutgendorf, *The Life of a Text: Performing the* Råmcartmånas *of Tulsidas*. Berkeley: University of California Press, 1991.

Regula Burckhardt Qureshi, *Sufi Music of India and Pakistan: Sound, Context and Meaning in Qawwali*. Chicago: The University of Chicago Press, 1995 (1986).

Richard Eaton, *The Rise of Islam and the Bengal Frontier, 1204-1760*. Delhi: Oxford University Press, 1994.

Sharma, Pushpendra K.: *Hindu Religion and Ethics*, Asian Publication Services, New Delhi, 1997.

Simon Coleman: *Pilgrimage: Past and Present in the World Religions*, Harvard University Press, Cambridge, 1995.

Subhan, John A.: *Sufism: Its Saints and Shrines*, Lucknow, 1938.

Trimingham, J. Spencer: *The Sufi Orders in Islam*, New York, 1998.

Index